For All
SEASONS

DERICK BINGHAM

AMBASSADOR

BELFAST ◆ GREENVILLE
NORTHERN IRELAND SOUTH CAROLINA

For All Seasons
© 1985 Derick Bingham
First published 1895
Reprinted 1987
This edition 1997

ISBN   1 84030 000 0

Published by
AMBASSADOR PRODUCTIONS LTD,
Providence House
16 Hillview Avenue,
Belfast, BT5 6JR
Northern Ireland

Emerald House,
1 Chick Springs Road, Suite 206
Greenville,
South Carolina 29609
United States of America

DEDICATION

This book is dedicated to Val English,
"who goaded me into writing it" and who takes time out
of the fast lane to eat strawberries.

INTRODUCTION

The fast lane is not what it used to be. Remember those times when you could coast downhill on your bicycle, the wind at your back, the blood tingling in your veins, the hedgerows whizzing by? Bliss!

Not so, today. The motorway has made the whole country a neighbourhood but certainly not a brotherhood. A huge number of people travel on the fast lane and when you join them there is always someone behind flashing lights, beating a horn, scowling and mouthing words trying to get past. When he does he almost gnashes his driving mirror as he glares at you on passing!

I am saying in this book: Slow down. Pull over. Ease the pace. Let others blast on up the fast lane. Let them go. God wants you to notice the seasons of life. He created them. His Word has truth for every one you will pass through. Trust Him and that pounding heart of yours will beat more gently: That ashen face of yours will begin to fill with colour. Let's put the car in the garage and walk through the seasons together. I would love to have the privilege of pointing out a few things on the way. Coming?

Derick Bingham

JANUARY

Short days and long nights. Slowing down time to take a stare at a new year crackling in a log fire. Ice, snow, and wind most mornings on the way to school, work or the Supermarket. Winter without Christmas. Flat batteries, de-icers, and soup coming into its own. A million snowballs thud in a million gales of child and student laughter.

Amid January's icy grip let's drive a few rivets into life's toboggan. I know a master riveter who fastened three thousand rivets in his time. His choicest collection is called Proverbs. His name was Solomon.

JANUARY 1

"Go to the ant . . . and be wise."
Proverbs 6 v 6

No better way to start a new year than a visit to Antshillvania. In an ant colony work is allocated and the guards would die for the guarded. Ants can carry twice their own weight and they can't be deterred or diverted. Present them with a problem and they'll find a way around it. They gather summer and autumn harvest for their winter needs and, incidentally, when they have nothing to do they groom themselves! All this with no guide, and no ruler to give account to. Amazing, that man, created in the image of God, should have to be sent to the tiny ant for instruction. Be wise. Go there often.

JANUARY 2

"Answer not a fool according to his folly."
Proverbs 26 v 4

So a fool has been criticising you. It hurts. You long to silence him. You want to baffle him. The best way to do that is to let him drive you to God and your duty. A man called Rabshakeh intended to frighten a king called Hezekiah from the Lord but, in fact he frightened him to the Lord. Let God shut the fool's mouth, not you. Remember how Joseph handled his brothers? Study Esther handling anti Jewish racism. As a swallow flying up and down will never land on us, so the words of a fool will not hurt us if we are driven to the Lord by them.

JANUARY 3

"How long, ye simple ones, will ye love simplicity?"
Proverbs 1 v 22

Satan knows where I live. He is no fool and he is a
dirty fighter. Let me never say 'But I never thought
he would attack me from that angle.' Don't be naive! We
are not to be ignorant of his devices; he will use
anything or anybody to do his deadly work. Ruin was at
Samson's door but he naively refused to admit it. He fell
from the highest office in the land to be the bald-headed
clown of Philistia. The track is littered with men like
him; Esau, Gehazi, Joab, Judas, Demas. We have been
warned. A prudent man forseeth evil and hideth
himself, but the simple pass on and are punished.

JANUARY 4

*"A fool hath no delight in understanding, but that his
heart may discover itself."*
Proverbs 18 v 2

Listening. It is an art much despised in the western
world. We have two ears and one mouth and should
listen twice as much as we speak. All a fool is interested
in is speaking what is on his mind. Too many people,
unwittingly, join him. Recently at the Crescent Church
in Belfast an Indian answered a question on the problem
of the servant of God and 'crossing cultures'. He
answered; 'You listen first and tell everything
afterwards!' It was excellent advice which we could do
well with heeding.

JANUARY 5

"Death and life are in the power of the tongue: and they that love it shall eat the fruit thereof."
Proverbs 18 v 21

Who would not be careful what seed he puts into a field when he knows that his harvest will be according to his seed? When will we ever learn that an unbelievably rich harvest can be reaped by a single kind word spoken to someone today. Notice in our text there is no middle road: nothing but extremes. Life or death. So Mary said, 'Well if that's true I'll never speak to her again,' 'Nor me either.' 'and I'm telling the elders,' 'If nothings done I'm leaving the church.' 'And me too and my family including my uncle and my cousins.' And all because Mary said. What if Mary had only said good things?

JANUARY 6

"Wine is a mocker, strong drink is raging: and whosoever is deceived thereby is not wise."
Proverbs 20 v 1

A leading surgeon in Belfast's Royal Victoria Hospital recently spoke on the subject of alcohol. 'If you could see inside as many people as I have seen and witnessed what alcohol has done to them, you would not touch it.' he said. Direct talking? Yes. But real. Victims are convinced too late that they have been mocked and grievously deceived. It is frightening to look around the world and see tremendous talents

brutalised by alcohol. We must never forget that the
biblical examples of Noah and Lot are not recorded as
laugh for the ungodly but as a beacon for the saints.
'Drink has drained more blood,' said Evangeline Booth,
'hung more crepe, sold more homes, plunged more
people into bankruptcy, armed more villains, slain more
children, snapped more wedding rings, blinded more
eyes, twisted more limbs, dethroned more intellects,
wrecked more manhood, dishonoured more
womanhood, broken more hearts, blasted more lives,
driven more to suicide, and dug more graves than any
other poisoned scourge that swept its death dealing
waves across the world.'

JANUARY 7

*"A good name is rather to be chosen than great riches,
and loving favour rather than silver and gold."*
Proverbs 22 v 1

Jack London was the world's first millionaire novelist.
'I believe life is a mess.' he said. He was discovered
comatose on the floor, after apparently injecting himself
with an overdose of morphine. Elvis Presley was the
highest paid performer in history. He took pills to get to
sleep. He took pills to get up. He died at forty-two with
ten different drugs in his bloodstream. Marilyn Monroe
said, 'Yes, there was something special about me, and I
knew what it was. I was the kind of girl they found dead
in a hall bedroom with an empty bottle of sleeping pills
in her hand.' She was. At thirty-six. Aristotle Onassis
said: 'I climbed to the top of the financial tree and when
I got there I found nothing.' You have been warned.

JANUARY 8

"By humility and fear of the Lord are riches,
honour and life."
Proverbs 22 v 4

The fear of the Lord is not being scared of God. It is, rather, a wholesome dread of displeasing Him. It is a childlike spirit. It shuts out any terror of conscience. For one who has trusted the Lord Jesus as Saviour the ground of their confidence is their acceptance. They serve Him, not with slavish fear, but, with a happy confidence. It was the fear of the Lord that took the three men with unshaken confidence into the fiery furnace. It was the same fear that caused the paralysed Joni Earickson to cry 'Oh God if you won't let me die. Teach me how to live.' and He did.

JANUARY 9

"It is better to dwell in a corner of the housetop, than
with a brawling woman in a wide house."
Proverbs 21 v 9

It can be very cold on a housetop; every kind of wind and weather fall on it. Better to be there than exposed to a lovely home in an atmosphere of contention. A solitary life upstairs would be better than a quarrelsome life downstairs. Someone has said, 'One never realises how the human voice can change until a woman stops scolding her husband to answer the phone!' So many plunge into marriage never seeking direction in their important choice, and the wife not being sought from the Lord, doesn't come from Him and brings no favour. The epitaph read: 'Beneath this stone, a lump of clay, lies Arabella Young, who on the twenty-fourth of May, began to hold her tongue.' Some women we would be better not knowing!

JANUARY 10

*"A man that flattereth his neighbour spreadeth
a net for his feet."*
Proverbs 29 v 5

You walk into a fearful net if you walk before men rather than before God. Beware of the flatterer! The parasites of Darius made him a god for a month to make him the tool of their malicious plot. David endured Shimie's curse but Ziba's smooth word drew him into an act of heartlessness. Ahab listened to the flattery of lying prophets to his own ruin. Gossip is what you say behind a persons back that you would never say to their face and flattery is what you would say to their face that you would never say behind their back. The flatterer will trap you.

JANUARY 11

*"Withdraw thy foot from thy neighbour's house; lest he
be weary of thee, and so hate thee."*
Proverbs 25 v 17

This is not an anti-neighbour proverb. It is saying that familiarity breeds contempt. Insensitive interruption to our friends' time, frequent visits without call or object, interference with his necessary engagements or family comforts bring weariness, disgust and even hatred. Make the sound of your footstep be more precious by withdrawing it from your neighbour's house more often. Better to ere on the side of reserve than to bring contempt by the opposite. Love your neighbour by letting him see less of you.

JANUARY 12

"Hope deferred maketh the heart sick: but when the desire cometh, it is a tree of life."
Proverbs 13 v 12

Is your heart sick with disappointment? Abraham waited a long time for God's promise of Isaac to materialise. Hagar started out for Egypt but the angel turned her back for a thirteen year wait. What about Israel's seventy year captivity? What of the waiting disciples? But Abraham laughed. Hagar eventually escaped. The Lord turned the captivity of Zion and they were like unto them that dream! The disciples believed not for joy and wondered. Do not despair. The Christian is often tried in his faith but never disappointed of his hope. Never.

JANUARY 13

"The heart knoweth his own bitterness; and a stranger doth not intermeddle with his joy."
Proverbs 14 v 10

Life is, in measure, a solitary path. We are often misunderstood. You know when your heart is wrung. Like Hanna. Like Job. Yet the Lord bears our grief's. His sympathy is no fiction. And joy? Our hearts often know deep down joy, Michal, David's wife, could understand David's bravery but not his joy. She knew him as a man of war, not as a man of God. If you can understand a persons hurts and joys, you will not be strangers any more. Try to.

JANUARY 14

"It is not good to eat much honey: so for men to search their own glory is not glory."
Proverbs 25 v 27

My father-in-law has a little statement which, I often think about. He says 'Some men were great until they discovered they were great and then they were great no longer'. It is victory in essence to be able to trample man's judgement under your feet and eye only God's approval. Honey is good and so is a good name and reputation. But as a dead fly can fall into honey so it will be if you force yourself upon public attention and search out your own glory. James Galway, the world's greatest flautist lay in hospital in Geneva once and said he had learned much from the accident he had just had; 'I was beginning to believe what the posters were saying about me!', he humbly commented. Those who think too much of themselves don't think enough!

JANUARY 15

"It is an honour for a man to cease from strife: but every fool will be meddling."
Proverbs 20 v 3

It is far more difficult to gather back waters once let out than to keep them within bounds. Remember Abraham and Lot? Who won in the end? Abraham gave what he couldn't keep to gain what he couldn't lose. You can feed strife by pride of wanting to strike the last blow instead of extinguishing it by a peaceful loving spirit. The greatest remedy for anger is delay and to keep away from strife is high honour. It is much better to swallow angry words than to have them to eat afterwards.

JANUARY 16

"The sluggard will not plough by reason of the cold;
therefore shall he beg in harvest, and have nothing."
Proverbs 20 v 4

Tell me, when your heart is cold in the service of God does not the most trifling difficulty hinder you? The world can get most of what we have got but God gets mere teaspoonfuls of service from our cold hearts at times. Remember! God can never thank us for service He never saw us doing. What we need in service is a new appreciation of our lovely Lord. Seminars, conferences, meetings, Christian study guides, daily thought calendars will never completely set us ploughing successfully for our Lord. But if we love Him: no valley will be too deep, no mountain too steep, no road too rough, no night too dark, no day too cold to do service for Him. Show me a heart that loves the Saviour and I'll show you a straight furrow ploughed and an eventual harvest that there is not room enough to contain.

JANUARY 17

"Every wise woman buildeth her house: but the foolish
plucketh it down with her hands."
Proverbs 14 v 1

Who would ever estimate the influence of a Christian mother who builds her house to God's glory? If a Christian church is only as good as its women will let it be, what of a Christian home? God put homes together long before He put churches together and a hearth is no hearth unless a woman sits by it. The ship's place is in the sea, but God pity the ship when the sea gets into it: so a foolish woman in a home will wreck it. She is idle. She wastes. She loves pleasure. Her cry seems to be 'In our house, my children rule, OK?' her children's souls are neglected and their happiness ruined. Children have more need of models than of critics and the parent's life is the child's copybook. What will they read in your home today?

JANUARY 18

"Riches profit not in the day of wrath: but righteousness delivereth from death."
Proverbs 11 v 4

A friend of mine was in charge of supervising the technology involved at Belfast Crematorium one day. He stood watching as the ashes came through and there he found what was then called 'a thrupenny bit'. Quietly he said to a colleague, 'One thing is for sure, you can't take it with you!' Fools they are who trust in riches. In the day of wrath a great ransom will not deliver them. If we are hidden in Christ, his righteousness covers us and we have a hope which is an anchor of the soul, both sure and steadfast and entereth into that within the veil. For a believer, death is but a passage out of a prison and into a palace and death stung himself to death when he stung Christ. No Christian has ever been known to recant on his death bed and if we are ready to die we are ready for anything. What hoot of a difference do riches make?

JANUARY 19

"He that hath pity upon the poor lendeth unto the Lord;
and that which he hath given will he pay him again."
Proverbs 19 v 17

Ever heard of a God who puts a desire in your heart, opens the opportunity to fulfil it, and afterwards accepts the act as if it were his own perfect work and you get the reward! Mind bending? Sure it is! Read the proverb again until it gets into your very bloodstream. Give to the poor and the Lord will take the debt upon Himself and give you the bond of His Word in promise of payment. He becomes a debtor of His own even though He has the right to everything! Some people would rather lend to a rich man on earth than to the Lord of heaven. They must be blind to eternal interest rates.

JANUARY 20

"As in water face answereth to face, so the heart
of man to man."
Proverbs 27 v 19

How many times when counselling people, I have heard them say, 'No one knows what I am going through.' They may be surprised. Open up your heart to someone and compare notes and they will immediately identify your complaints. Eternity is in everybody's heart. I once flew 15,000 miles from home to a city in the Far East and preached, amid sweltering heat, soon after getting off the plane. I was exhausted and wondered if the interpretation of my message meant anything to my audience. A man was converted! Well, you could have bowled me over easily. I couldn't believe it. First message and a conversion! Yet, why not? Far Eastern hearts are no different to Irish ones; they all need a Saviour. Sow God's good seed today, it grows in any climate.

JANUARY 21

"Buy the truth, and sell it not."
Proverbs 23 v 23

'Buy off me gold', said the Lord in Revelation 'That thou mayest be rich'. But the rich young man wouldn't buy, would he? Nor Herod either because he wanted to be King, now. Nor Agrippa, nor Demas, nor Judas, nor Esau. But Moses did and gave up the treasures of Egypt for it. Paul counted everything but rubbish compared with it. The Christian martyrs loved not their lives unto death because of it. Trust is not a feeble thing. Truth is power and he is wise who trusts it. There is no stronger argument. It may be daunting but there is nothing better worth knowing. I'll buy this spiritual gold. Will you?

JANUARY 22

"Better is a dinner of herbs where love is, than a stalled ox and hatred therewith."
Proverbs 15 v 17

This proverb is not against that delicious steak dinner you had the other winter's night. It is not meant to put Stakis out of business but it is saying that love sweetens even the meanest food. A celery consommé with your Mary would beat a Steak Diane with a godless crew boozing the night away, would it not? The universe would not fill a worldly heart while a little will suffice a spiritual heart. Love sweetens the meanest meal. The two at Emmaus didn't have much to eat but their Lord was there. It became one of the most satisfying and memorable meals in history. Meat with hatred suffices no one.

JANUARY 23

"As a bird that wandereth from her nest, so is a man that wandereth from his place."
Proverbs 27 v 8

A bird's instinct teaches her that the nest is her base. If she wanders too far from base, danger awaits her. Would that every person heeded this proverb. In this restless, foot-loose-and-fancy-free society, let us be content to remain where God has called us. A person wandering from their place is useless, restless, discontent and exposed to constant temptation. In fact, a lot of people are spiritual gypsies. They want to hear from all but learn from none. Let's do our own work, in the place the Lord has directed us, and stop wandering. Enrich and concentrate your gift today. Don't wander all your life trying to find somebody else's.

JANUARY 24

"To have respect of persons is not good."
Proverbs 28 v 21

'I have known', said an old friend of mine, 'Long haired saints and short back and sides rascals'. Often I think of those wise words. When will we ever learn that things are never as they seem? We go through life having respect of persons and it is not good. The farmer Gideon didn't look much of a military strategist. David didn't look like a king. Ruth the gleaner didn't look like one of Christ's royal line. The fisherman weeping outside the judgement hall didn't look like the mighty evangelist of Pentecost. Saul watching Stephen's martyrdom didn't look the future Paul at Mars Hill. The Indians say, 'Don't criticise a man until you have walked in his moccasins for two moons.' Try it.

JANUARY 25

"Seest thou a man diligent in his business? he shall stand before kings; he shall not stand before mean men."
Proverbs 22 v 29

Henry Martyn of India was known as 'the man who had not lost an hour'. Millions were blessed as a result. I care not where you go, in whatever walk of life, a person who is diligent in the work they have in hand will prosper. Look at Joseph, Daniel, Nehemiah, Paul. Kings took note of them. Even diligence is recognised as virtuous in the world. Did not Scott Fitzgerald, the great novelist, paper his room with rejection slips? He kept at his work though, and prospered. 'What is it like to preach before the Queen?', reporters asked Billy Graham at Sandringham in 1984. 'I preach before the King of Kings every day', answered the mature farm boy from North Carolina. Little is much if God is in it.

JANUARY 26

"A soft tongue breaketh the bone."
Proverbs 25 v 15

The power of gentleness is underestimated. The silent preaching of a lovely life, backed home by gentle words has touched some of the very hardest of hearts. Gentle words also stop future trouble. Is there something you can intend to ultimately deny. Better to break a bone with a soft tongue now than break a few in anger later. Soft words and hard bones may seem a paradox but it is a perfect illustration of the power of gentleness over hardness and irritation. 'Will we see Wesley in Heaven, Mr Whitefield?', asked a critic of Wesley's. 'No,' replied Whitefield, 'he will be so near the Saviour and I will be so far back I shall scarce get a glimpse of him.' Crunch!

JANUARY 27

"Let another man praise thee, and not thine own mouth."
Proverbs 27 v 2

You remember John the Baptist? He was the Morning Star. When you saw his solitary light you knew that the greater light of the Son of God was coming. 'I am unworthy to unloose the latchet of His shoes' he declared. He shone like a Morning Star does with the sun for just a little while and then his light was overwhelmed by the greater light. He was the preacher who lost his congregation. Was he annoyed? 'He must increase and I must decrease', said John. Never a word of praise about himself. Did another praise him? The Saviour said that those born of woman there was none greater than John the Baptist. So, if the Lord blesses me let me remember that I am only a beggar telling other beggars where to find bread. I have found that people are not so concerned about the name over the baker's shop as they are concerned about whether or not you have any bread.

JANUARY 28

"My son, give me thine heart."
Proverbs 23 v 26

'Bingham,' said my English teacher at school when advising me on taking part in the school Debating Society. 'only speak on the subjects your heart is in. If your heart is not in it you are not a good speaker.' No fellow would tell a girl, 'I love you with all my feet', would he? It is not my money, or time, or talents God asks for. He does not ask for pious ceremony and impossible sacrifices. Nor is it my hands or my feet, my ears or my mind. No, it is my heart. Lot's wife had no heart for the separated life and Orpah stopped at the border. God spurns a divided heart but a broken and contrite one He will not despise. Give that and He has all else.

JANUARY 29

"There is that scattereth, and yet increaseth; and there is that witholdeth more than is meet, but it tendeth to poverty."
Proverbs 11 v 24

Misers; they are poor! 'Why', said a friend of mine from County Armagh as she and her husband set off to serve the Lord in France after selling up home and hearth, 'Some Christians are so poor all they have is money!' I know what she meant. Give and you will receive, good measure, pressed down and running over. Hoard and you will lose everything anyway. Think of Lot, he chose the well watered plains. Nothing wrong with well watered plains if God sends you there. But he went without asking the Lord about it and he lost his home, his wife, and his testimony. Abraham scattered and did he increase? World history has never been the same since.

JANUARY 30

"Rejoice not when thine enemy falleth, and let not thine heart be glad when he stumbleth: Lest the Lord see it, and it displease him and he turn away his wrath from him."
Proverbs 24 v 17,18

Private revenge is a canker. Injuries in fact cost more to avenge than to bear. As the fellow said, 'If you lift mud to throw at your enemy you are the one who is losing ground!' It is natural to be happy when our enemy goes under and if we are, the Lord may turn His wrath away from the enemy to the mocker. If we want to hit our enemy with a knockout blow let us hit him with an act of loving-kindness. Come on, let us obey the Lord in this. Let us ask Him to let our enemy cross our path and to set up a circumstance where we can do our enemy good without being in any way condescending. We might be very surprised who will cross our path today in answer to our prayer.

JANUARY 31

"She is not afraid of the snow for her household: for all her household are clothed with scarlet ... Her husband is known in the gates, when he sitteth amongst the elders of the land."
Proverbs 31 v 21-23

On this last day of January we are not reading a proverb about a recluse. Study this character and you will see that she is out and very much about. When the going gets tough, she being tough, gets going. But she is not only tough she's tough and tender. She's got class. She is early and late at her work. She does not look like an unmade bed all day. Her husband is what he is because of her alignment with him. Here is no withdrawn, holier-than-thou individual. Her secret is that she fears the Lord. Rubies couldn't buy her. She is calm and in control amid hectic days. I'm very glad she lives in my house.

FEBRUARY

Always a kind of impatient month. Primroses here and there, snowdrops, willows and catkins. The world of green wishing to break through but, no, not yet, for all the months of the year curse a fair February. We must wait for Spring and waiting is not easy. We will look from the promise to the promiser. And waiting is our theme this month. Have the Scriptures much to say about it? Come and see.

FEBRUARY 1

"Lord, if thou hadst been here, my brother had not died."
John 11 v 32

Imagine scolding the one who never let a planet move, or a star shoot, or a primrose grow one second out of His plan. Why did the Lord Jesus delay to visit the bereaved women at Bethany? Because He wanted to show them that He not only had power over death; He had power over decomposition too. 'Lazarus come forth', He cried. If He had not said 'Lazarus' the whole graveyard would have come forth! His delay became a delight. It always does. So don't, please don't, scold the Lord for delaying on your requests.

FEBRUARY 2

"Because I saw ... that thou camest not within the days appointed."
1 Samuel 13 v 11

Saul, How did the big-souled king become such a shrimp? Good looking, shy, humble, astute and godly he became a raving, jealous, ungodly occult-dabbler. What happened? He was impatient. His men were leaving him and the Philistines were massing and he must DO something! But God's prophet had said, 'Wait for me.' But Saul couldn't wait and rushed in where the prophets fear to tread and went down a slope which slid year by year to a suicides grave. Impatience; it has been the undoing of kings never to speak of their subjects. If the Lord says wait, for any sakes, wait. Cool it, stand back. Let those who may run on and impress everybody. Wait, I say, upon the Lord.

FEBRUARY 3

"They that wait upon the Lord shall renew their strength; they shall mount up with wings as eagles."
Isaiah 40 v 31

Is your activity born out of communication? This verse in no way implies that those who wait upon the Lord aren't busy. Was Nehemiah busy as he waited on the Lord in Shushan? Was Paul busy when he waited on the Lord for guidance about going to Asia? Was Ruth busy as she waited on the Lord for guidance for her future life? Was Eric Liddel busy while he waited for the time to serve God in China? But they all soared. The young eagle flies on air currents created by his parent flying behind him. The will of God for you is to do the legitimate duties of today. God's air currents will carry you far.

FEBRUARY 4

"So Jonah went out of the city ... and there made him a booth, and sat under it in the shadow, till he might see what would become of the city."
Jonah 4 v 5

Reputations are dangerous things and Jonah had one. He was ripping mad that the Lord had not sent destruction upon the city of Ninevah. He should have known that repentance on the part of the people would have brought their reprieve, for this is always implicit in God's warnings. And the Ninevites repented. But Jonah waited and waited and he might as well have caught the next camel home. No point in waiting to enhance your reputation when even the character of God will not allow what you are waiting for.

FEBRUARY 5

"My little daughter lieth at the point of death: I pray thee, come and lay thy hands on her, that she may be healed; and she shall live."
Mark 5 v 23

Poor Jairus. Surely the Master would heal his little girl immediately? But no, he stopped to speak of faith to a woman with a problem. In the mean time , a servant informed him, his child had died. Had waiting meant disaster? Waiting on God never means disaster, no matter how contradictory the circumstance. Jairus found out that the Lord had more than power over illness; He had power over death. Do not panic, spin-dryer stomached friend, God wants to show you more about Himself through holding up on you. There's more, there's more. Ask Jairus.

FEBRUARY 6

"The Lord is good unto them that wait for him."
Lamentations 3 v 25

Elizabeth waited. Mary waited. Hanna waited. Ruth waited. The Bible is full of 'waiters'! Was the Lord good to them? Elizabeth's child turned the people's hearts upside down. Hanna's child turned Israel's history upside down. Mary's child turned the world upside down. Ruth's grandchild was David. And David? He had been promised the kingdom and although he had only been made King of Judah he did not panic, connive or complain. He just sat in Hebron and waited. He never even lifted a finger to claim his rights. And he waited for God to turn events for seven and a half long years. 'And then came all the tribes of Israel ... and anointed David King over Israel'. Beautiful! God will do better for us than we ever can for ourselves. If only we wait for Him!

FEBRUARY 7

"But when the Philistines heard that they had anointed David king over Israel, all the Philistines came up to seek David; and David heard of it, and went down to the hold."
2 Samuel 5 v 17

Nicely settled? Good. God's promises kept in your life? Great. But what now? Napoleon was once approached by an officer who asked him to honour a soldier who had shown outstanding bravery in a recent battle. 'And what' asked Bonaparte, 'did he do the next day?'. David was no sooner settled in Jerusalem than all the Philistines came to get him and not to ask him to a summit at the Gaza Hilton either! Did he get impatient? No. He went to 'the hold' generally reckoned to be the cave of Adullam, and 'enquired of the Lord'. He was back to waiting again but he got his directions and a great victory. So what if you have a sudden reversal in your circumstances today? God is only taking you on a new route to greater blessing.

FEBRUARY 8

"My strength is made perfect in weakness."
2 Corinthians 12 v 9

She lost her foot. Then her leg. Then her arm. What could she do? She wrote with a pen in her mouth and one thousand were led to Christ through her letters from that room in Australia. When asked, 'How do you do it?' she replied, 'Well, you know, Jesus said that they who believed in Him, out of them should flow rivers of living water. I believed Him.' Chained in, hurting one? Don't be like Sir David Baird who was captured and chained to a guard. When his dour old Scots mother heard of it; knowing her son she said, 'Well God have mercy on the poor chap that is chained to our Davy!'

FEBRUARY 9

*"Fear thou not; for I am with thee: be not dismayed;
for I am thy God."*
Isaiah 41 v 10

Gloom? With you. Enemies? Be not dismayed. Not feeling well? I will strengthen you. Insurmountable difficulties? I will help you. Wandering and falling? I will uphold you with the right hand of my righteousness. God has not brought you across the Atlantic to drown you in a ditch.

A friend of mine was badly hurt in the face after a bomb explosion in Ulster. 'What have you learned from it?', I asked him. 'I have learned that if God can bring order out of the chaos of the cross he can bring order out of the chaos of my face.' he replied. Dismay must never be allowed to rule in our lives and lead us to panic. Never.

FEBRUARY 10

*"To Him who is able to do exceedingly abundantly
above all that we ask or think."*
Ephesians 3 v 20

You wouldn't think it to look at us! A lot of us live like sons and daughters on a Sunday and like orphans the rest of the week. Relating to the Lord Jesus the Christian finds that the Lord meets his need fully and eternally. That is why he should be at peace. Physical needs? The Lord says he will have food, clothing and shelter. Security? Christ died for him. Purpose? For him to live is Christ and to die is gain. Loved? God's thoughts about him are more than the sand on the seashore. Live today as if you really believe today's verse and, a wee word in your ear; 'Go and count a handful of sand!'.

FEBRUARY 11

*"Bel boweth down, Nebo stoopeth ... they could not deliver
the burden ... even to hoar hairs will I carry you ... even
I will carry, and will deliver you."*
Isaiah 46 v 1-4

Those Israelites waited seventy years for Bel and
Nebo, the Babylonian gods to fall. And fall they did.
They were pitched into the back of wagons and were
carried away. Those gods were no burden bearers but
ours is.

'It's the people with the money who are the royalty
now', said Aristotle Onassis. 'We are more popular than
Jesus Christ', said John Lennon while travelling in
America's Bible belt. Ah! but where, oh, where are they
now? God will never fail. He assumes the responsibility
of carrying the burdens of those who wait for Him. The
burden of existence, of sin, of responsibility for others, of
our life's work. He posted us to our duty and He is
responsible for all that is needed for accomplishment of
His purposes. He will not forsake the work of his own
hands. Trust Him.

FEBRUARY 12

*"Yet did not the chief butler remember Joseph,
but forgat him."*
Genesis 40 v 23

Joseph had waited. Years had gone by but now
suddenly, there was a ray of hope. The butler would
pass the word. Joseph had interpreted his dream and in
three days the butler was restored to his former
employment. Surely a couple of days would see Joseph
reprieved. But no word came. Days passed. Months.

Two full years. The fact that the Lord gave Joseph an ability to predict someone else's future didn't mean he had supernatural ability to predict his own. His hope lay in fact, not in the butler, not in Pharaoh or Potiphar, but in God. This enabled him to endure. Don't hope too much in those people you have helped. You are convinced they will help you. They will probably forget all about you. Don't wait for them. Wait for God.

FEBRUARY 13

"But the Lord had shut up her womb."
1 Samuel 1 v 5

Do some childless eyes scan this book today? Time, who heals so many sorrows keeps yours ever freshly aching. Day and night, asleep or waking, you mourn your loss. You have waited long but the Lord has said 'No'. Yet, have not childless people become some of the greatest youth workers in the world? In ministering to the world's childhood they have lost their own loneliness and longing. There are children without fathers and mothers but there are certainly children who would be better off if they had none. Such children call not for sorrow but for service. Go to it.

FEBRUARY 14

"Be still, and know that I am God."
Psalm 46 v 10

All-work-and-no-play makes me happy. That's what a lot of folks believe. Is it true? Look around you. It isn't. There are millions of people, and particularly

Christian people, who think that to relax and stop is almost a sin. They feel guilty about it. The big word in these days is 'Are you busy?'. If you reply 'No, I'm just eating my Aero bar', they think, 'What a lazy fellow'. The ultimate 20th century comment is 'I don't know how she gets so much done' or 'He's a very hard man to get'. It's all wrong. Snapping at your children? Choking food down at meal times? Hate interruptions? Can't wait? In the final analysis it will be your use of leisure that will be far more important than the hours you spend working.

FEBRUARY 15

"Wise men, which knew the times."
Esther 1 v 13

'If you preach the Gospel in all aspects with the exception of the issues which deals specifically with your time, you are not preaching the Gospel'. Did some American T.V. preacher, hot foot from the studio lights say that? Was it some teenager who was trying to act smart with his peers? No. Some young preacher, perhaps, fresh out of school? No. It was Martin Luther the sixteenth century monk. So we need, Mr. Preacher, your God given gift to put the hay down where the sheep can get at it. Miss doing this and you'll miss reaching your generation for Christ. Are you a Sunday School teacher: freshen up on your communication! Children need it too. Wait a while to listen to what the people are saying and take note of what is worrying them. Then, get in there with the message of God's word where the people are hurting.

FEBRUARY 16

"He that waiteth on his master shall be honoured."
Proverbs 27 v 18

Fidelity is hardly an honoured word in our society. No matter what the storm, the Christian must always be true to the Lord. He will guide us with his eyes, like a surgeon guides a nurse in an operating theatre or like a father guides his child by a look. Think of that amazing character sent to find a wife for Isaac, by his master. Eliezer's task must have been one of the most difficult ever. How would you have fared in his sandals? You say 'I found it hard enough to find a wife for myself never to speak of one for someone else!'. But he listened to and waited on his master and obeyed him to the letter and Rebekah was found. There are no exceptions in the service of the divine master. We are His servants, we wait on Him and His honour is ours. Who cares who gets the credit as long as God is honoured? Waiting on Him glorifies His name.

FEBRUARY 17

"Jesus wept."
John 11 v 35

All this teaching on waiting on the Lord may give some the impression that the patient Christian would never give way to tears. The idea does get thrown around. A lady said to me recently 'Some Christians say that I was letting the Lord down because I cried so much at my husbands death'. The Bible knows nothing of such dehumanising rubbish. 'Weep with those that weep' it demands. Often our embarrassment in the presence of mourners betrays a failure to do just that. Grief, to be cured, has to be expressed. The example of our Lord Jesus and His tears, stands. Stoicism (the 'stiff upper lip') is a heathen philosophy.

FEBRUARY 18

*"And there was a famine in the land: and Abram
went down into Egypt."*
Genesis 12 v 10

M ark my words: the circumstances of life often
seem to contradict the promises of God. The land
was promised to Abraham, the stars were as many as
his promised children. After years of waiting he got
the land, and there was a famine in it! He panicked and
rushed out of God's will to Egypt where he lied and
very nearly wrecked his life. When will we ever learn
that waiting is winning? Walk in the conscious
knowledge that you are beloved of the Lord. He turns
famines into feasts. He makes crooked places straight.
He makes mountains into molehills. Don't be like
Abraham who had to learn the hard way. Please.

FEBRUARY 19

*"God .. made .. a woman, and brought her unto
the man."*
Genesis 2 v 22

A wife is not meant to be her husbands echo. She is
his counterpart. She provides the missing pieces to
the puzzle of his life. Without her he is incomplete and
he should never deny it. His helpmeet does not mean his
skivvy but the one who assists to complete fulfilment.
Subjection to a husband should never mean slavery. The
way some men behave one would think it was a sign of
incredible weakness to wash a dish. Marriage is not the
federation of two sovereign states, it is the coming
together of two tributaries. It's worth waiting for.

FEBRUARY 20

"Go after that which is lost."
Luke 15 v 4

Dr. Leighton Ford recently told the story about his little girl Debbie. Debbie failed to return home from school and there was a frantic panic until she turned up two hours later having been eating ice-cream at a relative's! 'The thought struck me afterwards' said Dr. Ford, 'I had letters to write, phone calls to make, preparation to do and yet all I could think of for those two hours was that my little girl was lost'. It is true. Sometimes legitimate things will have to wait because we have a higher priority. If you were sinking on the Titanic would you spend your time re-arranging the deck chairs?

FEBRUARY 21

"And it came to pass after a while that the brook dried up."
1 Kings 17 v 7

Has your brook dried up? Should you wait for it to fill again? You might be dead before it does. There is a time to wait and there is a time to go. God commanded Elijah to move on and ask for help. Elijah obeyed, went to Sareptha in God's will and a miracle occurred as a result. It may be time for you to move on too, in the will of God, and unashamedly ask for help. 'Never!' you might say, 'I never make my need known'. Be careful my friend, there is a time to wait for help and there is a time to go and ask for it. There may be someone today who is longing to help you and you're denying them that opportunity. Share your heartache with a trusted friend. You may be amazed to find that it is the greatest compliment you could ever pass them.

FEBRUARY 22

"Unto thee will I cry, O Lord my rock; be not silent to me."
Psalm 28 v 1

While waiting for God's guidance in a matter, have you ever experienced the silence of God? We sometimes interpret it to mean that God is angry with us. This is not necessarily so. God was silent to Job and could not have been more for him. God was silent to John the Baptist regarding John's execution but said that there was none better than John. God was silent to Paul about the meaning of his illness but blessed him immensely. If you have heard God speak you can bear His silences. Anyway, speech is only good when it is better that silence.

FEBRUARY 23

"The meek .. shall inherit the earth."
Matthew 5 v 5

'Glory to the microchip in the highest. See what it has done.' This seems to be the 20th century motto. From space walking to microwave ovens in the kitchen the microchip is the nation's shepherd, Silicon Valley software its fold. A Christian on his knees seems no programme at all. To turn the other cheek and to return good for evil seems mild in comparison with Star Wars. The all powerful Herod and the invincible Romans seemed so strong in comparison to a Saviour hanging on a cross. He had the power to wipe them out but he didn't use it. If you think meekness is weakness try being meek for a week. But where is Herod now? Rome is Mediterranean rubble. The meek shall inherit the earth. Just wait.

FEBRUARY 24

"Love the Lord thy God with all .. thy mind."
Matthew 22 v 37

Not to think and use your mind is a sin. God's promise of guidance are not given to save us the bother of thinking. Sow a thought: reap an act. Sow an act: reap a character. Sow a character: reap a destiny. And all because of a thought. Thoughts in fact, are heard in heaven. So we must let the Holy Spirit move in our minds and be president of our thinking because five words in the Spirit are better than ten thousand in an unknown tongue. As you wait upon God today ask Him to control your mind until every thought is brought into captivity. If that happens I would just love to be in your company today. You would be worth talking to.

FEBRUARY 25

"And to wait for his Son from heaven."
1 Thessalonians 1 v 10

'At what time do you think the Lord will return?', asked Robert Murray McCheyne. 'Oh, I think in the morning', said one. 'I think at night', replied another. 'I think perhaps in the afternoon', quipped a third. 'Ah!', said Robert, 'Remember that Jesus said at such a time as you think not, He will return'. Every day we must be found waiting, not star gazing. We are not waiting for death, we are waiting for Him. Many will be surprised at His coming but no one mistaken. So while waiting for the King, His subjects get busy. Because He is coming that vicious vindicating letter is never written, the hard word remains unsaid, the split in the church never comes from our corner, the phone is never used to 'tear strips'. The Judge is at the door. He'll handle it.

FEBRUARY 26

"The love of God is shed abroad in our hearts."
Romans 5 v 5

'They have not got the love of God in their hearts', said my friend Muriel commenting on such unchristian behaviour. Often I think of her words. As that man swears, remember he often does not know what he is actually doing. As that girl smokes herself to death, it may be the only comfort she knows. As that fellow raves and rages, he has Satan controlling his heart. As that drunk curses you, he may have never tasted living water. Christians often forget their privileges and that they now have the advantage of God's love in their hearts. Be patient. Communicate God's work at all levels and don't give up sowing seed because the conditions are poor. Bigots become gentle Christians. Ask Paul. Drunkards become church elders. Ask the Corinthian Christians. Sceptics become worshippers. Ask Nathaniel.

FEBRUARY 27

"Go thy way for this time; when I have a convenient season, I will call for thee."
Acts 24 v 25

Let us balance this teaching on waiting. Felix put off obeying Paul's message because of procrastination. Waiting is important but there are certain things which must be dealt with now. Procrastination is a slick operator and you would walk with him arm in arm to ruin. He can steal an incentive and strip you of your priceless treasures. 'You have bought some land so you can't go', he says. 'You have bought some yolk of oxen and you must needs prove them', he whispers. 'You have married a wife therefore you cannot go', he finalises. He did not tell Felix there was no Hell he just said there was no hurry. Kill time and you murder opportunity.

FEBRUARY 28

"Twenty and five years old was he when he began to reign .. after him was none like .. for he clave to the Lord .. and the Lord was with him; and he prospered."
2 Kings 18 v 2-7

We finish February's readings with Hezekiah: soldier, statesman, architect, poet and saint. He was the only man who ever knew just how long he had left to live. God told him he had fifteen years left and after waiting for the Lord's directions he went into action. In those fifteen years he arranged for the transmission of the Old Testament scriptures and formed a special guild of men specially set apart for such devout literary work. He shaped, among other things, the book of Psalms and Proverbs. Every time people lift the Scriptures today they are indebted to the way Hezekiah spent those fifteen years.

As we have waited on God so now we must go God. Our time is short. We must live, like Hezekiah, so as to be missed. Our motto as we go into March should be: the will of God, nothing less, nothing more, nothing else, and at all costs, for lost time is never found.

MARCH

The Anglo Saxons called it 'Hlyd Monath': the stormy month. As the man said 'March'll search you'. She comes in like a lion and few speak in praise of her. But the lion goes out like a lamb and from her springs Spring. 'Daffodils come,', said one William Shakespeare, 'before the swallow dares and takes the winds of March with beauty'. So, this month, we shall study just about the most neglected book in the Bible, Job. His life comes into Scripture hounded by the lion of trouble but goes out like a lamb of incredible beauty and gentleness. Job, like the thrush of March, sang his song twice over 'Lest you should think he never could recapture that first fine careless rapture'.

MARCH 1

"Doth Job fear God for nought?"
Job 1 v 9

He was a very unique man. 'None like him', said God. '£395,000 at today's prices', has been the estimated value of his livestock. He also had a happy family whose value cannot be valued at any price. Then Satan hit him where it hurt. The arch cynic said he-was-in-it-for-the-money. His godliness was artificial. Who would not serve so munificent a God? Take away his gains and see if his goodness went with them. Till Christ came no soul ever made such a battleground between Heaven and Hell as Job's. Is Satan trying the same tactic with you? God allowed Satan to attack and it was no cruel experiment. The path of danger was the path of honour. Job was to prove that a person is capable of loving right, simply because it is right, and hating wrong, even though he didn't gain by it, but lose. Care to join him?

MARCH 2

"The Sabeans fell upon them .. the fire of God (lightening) is fallen .. there came a great wind .. and smote the four corners of the house, and it fell upon the young men, and they are dead."
Job 1 v15-19

Never forget God initiated the whole drama of events that hit Job, not Satan. The terrorism, the lightening, the cyclone, they all appeared to be so natural to every day life in the East that the hand of God was concealed. Financial collapse and death by storm are not a problem to the atheist, the fatalist or the materialist. A tragedy, yes, 'But sure they happen every day,', they will tell you, 'you win some and you lose some.' It is a problem for the believer in a good and almighty God though. Ethiopian famine? Mrs Ghandi? Brighton? South America? If all of life were rational and could be explained there would be no gap between God and man: that gap only the Cross of Calvary can span. God does not always explain himself and He never did so with Job. A night of pain will bring you closer to God than years of ordinary living. Suffering is God's megaphone to the deaf.

MARCH 3

"Skin for skin, yea, all that a man hath will he give for his life."
Job 2 v 4

L et no one fool you. The devil is a real person, not just a mere evil force. His single ambition is to turn us away from God. He strikes all the harder at those who are walking with God and the closer you walk the harder he strikes. But his power is limited. Submit to God and resist the devil and he will flee from you. Watch Job resist. 'As long as Job walks in his skin you'll never know his true nature', sneers Satan. 'He doesn't care much that the business went down or that his family is dead: take his health away and you'll see the selfish nature of his faith.' His health goes but his faith held. Remember that it is not the will of God that we should all be healed of our diseases. Through these skin diseases of Job's untold millions were to be blessed as a result of his faithfulness in illness. God will either lead us out of our affliction, or, give us grace to bear it.

MARCH 4

"Then said his wife unto him .. curse God, and die."
Job 2 v 9

Satan controls people (John 8 v 44), tempts people
(John 13), sifts people (Luke 22 v 31), overcomes
people (2 Corinthians 2 v 11), devours people (1 Peter 5
v 8), hinders people (1 Thessalonians. 2 v 18), falsely
accuses people (Revelation 12 v 10), deceives people
(Revelation 20 v 10) and can cause a man's wife to ditch
him. It is amazing how that by one statement one person
can be remembered. Satan's open temptation could not
bring Job down so he came more subtly through the lips
of a loving wife, half maddened by intolerable misery.
Job's wife represents the person who speaks well of God
when all is going smoothly, but, when trouble comes,
they forget all about the Lord's unfailing grace. How
very different the words of Catherine Booth who said,
when dying, 'The waters are rising but I am not sinking!'
Are you a fair weather Christian?

MARCH 5

*"What? shall we receive good at the hand of God, and shall
we not receive evil (adversity)? In all this did not Job sin
with his lips."*
Job 2 v 10

The going now gets really tough for Job. His trials
were rough up until now but the pressure of his
wife and his three friends put him under is more than all
the other things that have happened him so far. Get a
grip on that word 'receive'. It is a good, active word

implying co-operation with God, not just mere submission. Such faith turns everything it touches to spiritual gold, for when smooth as well as rough times are received at the hand of God, every experience of life becomes an occasion of blessing. But the cost is great. It is easier to lower your view of God than to raise your faith to such a height. The word 'chance' is a non-starter for the Christian. It might be used in a game of Monopoly but it won't do on the royal route to Heaven. Nothing, no nothing, happens to the Christian by chance.

MARCH 6

"Now when Job's three friends heard of all this .. they sat down with him upon the ground seven days and seven nights, and none spake a word unto him: for they saw that his grief was very great."
Job 2 v 11-13

The stage is now set for a 'fierce' argument. These men were genuine and sincere but their theology was poisoned. The disfigured, unrecognisable Job was at rock bottom so they said nothing for seven days, but, when they were to get going their poisoned theology was to nearly tear him apart. They believe that God afflicts men only for their sins: God is good to the good and bad to the bad. But Job believes God is not punishing him for his sins and brings him to this dilemma: 'Is God unjust?' These fellows only questioned Job's integrity: Job was concerned about God's. Through it all Job was to find God true and was to cleave to and trust the one he could no longer comprehend. So must we.

MARCH 7

"After this opened Job his mouth and cursed his day .. and said let the day perish wherein I was born .. wherefore is light given to him that is in misery, and life unto the bitter in soul."
Job 3 v 1-3,20

Ever feel you want to die? You are not the first. Poor Job, he found life at this stage intolerable and death desirable. To curse in Hebrew means 'to wish a catastrophe on'. The Western practice of cursing i.e. profane language is never referred to in the Scriptures. Job is talking about how wretched human existence can be. Job had not cracked under the strain and, in fact, self control is something quite different from showing one's emotions. At the end of this speech Job says, 'I cannot relax! I cannot settle! I cannot rest! Agitation keeps coming back!' Job is looking in and if we do that we are trapped and we will be in a muddle. We need an intention. We need a goal. Let's not lose it. I've heard of people who cursed the day of their birth but I've never heard of any who cursed the day of their new birth. Have you?

MARCH 8

"Behold, thou hast instructed many, and thou hast strengthened the weak hands. Thy words have upholden him that was falling .. but now .. it toucheth thee, thou art troubled."
Job 4 v 3-5

Eliphaz is Job's first friend to speak to him in his trouble and, frankly, a little sympathy from him would have been worth a good deal of theology.

Bystanders are always of a more logical turn. This jibe must have hurt Job severely. It implies that he had failed to live up to what he had taught. Has such a jibe been driven into your heart? Maybe at school, or work, trouble has come to you and they say, 'Let's see how you react Christian!'

A Christian had a deformed child born to him and his workmates jibed, 'But we do not believe in God and look at our healthy children!' Quietly the Christian replied, 'Isn't it a good thing, then, that when God allowed such a child to be born, he allowed him to be born of me?'

MARCH 9

"Although affliction cometh not forth of the dust, neither doth trouble spring out of the ground; yet man is born unto trouble, as the sparks fly upward.'
Job 5 v 6-7

Testing in life and trouble do not merely happen, they are to be expected. Some people get all excited when trouble comes as though such a thing is unusual. 'Why,' said Peter, 'think it not strange concerning the fiery trial which is to try you, as though some strange thing happened unto you?' We may say, 'Why can't He change things? Why doesn't He relieve any suffering?' He could change all of it if He wanted to and, if it were for our good, He would. The fact that we are not receiving immediate relief from our suffering, strongly suggests that there is some hidden mission. God wants to work in us so that some new power of usefulness and service will be gained through our trial. Accept your trial from the hand of God.

MARCH 10

"My brethren have dealt deceitfully as a brook, and as the stream of brooks they pass away."
Job 6 v 15

Ever learn about wadi streams in Geography at school? In the East a sudden rain can fill a dry creek with rushing flood water. The problem is it vanishes just as quickly into the porous rock. Job's friends seemed so full of tender, considerate kindness but like the wadi stream they cheated and mocked all those who trusted in them. Like the Eastern caravans, cheated by the treacherous torrent, there was nothing left but to return to the desert and die, so, Job, shrinks back into his misery. For any sakes, do not put all your trust in people. They can be treacherous, they can fail to deliver. How different are Isaiah's words to all who trust the Saviour: 'and a man shall be as an hiding place from the wind, and a covert from the tempest; as rivers of water in a dry place, as the shadow of a great rock in a weary land (Isaiah 32 v 1-2).' Hide in Him today no matter what.

MARCH 11

"Let me alone; for my days are vanity."
Job 7 v 16

Depression is a giant in so many lives. In fact, the Christian's chief occupational hazards are depression and discouragement. How many people have reached the point Job reached when he reckoned everything was pointless and all he wanted to do was to be left alone? Are you in despair today? Despair cuts the sinews of endeavour. Job could not see as yet that many of the calamities which come on people are only undeserved in the sense that the people have not and cannot deserve so great a blessing as they disguise and contain. Caleb waited forty five years to realise God's promises to him despite giants in the land. Difficulties are God's errands and when we are sent upon them we should esteem it as proof of God's confidence. Let me alone? Thank God, you never will be.

MARCH 12

"Behold, God will not cast away a perfect man, neither will he help the evil doers."
Job 8 v 20

This is Bildad's God-is-good-to-the-good-and-bad-to-the-bad theology and he is telling Job that his calamities are because he has sinned. Let's nail this beggarly theology once and for all. Always remember that good does come to the good and bad does come to the bad but it is also true that what may seem terribly evil in itself is allowed to come to the good and good does come to evil people in order that they may renounce evil and cleave to the good. Bildad's statement is just a platitude and platitudes can be trite and cruel things when spoken to people in trouble. Was not Bildad's platitude the very thing they cast at the Saviour as he hung on Calvary? 'He trusts in God, let Him deliver Him.' Because God did not deliver Christ did not mean he had sinned. Seeming dereliction does not imply error on your part. Don't listen to Mr. Bildad on the reason for suffering. Please.

MARCH 13

*"For he is not a man, as I am, that I should answer him ..
neither is there any days man betwixt us, that might
lay his hand upon us both."*
Job 9 v 32-33

The continual problem of the book of Job is not the
problem of suffering and a looking for the ultimate
intellectual answer to explain it. No. It is a right
relationship with God for which the hunt is on. If that is
in order then you can bear suffering: it makes it
acceptable. Job is looking for an umpire, a mediator, a
common friend who can reach both God and himself
and impose his authority. Amazing that here, reverently
speaking, in an alley of an ancient book is a theme which
joins up with the road which joins up with the motorway
which leads to the heart of the metropolis of all
Scripture: the Lord Jesus. I have a great need for Christ
then I have a great Christ for my need!

MARCH 14

"My soul is weary of my life."
Job 10 v 1

Nobody can tell me the Bible is an unreal book. As
this month of March howls along we have been
studying the very soul of a man going through tough
times. Here Job speaks of his utter weariness of life. How
can I tell whose eyes will scan this reading? Maybe
someone ready to cave in, utterly weary of life, hurting
until there seems no more new hurts which can be
invented. The burden of children, work, bills, repairs,
sickness and impossible people are all piling in. Weary
one, remember John Calvin's word: 'Afflictions ought
ever to be estimated by their end.' It will pass and when
your trials are through you will find you have learnt more
under the rod that struck you than under the staff that
comforts you. Job will soon change his tune. You'll see.

MARCH 15

"Should a man full of talk be justified?"
Job 11 v 2

Zophar, Job's third friend, now enters the fray. He
calls Job a babbler, a 'from-the-teeth-outward' sort
of man. How very easy it is to shoot at a skylark but
how very difficult to produce its song. To speak ill of
others is often a dishonest way of praising ourselves.
Zophar is a man who bigoted and takes up the options
in vogue at the time and delivers them as his. Since his
neighbours agree with him then it must be right, he
thinks; but it wasn't. He was often way out of line in his
talk. Let's not be like him with these judgements on
others. Let's remember that the best place to criticise
your neighbour is in front of your own mirror.

MARCH 16

*"The Lord .. in whose hand is .. every living thing, and the
breath of all mankind."*
Job 12 v 9-10

We have lost our sense of worship. The God we
present to the people rarely astonishes anybody.
We go to Him like we go to the supermarket: he is 'the
need meeter'. The last thing in the world the devil
knows we are liable to be in our public services is to be
'lost in wonder, love and praise'. We are no longer
fascinated, captivated, nor entranced with him. Do we
love God with fear and wonder and yearning and drive?
Job shows himself to be more than an honest observer.
Read Job chapter 12, and your mind will reel at his
immense concept of God. With Job's appreciation of God
ringing in our hearts let's test the soundness and
ultimate worth of everything by the place our Lord
occupies in it. It will make a difference to our day for
sure. Try it.

MARCH 17

"O that ye would altogether hold your peace! and it should be your wisdom."
Job 13 v 5

Better to be thought a fool than to open your mouth and remove all doubt. Even a fool, Solomon noted, when he holds his peace is counted wise. Job is devastating in his condemnation of his friend's multitude of words. Why is it that we have to be always giving our opinion? If we had the slightest clue as to the incredible power of words we would chose them carefully to the ultimate good of those around us. Think all you speak but do not be like Job's friends and speak all you think, for speech is the index of the mind, and, uncontrolled tongues are the devil's bellows.

MARCH 18

"So man lieth down, and riseth not: till the heavens be no more, they shall not awake."
Job 14 v 12

Some try to prove from this statement of Job's that there is no Hell, that people become extinct after death. There is nothing like that stated here. It is only the body that lies down and goes back to dust. The soul leaves the body at physical death, 'For,' James said, 'as the body without the spirit is dead, so faith without works is dead also.' The message of the Gospel is not a helpless child in it's mother's arms, a dead man upon a cross, or a stern Judge in the future, so often depicted by Christian artists. The message is an empty tomb! The best news the world ever heard came from a graveyard. And because He lives, we shall live also.

MARCH 19

*"Hast thou heard the secret of God? .. What knowest thou,
that we know not?"*
Job 15 v 8-9

Eliphaz has been stung by Job's answers to his
pontifications. He is ripping mad and at the
beginning of his speech had called Job a wind bag. Now
he takes a figure from the divan of an Oriental prince on
which state secrets were discussed and the sarcastic
insinuation of it is that no man could be so wise as Job
pretended to be unless he frequented the council
chamber of the Almighty. It is an attitude many a
Christian has to bear from his enemies today. Yet, did
not the Almighty withhold state secrets from the High
Priest Eli and reveal them to little Samuel? God hides
things from the wise and prudent and reveals them even
to babes. Do you have his ear today? Have you heard
the secret of God? You can.

MARCH 20

*"My friends scorn me: but mine eye poureth out tears unto
God. O that one might plead for a man with God, as a man
pleadeth for his neighbour!"*
Job 16 v 21

Here we see Job struggling with two Gods. There is
the God of imaginary current theology who afflicts
him because He hates him and the real and only true
God who loves him while He afflicts him. This true God
is witnessing to Job in Heaven while here on earth He is
striving with him. That is the God to whom Job appeals.
Job is struggling towards the light and it is coming: it is
that the true God is far beyond such poor conceptions of
Him as we might have. Job has all along been appealing
from God to men, now he appeals from men to God.
Men mock his innocence so he turns from them to Him.
So must we.

MARCH 21

"Who is he that will strike hands with me?"
Job 17 v 3

This verse is somewhat akin to the old method of bargaining by striking hands, still alive at livestock fairs in Europe. The 'striking hands' confirm the agreement. But no one will strike hands with Job. His friends disagree with him. The bitterest hurt in life is to be wounded 'in the house of your friends'. There is always an intangible something which makes a friend: it is not what he does but what he is. To be with him is ease, it is for the better. A friend has a reverent sympathy with what he does not understand but Job's friends have stopped giving him this kind of sympathy. They know it all so they babble on. Is that what we do?

MARCH 22

"Shall the earth be forsaken for thee? and shall the rock be removed out of this place?"
Job 18 v 4

Mr. Bildad now continues his withdrawal of sympathy from Job and covers his retreat in a cloud of rhetoric. 'Do you want the whole universe to be reconstructed to suit you Job?' he asks. A speaker who has run out of ideas can always resort to satire. Bildad is no pastor nor skilled counsellor. In fact, in this world there are few. Kindness and compassion should rule all pastoring of suffering people. The deaf can hear kindness and blind can see it. 'Biblical orthodoxy without compassion is surely the ugliest thing in the world', wrote Francis Schaeffer. How much uglier are the Bildads who think they are full of the orthodoxy and compassion and they have neither? If we could see ourselves as the others see us we would do a U-turn!

MARCH 23

*"Have pity upon me, have pity upon me, O ye my friends;
for the hand of God hath touched me."*
Job 19 v 21

Oswald Chambers, writing of the Great War, said an amazing thing. He said, 'There is no reasonable hope for countless lives on account of this War and it is shallow nonsense to tell them to 'cheer up': life to them is a terrible darkness of the most appalling order. The one who preaches at such a time is an impertinence but the one who says 'I don't know why you are going through this, it is black and desperate but I will wait with you' is an unspeakable benediction and sustaining'. Job had no one to do that for him. Has your suffering friend got one?

MARCH 24

*"For I know that my redeemer liveth, and that he shall
stand at the latter day upon the earth: and though after my
skin worms destroy this body, yet in my flesh shall I see
God."*
Job 19 v 25-26

This is Job's greatest statement and millions of people believe it to encapsulate everything they believe about immorality. In this study of Job we have seen God as umpire, judge, advocate, witness and sponsor. Here Job speaks of God as the redeemer. God will interpose and rescue Job and so Job plants the flag of victory upon his own grave. 'This is the victory that overcometh .. even our faith' and it means that we must live as a people who are prepared to die and die as a people who are prepared to live. A faith like Job's is bound to win through. Have you got it? Don't be like the folk one minister of my acquaintance described: 'Why Derick,' he said, 'some of them are spiritual atheists.'

MARCH 25

"Hearken unto this, O Job: stand still, and consider the wondrous works of God."
Job 37 v 14

Enter Elihu. Not mentioned with Job's true friends earlier in the book he has, nevertheless, been listening to all the talk. He is the youngest speaker and tries to act as mediator. Some have called him a conceited young philosopher, others an impudent intruder. All I can say is that today's verse is very good advice. If I were to walk into your home today I could learn a lot about your tastes and interests by the colours and objects you have chosen for your interior decoration. So it is in God's creation. When you look at the stars you are thinking God's thoughts after Him. When you smell a rose you are learning what kind of delicate touch He is capable of. How can you say he is narrow minded? 'Go stand and stare awhile, Job' advises Elihu. Good advice for 20th century workaholics too. Even joggers won't stand still to let your car past!

MARCH 26

"Then the Lord answered Job out of the whirlwind, and said .. who shut up the sea with doors .. who .. divided .. a way for the lightning or thunder .. who hath given understanding to the heart?"
Job 38

It's been a long time, in our study of the book of Job since we have heard God actually speak to Job. Some of the most difficult questions in all the universe have been grabbed by the throat and hurled skywards in all the discussions of the five men in the book of Job. Now comes the answer. Is it academic? Is it a deep and involved theological argument? Would you need a course in semantics to understand it? Never! 'See what I have DONE', says God to Job. From chapter 38-41 what He has done covers everything from the eagle in flight to the cedar tree, from a horse in battle to the whale in the ocean, from lightening in the sky to the human heart. It seems to me that what the book of Job is saying to us all is that we ask too many questions and don't worship enough. True?

MARCH 27

"Then Job answered the Lord, and said, Behold, I am of small account; what shall I answer thee? I will lay mine hand upon my mouth. Once have I spoken, but I will not answer: yea twice; but I will proceed no further."
Job 40 v 3-5

My, what a contrast! Thousands upon thousands of words have poured out of Job regarding why he has suffered and now, after God has given him a conducted tour of His creation, Job is speechless. Will this not be the way we react when we see God face to face? We will not say: 'Why did I not get that employment? Why was I ill? Why did the firm I booked my holiday with go broke? Why did our Jane fail her exams? Why did Tom never ask me to marry him?' We will see God, then, and questions will be superfluous. Meanwhile, He comforteth.

MARCH 28

"I have heard of thee by the hearing of the ear: but now mine eye seeth thee."
Job 42 v 5

This majestic statement of Job's shows just how finite our knowledge of God is. We speak of Him. We sing of Him. We worship Him. We think we are beginning to know Him. Yet, we are as one who has but heard of someone. Wait, oh wait, until your eyes behold Him. God is the cause of causes. If He were not, nothing could be. He can make a straight line with a crooked stick and He is faithful to all who trust Him. But, oh, to SEE Him. Soon and very soon, we are going to see the King. Hallelujah!

MARCH 29

"And it was so, that after the Lord had spoken these words unto Job, the Lord said to Eliphaz .. My wrath is kindled against thee, and against thy two friends: for ye have not spoken of me the thing that is right, as my servant Job hath."
Job 42 v 7

Eliphaz got a mighty shock. The thing reeled in his mind: all his talk of God was not right! The poor, despised, suffering, bewildered, questioning Job had spoken truth about God after all. And God was well pleased.
In a cemetery in Bangor, Co. Down, stands a grave stone I quite often visit. The wording on it draws me there. It reads; 'William Patison Nicholson, Evangelist. The man did no miracle but all the things that he spake of Him (Jesus) were true. And many believed on Him there.' It is, in my view, an epitaph of epitaphs. Agreed?

MARCH 30

"And the Lord turned the captivity of Job, when he prayed for his friends."
Job 42 v 10

Imagine praying for three friends who had, in fact, brought you more trouble than all of your other troubles combined. The Irish hymn writer, Joseph Scriven, who himself suffered great personal loss, certainly caught the spirit of today's text in his lines: 'Do thy friends despise, forsake thee? Take it to the Lord in prayer.' You see, the person who trusts in God and knows Him can afford to be magnanimous. Let's not allow the bitterness of others steal our job, the rancour of others steal our capacity for kindness and the hurtful actions of others make us hurtful in return. It's not worth it. Do what Job did. Take them to the Lord in prayer and see what happens. Go on.

MARCH 31

"Also the Lord gave Job twice as much as he had before .. after this Job lived 140 years and saw his sons' sons, even four generations. So Job died being old and full of days."
Job 42 v 10-17

God is no man's debtor', my mother used to tell me as a child. I knew it then but I know it better now. Abraham fed three angels and they told him a son would soon be born in his house. The starving widow fed the Godly prophet and found she suddenly had oil in the house, day after day. Peter lent his fishing boat and before the Lord was through it nearly sank with fish! The lad gave his lunch and 5,000 lunches materialised. Job had a lot of patience and trouble that came in like a lion went out like a lamb. He lived to see another day: a much better day. So will you, my friend, so will you. So don't quit. Remember in the dark what God taught you in the light. Springtime is coming. A double portion awaits you.

APRIL

Bluebell lights everywhere. The lambs are bleating, the birds are chirping and the flowers are blowing in the wind. What colours? Violet, Milk white, Golden yellow, Purple. There is a treasury of bursting wealth in every hill and dale. From Tollymore to Tillicoultry. From Braemar to Ballywillwill. From the Rhonda to the Rasharkin. From Salford to Sevenoaks. From Dallas to Dusseldorf. From Paris to Pucket's Creek. We all fall into April's aproned lap. 'For lo, the winter is past, the rain is over and gone; the flowers appear on the earth; the time of the singing of the birds is come .. the vines with tender grape give a good smell. Arise, my love, my fair one, and come away!' Nice? More than nice; majestic! Solomon again. The Song of Solomon, in fact. And we shall study it through this Springtime together. Come away.

APRIL 1

"The song of songs, which is Solomon's."
Song of Solomon 1 v 1

Near my home is a stately and beautifully walled garden. Often I would wander there gazing in on its lawns and flowers and trying its locked gate entrance to no avail. One day I made a discovery. When the gardener was present one could enter. He had the key and let me in. To many the Song of Songs is like a locked garden. People find it very difficult to understand. But the Divine Gardener will open up its beauties for us for He is the key to this garden of verse. The song is, on one level, about marital love but on another level come great themes which point to the great lover of souls, our perfect Lord Jesus. When the going gets rough He is our quiet bower. He is no April fool who rests in Christ.

APRIL 2

"For thy love is better than wine."
Song of Solomon 1 v 2

Ever been in love? The woman of Solomon's song certainly was. She preferred the one she loved to wine. And so do we. Our love to the Lord is often not worth speaking of but His love to us can never be spoken of enough. I love those two words 'Better than'. What could be better than Christ's love for us? Go into this springtime day knowing that nothing is better than His love. It will spare you the heartache of discovering the hard way that none but Christ can satisfy. The world's love is an empty thing and that is why Jesus did not pray that His Father would not take Christians out of the world but that He would take the world out of Christians. Since we know His love better we worship Him alone. We must never have a divided heart.

APRIL 3

"Look not upon me, because I am black, because the sun hath looked upon me: my mother's children were angry with me; they made me the keeper of the vineyards; but mine own vineyard have I not kept."
Song of Solomon 1 v 6

A sun tan in a British winter is a great status symbol. People spend fortunes just to get one and fortunes trying to keep it! But a dark sun tan in the East is not a status symbol. A row at home had put this girl into the vineyards to work and her tan proved she was a woman of the fields. She complains to her lover that she feels dishevelled.

How many of us sit at the King's table on a Lord's day and feel the same way? 'I am dark Lord.' Yet, God sees a beauty in us that we cannot see. To be hidden in Christ is to be a joint heir with Christ. Live today as part of the Bride of Christ, His Church. Don't look in, look up and see Him there who made an end of all your sin.

APRIL 4

"While the king sitteth at his table, my spikenard sendeth forth the smell thereof. A bundle of myrrh is my well beloved unto me."
Song of Solomon 1 v 12-13

True love flows two ways. Watch any fellow who is in love with a girl who does not reciprocate his love. No matter what he does it all remains one sided. Look at such a theme on a spiritual level. It is a mystery of mysteries: God loves me. Who am I that a King should die for; who, for the joy that was set before Him, endured the cross, despising the shame. What joy? His people. Recently an ecclesiastical figure publicly denounced that anyone should make the Gospel so very personal. We were merely joined to a mainstream of a heritage that flows on and on, he said. How wrong can a man be? Paul confidently wrote: 'The Son of God Who loved me and gave Himself for me.' Our praise is a sweet smelling savour to Him. So is He to us. It flows both ways. Never, in rough times, lose a sense of the two sided relationship.

APRIL 5

"I am the rose of Sharon, and the lily of the valleys. As a lily among thorns, so is my love among the daughters."
Song of Solomon 2 v 1-2

The bride (called the Shulamite, in the Song of Solomon) does not feel herself to be special. There are many roses of Sharon, millions of them. There are a multitude of lilies in the valley. She feels she is only one of a multitude. But the Bridegroom does not see it that way. She is very special to him and he says so. She is not just like a lily, she is like a lily among thorns. Someone so described has just got to be special!
Why not tell the loved one in your life that you think she is special? It may be that today she is feeling very ordinary and needs encouragement, for encouragement is the oxygen of the soul. It could lift her day and give purpose to it. Most men are always in grave danger of taking their wives for granted. There is nothing more ungrateful than a man who takes his wife for granted and begins to treat her as ordinary. 'You always look good,' said a man taking his wife out one evening, 'but tonight you look terrific.' Thats the spirit!

APRIL 6

"I sat down under his shadow with great delight."
Song of Solomon 2 v 3

When Elizabeth Elliot wrote a biography about her
husband Jim, murdered by the Auca Indians as he
tried to reach them with the Gospel, she called the book
'Under the Shadow of the Almighty'. The biography
shows that for a Christian dwelling under such a
shadow the going is not necessarily easy as far as
circumstances are concerned. But the will of God is
good, acceptable and perfect. And in that order.
Amazing that, to my knowledge, the man who
murdered Jim Elliot is now a pastor and recently
baptised Jim Elliot's two grown children on the beach
head where their father entered heaven. 'Under His
shadow' is not easy in the sense of being free from
trouble but it always ends in blessing.

APRIL 7

*"The voice of my beloved! behold he cometh leaping upon
the mountains, skipping upon the hills."*
Song of Solomon 2 v 8

My friend Ian Barclay calls this the 'Healthy energy
of Heavenly love'. As the lover in Solomon's song
rushes to be with the one he loves, so God's love swiftly
moves to reach down to us. They that call upon the
name of the Lord shall be saved. Swift, immediate,
leaping over all international and cultural barriers,
skipping upon the hills. See it? Know it? Revel in it! Lose
yourself in it! It leaps. It skips. Tell everyone about it.

'Tell them it's true!' wrote W. E. Sangster of the Gospel to a great evangelist. Sangster lay slowly dying from muscular dystrophy at the time.
Enjoying success? Good. Let this love keep you balanced. Suffering heartbreak? Let this love comfort you. There is nothing that is greater, wider, higher or deeper. This is it. God is love.

APRIL 8

"Rise up, my love, my fair one, and come away. For, lo, the winter is past, the rain is over and gone; The flowers appear on the earth; the time of the singing of birds is come .. come away."
Song of Solomon 2 v 10-13

Spring has sprung! The Shulamite is called by her bridegroom to enjoy the Springtime; to snap out of winter thoughts. On a spiritual level a whole lot of people should do the same; snap out of negative thinking. To look at some it would appear that they were enduring God's salvation rather than enjoying it! According to Paul the first sign of a Spirit filled life is singing. Read Ephesians chapter 5 and there it is in black and white. 'Be not drunk with wine .. but be filled with the Spirit .. Singing and making melody in your hearts to the Lord', he said. The rain is over. The winter is gone. God's people should be rejoicing. Watch a crowd coming home from a football game and watch a crowd come home from many a church meeting. Different? One is excited about a bag of wind going between two posts and the other seems to get excited about very little. If the church doesn't come into a New Testament Springtime one of these days, the very stones will cry out.

APRIL 9

"Take us the foxes, the little foxes, that spoil the vines."
Song of Solomon 2 v 15

I often think of those men on the day King Saul became King of Israel. While there went with Saul 'a band of men whose hearts God had touched' there were a minority who dispised him 'and brought him no presents'. They are always around, the little foxes. I watched one the other night by my car headlights. Cunning. Slippery. Dodging in and out. The vines take a long time to mature but a little fox can ruin years of work in a moment. The Bible says 'But Saul held his peace', he did not let those 'foxes' spoil his coronation. Don't let them spoil your ministry either. At a later date another little fox entered Saul's vineyard and led him to suicide's grave. He was called Jealousy. Watch him. Take him before he takes you.

APRIL 10

"Until the day break, and the shadows flee away, turn, my beloved, and be thou like a ros or a young hart upon the mountains of Bether."
Song of Solomon 2 v 17

What does this text mean? It means that the bride did not want to go with the bridegroom at that particular moment. She was too lazy. 'Later' was her cry, 'You go where you like, as you please. I'm staying here'. The other classic Biblical example of this kind of laziness was Michal, David's wife. Beside him with joy at the return of the Ark of the Covenant from enemy hands, David danced in the streets and hurried home to sarcastic scorn from Israel's first lady. She learned to regret her behaviour. Enthusiastic support of legitimate enthusiasm in a partner's life is vital to any marriage. It particularly applies in spiritual enthusiasm too. How many a man or woman has been dragged away from serving the Lord because their partner in unenthusiastic? Too many. Don't be that partner.

APRIL 11

"I sought him, but found him not."
Song of Solomon 3 v 2

Too lazy and too late the Shulamite sought the one who had sought her. Her grief was raw, her spirits frantic. She couldn't find him. Many a person has treated their partner selfishly and then lost him. When they wanted to make restitution it was too late. Would you have said to your partner what you said this morning if you had thought he or she might not return this evening? Would we have written that 'ripping' letter this week if we had thought that the hand that was meant to open it, never would? Let's be careful. The bride of the song found her partner, he returned: ours might not. Chilling thought? 'Teach us, Lord, to number our days that we might apply our hearts unto wisdom.'

APRIL 12

"Who is this that cometh out of the wilderness?"
Song of Solomon 3 v 6

I shall never forget standing a few feet away from the Prince of Wales in a tumultuous crowd one morning. England's future Queen was radiant. The women around me were examining her engagement and wedding rings, and like me cheering themselves hoarse. Quite a morning! But what of that day the King of all Kings comes? The Shulamite describes Solomon coming up out of the wilderness with sixty of his valiant men around him. She describes his gold inlaid chariot as the multi-million-pound-a-year King returns. 'Who is this?' she asks. Yet, when the Saviour comes all earthly royalty will fade in comparison. Every knee shall bow and every tongue confess that Jesus Christ is Lord, to the glory of God the Father. Many people will be surprised when the Lord Jesus comes again but nobody will be mistaken. Perhaps today. Ready?

APRIL 13

"A garden inclosed."
Song of Solomon 4 v 12

The image is the epitome of how the Shulamite is viewed by her bridegroom. I often view my own experience of the Lord Jesus this way. When I first trusted Christ as a ten year old lad I was but coming through the gates of an enclosed garden. Millions pass this garden but those who enter discover an amazing thing: the beauties within unfold more beauties which, in turn, unfold more. Millions of believers have found that as every day passes there are more beauties in Christ than they ever dreamt of. Once they saw no beauty in Him until, through conversion, their spiritually sightless eyes were opened to see His loveliness.

It is my privilege nearly every day of my life to preach God's Word somewhere. Never does the Word of God grow stale. Never does it lose its power because it is all about the Lord Jesus. I used to teach about authors like Shakespeare, Shelley, Arthur Miller, Dickens, Thomas Hardy, Wordsworth, but never in my life did I see one of my pupils' lives changed by one line that any of these authors wrote. It is very different to teach God's Word and to see people enter 'the enclosed garden' to find refreshment beyond anything they could have asked or thought. And, as Corrie Ten Boom used to say, 'Out there beyond the eyes horizon: there's more.'

APRIL 14

"I sleep, but my heart waketh."
Song of Solomon 5 v 2

Some of the best times of meditation come when the house is silent, the children are asleep and you are in your bed. Here the Shulamite is asleep when she hears her beloved knocking. Her heart is awake. The night scenes in Scripture, when God spoke to people are numerous; there was Pharaoh, Samuel, Gideon, Daniel, Nicodemus, Paul and many others. David even wrote songs in the night. If you are bothered with insomnia even in the springtime, use the nightwatches as a time to pray. All the storehouses of God are open to the voice of faith in prayer. The goal of prayer is the ear of God. Talk to Him tonight. Pour into His ear your needs, your praise and your worship. The awakened heart sleeps better. Try it.

APRIL 15

"I rose to open to my beloved .. but my beloved .. was gone .. The watchmen that went about the city found me, they smote me, they wounded me."
Song of Solomon 5 v 5-7

Again laziness traps the Shulamite. She does not respond when needed and loses her opportunity. So it is in spiritual matters. The opportunity slips away and never returns. We are grieved by it, go searching for it but it has gone. Notice that the Shulamite got no comfort from the watchmen of the city because they did not understand her heart. They did not understand what had happened to her. Have we not found that when we get away from the Lord in our hearts and are inevitably miserable as a result that the unconverted have no sympathy with our moanings? How could they? They do not love our Lord. Let's not expect sympathy from them because we won't get it. Better to obey the Lord and be happy. As Oswald Chambers put it 'The best measure of a spiritual life is not its ecstasies but its obedience.'

APRIL 16

"What is thy beloved more than another beloved?"
Song of Solomon 5 v 9

The daughters of Jerusalem asked this question of the bride and many a non-Christian asks it of the Christian. In a recent broadcast I happened to quote the following statement and received marked interest in it. It surely answers the questions in today's text. Just what is our beloved Lord Jesus more than another beloved's? To the artist He is the altogether Lovely One. To the architect He is the Chief Cornerstone. To the astronomer He is the Son of Righteousness. To the baker He is the Living Bread. To the banker He is the Hidden Treasure. To the biologist He is the Life. To the carpenter He is the Rule. To the doctor He is the Great Physician. To the educator He is the Great Teacher. To the farmer He is Lord of the Harvest. To the geologist He is the Rock of Ages. To the horticulturist He is the true Vine. To the judge He is the Righteous Judge. To the juror He is the True Witness. To the jeweller He is the Pearl of Great Price. To the editor He is the Good Tidings of Great Joy. To the philosopher He is the Wisdom of God. To the printer He is the True Type. To the student He is Incarnate Truth. To the sinner He is the Lamb of God that taketh away the sin of the world. To Christians He is the Son of the Living God, the Saviour, the Redeemer and Lord.

APRIL 17

"The chiefest among ten thousand."
Song of Solomon 5 v 10

The expression has been used by millions to describe the Lord Jesus. He is the chiefest. He isn't just greater, He is the greatest. He isn't just higher, He is the highest. He isn't just better, He is the best. Write over every pub, novel, film, play, sport, these words: 'Whoso drinketh of these waters shall thirst again'. No matter what earth may offer, no matter even how legitimate its beauty or pleasures they all pass away. But the Lord Jesus? When aeons have passed He will be the same. As Napoleon put it, and he was no evangelical, 'Between Jesus and whomsoever else in the world, there is no possible comparison'. We don't just love the Lord. We adore Him. He is the chiefest. Let's make Him just that in all we do today.

APRIL 18

"He is altogether lovely."
Song of Solomon 5 v 16

Robert Murray McCheyne commented that one of the true tests of the depth of a person's Christianity is how they view the Song of Solomon. What he was implying was that how we view the Lord Jesus is all important. The older I grow the more convinced I am that the church must abhor a mere social Gospel, it must stop trying to be a political connivance, it must move away from denominationalism and preach Christ. When it does, the people will be drawn to the Altogether Lovely One and trust Him as Lord and Saviour. Then our society will be a better society.

A church building once had a text above its door. It read 'We preach Christ crucified'. As the ivy flourished the text then read 'We preach'. Eventually all that was left was the word 'We'. Soon that went too. The amazing thing was that people notice what the ivy had done highlighted the actual history of that local church. They stopped preaching Christ crucified and bit by bit they stopped altogether.

APRIL 19

"Whither is thy beloved turned aside? that we may seek him with thee."
Song of Solomon 6 v 1

We cannot help but influence others as we live our lives. A single word spoken can literally wreck or bless a nation. The person without influence simply does not exist. Here the Shulamite has spoken so much about the one she loves that the others around her wish to see him.

There is a little poem which often haunts, and I mean haunts my mind. I don't know where I read it first but it was used by someone writing of Peter when he denied the Lord. The girl, you remember had said to Peter, 'Thy speech betrayeth thee!' She knew he had been with the Lord Jesus. The writer wrote:

'O that it might be said of me,
Surely thy speech betrayeth thee,
Thou hast been with Jesus of Galilee,
With Jesus of Galilee.'

Does the way I talk give me away? Do people know that I have been with Jesus? As Jimmy Carter used to say 'If you were convicted in a court of law for being a Christian would there be enough evidence to convict you?'

APRIL 20

"I am my beloved's, and my beloved is mine."
Song of Solomon 6 v 3

Marriage is sacred. It is exclusive. Because it is so intimate and special, when it is broken in jealousy fire can start which many waters cannot put out. There was such a thing in the Old Testament as a jealousy offering. God knew very well that jealousy could arise. There would be something desperately wrong if one partner were unfaithful and the other did not feel jealous. Jealousy protects a marriage.

So it is with God and His people. God's name, according to the book of Numbers, is Jealousy. If his people flirt with other god's it provokes Him to jealousy. He will move to protect the relationship. He will chasten us, be sure of it. That is why Paul warned the Corinthian church that they had better be careful with the way they were behaving lest they provoke the Lord to jealousy. We are His and He is ours. Let us never by thought, word or deed provoke Him to jealousy. The sin of David's life was that by his adultery he had not only 'given great occasion to the ememies of the Lord to blaspheme' but that he had hurt God. The repercussions never left David's house. If we do the same, God forbid, the repercussions will never leave ours.

APRIL 21

"His desire is toward me."
Song of Solomon 7 v 10

Recently I watched a television documentary on the raising of a family of buzzards. It was fascinating. Just when the family were ready for their first flight a gust of wind blew a young buzzard off the edge of the nest to the ground. It was a sixty foot fall. The commentator explained how that the youngster was now in great danger as first flight from the ground level for a buzzard was extremely difficult. For about fifteen days the young bird stayed on the ground. Round and round flew its parents protecting it. Watching constantly for its enemies. Down they would swoop with food, regularly. The care shown was very moving. Then came the day when everything changed: the young buzzard took off to become a dot in the sky.

I thought about God. When my feet made haste to Hell, He moved in. There was one who desired to have me that He might sift me as wheat but God's desire was and is toward me. Down through the years in all sorts of dangers I have watched Him swoop in to feed me, protect me, care for me. Slowly as I tried to take flight for Him He was at my side. Always when I faltered, He encouraged me. When I fell, He picked me up. When I soared, I felt his pleasure. So it is, still. So it will ever be. Do you know Him?

APRIL 22

"Let us get up early to the vineyards; let us see if the vine flourish, whether the tender grape appear, and the pomegrantes bud forth."
Song of Solomon 7 v 12

Things have changed for the Shulamite. Industrious, eager, diligent, she works in the vineyard with her loved one. At the start her complaint was 'My own vineyard I have not kept' but now she has become more mature and confident in her love, caring for and giving attension to the development of the ground in her own life. Set free from selfishness, even the youngest and most tender plants draw her interest. Selfless love changed her. Love makes a big difference to all our lives. Christian's often take it for granted that they serve Christ because they love Him, but is the assumption always safe? I often detect in my own Christian service a coldness and aloofness. My service can so easily become mechanical, technical, theological, but dry. Why? Because my love for the Lord has grown cold.

An eminent pianist whose recitals crowded the most spacious auditoriums in Europe with ecstatic audiences, had one thing lacking in his life. The brilliant pianist was a lonely, taciturn man and a certain coldness and aloofness would steal into his playing from time to time. An equally brilliant but much older pianist once laid his hand upon the shoulder of the brilliant young performer and said: 'Will you let me tell you, my boy, that your playing lacks one thing. So far you have missed the greatest thing in the world. And, unless you fall in love, there will always be a certain cold perfection about your music. Unless you come to love another human being passionately and unselfishly, you will never touch human hearts as deeply as you might.' Solomon would have agreed with that pianist. What about you?

APRIL 23

"Who is this that cometh up from the wilderness, leaning upon her beloved?"
Song of Solomon 8 v 5

Learning to lean? One of the great lessons in the spiritual life is to learn to lean upon the Lord. When fear and distress of the future drew around John's heart in the upper room he leaned upon the Lord Jesus' breast. Lean on money, lean on intellect, lean on social position, lean on people and they will all fail you. Lean on Christ and you'll find more power than you've ever dreamed.

Faint? Yet pursuing. Spent? Yet renewing. Christ? Ever viewing.
The coachman on the Bath coach in the last century could not tell the names of the gentry who owned the various mansions along the road. But the coachman gave a fine answer to the angry passenger who asked, 'What do you know?' He quietly said, 'I know how to drive this coach to Bath.' We may not know a lot about this world's society but we know where to lean for all eternity. Praise His name!

APRIL 24

"Love is strong as death."
Song of Solomon 8 v 6

There are, of course, various kinds of love. There is affection. You could have affection, say, for a coffee shop. I have a great affection for one tucked away in a quiet place. The Lord alone knows how I appreciate the friendliness shown to me there on many a weary day. But the coffee shop affection is not as strong as death. There is eros. Wonderful thing, eros. Knocks you for sixty six! It is the state of being in love. There is friendship. Two people have the same outlook and are friends. Eros makes two people of the opposite sex think of each other primarily. They look at each other. Friendship is rather two people looking out on life in the same way. But Agape, that is something else altogether. Agape is God's love, which loves the unloveable. Eros, friendship and affection love those who love them. Agape can love and never have love returned. Christ, you see, died for the ungodly. No one was there to say thank you. He died, alone. His love for you was as strong as death. What a Saviour!

APRIL 25

*"Jealousy is cruel as the grave: the coals thereof are coals of
fire, which hath a most vehement flame."*
Song of Solomon 8 v 6

And it is. What does the grave do? It robs us of life,
of friends, of sympathy, of tenderness, of kindness:
it cuts off, it separates. No strata of society from Queen
on the throne to child in the backyard is exempt from its
cruel influence. So it is with jealousy. It eats church
fellowships alive, it reaches out and brings great
ministries to nothing, it empties lives of vibrancy and
enthusiasm and replaces them with bitterness, criticism
and hardness. There is only one way it can be defeated.
If the hell-spark of jealousy arises in your heart
extinguish it in a sea of prayer.

APRIL 26

*"Many waters cannot quench love, neither can
the floods drown it."*
Song of Solomon 8 v 7

Waters will quench fire but many waters cannot
quench love. Think of the floods of sorrow, pain,
agony, deprivation and loneliness which the Lord Jesus
waded through for us. We must not allow anything to
entice us from loving the Saviour. As we walk these days
through April showers lets remember today's text.
Human love is a wonderful thing in that it will go
through anything and remain intact. It is the material
that moved Tolstoy to write 'War and Peace' where a

Natasha and Pierre survive the Napoleonic wars in Russia and their love survives too. It is the material used from 'Romeo and Juliet' to a Broadway hit like 'West Side Story'. Yet when a fellow or girl, man or woman loves the Lord Jesus a real love story begins to which there is no end. It is love on another level altogether. Through wars and rumours of wars the Gospel of Christ survives, making all who believe it look back and say 'No sacrifice is too great for Him'. Ask them why. They will, without exception answer 'We love Him because He first loved us'.

APRIL 27

"If a man would give all the substance of his house for love, it would utterly be contemned."
Song of Solomon 8 v 7

Money is not the natural reward of love. A man who marries a woman for her money would be contemned by all of us. People may accuse us of serving the Lord Jesus because of what we get out of it but did we not study Job together last month and find that it is possible for a person to love God even though he may not seem to gain by it but rather in the immediate circumstance, lose? Becoming a Christian has just got to be deeper than wanting to escape from Hell. We trust the Lord Jesus as Saviour because He is worthy of trusting. His love cannot be bought. It is not mercenary. We worship God because He is God and there is none other. He is worthy. Knowing Him is reward enough. Money has, praise His name, nothing to do with it. In fact, God thinks so little of money that He uses it for tarmac in the New Jerusalem!

APRIL **2 8**

"We have a little sister .. If she be a wall, we will build upon
her a palace of silver: and if she be a door, we will inclose
her with boards of cedar."
Song of Solomon 8 v 8-9

The young folk: let's never forget the young folk.
From what may appear to be very ordinary,
extraordinary things can come. Many people when they
get rich, or successful in business, or whatever, just get
carried away and care for no one, not even members of
their own family. Be careful to those on the way up for
you might have to pass them on the way down. That
little sister might suprise you, yet!
It is moving as this Song of Solomon reaches its
conclusion that the Shulamite, so blessed with love did
not forget her sister. Her sympathy was with the
younger one coming up. It was George McDonald who
said 'When we are out of sympathy with the young, then
I think our work in this world is over.' Sobering words.
The person who misses his or her opportunity to
influence the young for good misses their opportunity to
influence for good.

APRIL **2 9**

"Thou that dwellest in the gardens, the companions hearken
to thy voice: cause me to hear it."
Song of Solomon 8 v 13

I often think it would be just great to have the Lord
sitting in my sitting room in person. Oh! the questions
I would ask Him. Oh! the guidance I would seek. 'Can I

do this?', 'Is that Your will for me, Lord?', 'Where do I go from here?' But no, He is not here, physically. I must seek to hear His voice in prayer. I must seek to know His will through His word; He has His own ways of talking to me. I have the Comforter, the Holy Spirit, Who will lead me into all truth. Through circumstances, through a friend, in a letter, a 'chance' meeting, in a thousand ways He speaks to His own. Sometimes He nudges. Sometimes He speaks loudly but quietly and surely I hear Him say, 'This is the way, walk ye in it'. The Shulamite's bridegroom was obviously away at this time and she longed to hear his voice again. Let this be our prayer as soon as we head on out of April: 'Cause me to hear Thy voice, Lord'. One word from Him and the day is strangely and gloriously different.

APRIL 30

"Make haste, my beloved, and be thou like a roe or to a young hart upon the mountains of spices."
Song of Solomon 8 v 14

We now leave this love song with a cry for the speedy return of the Bridegroom. How often nowadays do we hear that greeting word of the early Christians, 'Maranatha!'? Everywhere they met the early Christians used it. It was an Aramaic word meaning 'Our Lord comes!' Do you greet the imminent return of Christ with joy or fear? The second coming is not a theory to be discussed but a truth to be lived. 'Even so come, Lord Jesus', cried John from the Isle of Patmos. 'The Spirit and the Bride say 'Come'.' From the mountains of spices He comes, from a land where eyes have not seen, nor ears heard, neither has it entered into the heart of man the things that God has prepared for them that love Him. As you live this last day of April amidst springtime glory just remember, reverently speaking, 'You ain't seen nothin' yet.'

MAY

My mother felt her horizons needed to be widened. Was Aughlisnafin, nestling near the mountains of Mourne, all that life offered? So, at nineteen years of age she set off for 'the New World' and started a doughnut shop in Boston! But the call of His home is deeper than we ever imagine: a few years later she took a return ticket and headed home on the Queen Mary. Soon Southampton gave place to Belfast and a bus 'dropped' her at McIllroy's Store in Aughlisnafin. She often told me that as she walked along the quiet country road she smelt the hawthorn as it bloomed in the hedgerow and determined in her heart to stay. And she did. The hawthorn led her home. The swallow had returned.

'Among the many buds proclaiming May
Decking the fields in holiday array,
Striving who shall surpass in braverie,
Mark the faire flowering of the hawthorn tree
Who finally clothed in a robe of white,
Fills full the wanton eye with May's delight'
- Chaucer

So it was with Israel. For seventy years Israel had been in Babylonian exile and then, one day, God sent a very sensitive and Godly man called Isaiah with a word about home. Israel was like those who dream; but it was true; the exiled nation was to go home. This month we will study Isaiah's words of comfort together. Hawthorn month will be home thoughts.

MAY 1

"Comfort ye my people, saith your God."
Isaiah 40 v 1

What Tolstoy is to the novel, what James Galway is to the flute, Isaiah is among the prophets. Energy, dignity, liveliness, variety, boldness, tenderness, spirituality, reverence, all these characteristics mark the writer of writers. But his message? At this stage in his life, when we home in on him, God has given Isaiah a message of comfort for His people and His message is not just localised for his day but is the thrilling message for our day. Be sure of one thing, God sends comfort to His people.

I issue a challenge to you. Are things difficult for you? Are you having tough times? If so, make a mental note of all the ways God sends comfort to you, this month. You'll be amazed at the means God uses; a friend, a phone call, a letter, a book, a message from His word, the smell of hawthorn in a hedgerow. In an amazing variety of ways the Lord comforts and guides. When you have made a mental note of these ways then, down the line of your life, when you meet someone in exactly the same state you are in now, pass on the details of how God comforted you. You will then become a comforter. And don't tell me they are not desperately needed.

MAY 2

"Prepare ye the way of the Lord, make straight the desert a highway for our God."
Isaiah 40 v 3

Between Babylon and Palestine lay a great desert of more than thirty days journey. The captives were held by a proud monarch. There was no way they could escape. But, when God arises to deliver His people in answer to their cry mountains swing back and iron gates yield. God will set you free from that narrow circumstance, my friend. You'll see. Red Seas and Jordans become pathways. Rough, hurting, places become smooth. Is your local church rent apart by division, bickering and jealousy? Fear not. God will turn the tide. A little Samuel, a young David, a Lydia will arise and be a source of spiritual revival. Don't run away. Stick it out. Pout all your heartache into your Father's ear. Remember the darkness of Calvary and what it led to. Go on for Him. Trust Him. Don't quit. Got any rivers you think are uncrossable? Got any mountains you can't tunnel through? God specialises in the things thought impossible. He does the things others cannot do.

MAY 3

"The grass withereth, the flower fadeth: but the word of our God shall stand for ever."
Isaiah 40 v 8

The old minister was given three gifts at a special service marking his retirement. He was given a wallet full of notes, a watch and a Bible. A few years later a friend, reminding him of the evening, asked him how things were 'Well,', he said, 'the money is all gone the watch is still going, but the Word of the Lord endureth forever.' Isaiah and that minister are from the same neck of the woods. Are you?

MAY 4

"Behold your God! Behold, the Lord God shall come with a strong hand, and His arm shall rule for Him; behold His reward is with Him and His work before Him. He will feed

*His flock like a shepherd: He will gather the lambs with
His arm, and carry them in His bosom, and gently
lead those who are with young."*
Isaiah 40 v 9-11

W hat is God like? He is like a shepherd. Do not be
afraid of Him. He has a shepherd's heart and
skill. He will not overdrive. If the track is rough, do not
panic; He knows what He is doing. He is leading you to
higher ground. When your strength fails, He will carry
you. He never sends you over ground unnecessarily. He
always covers the ground Himself before He asks you to
tread it. Sheep can, if left alone ravage a countryside and
get into dreadful ruts. He stirs up His flock and leads
them on to fresh ground. It is usually higher ground. He
gathers the lambs with His arms. There is no gentleness
like His. The sheepdogs, Goodness and Mercy, will
follow all the days of your life. Relax, my friend, you are
under new management.

M A Y 5

*"Why sayest thou, O Jacob, and speakest, O Israel,
My way is hid from the Lord, and my judgement
is passed over from my God?"*
Isaiah 40 v 27

G od has forgotten you? You are too insignificant for
the creator of stars? He's too busy to care for you?
What are you saying! That head of hair, lady, over which
you rightfully spend a lot of time; have you counted
how many hairs you have? He has. That girl you love,
fellow, you think about her a lot. She is almost in your
bloodstream, is she not? Has it ever occurred to you that
God's thoughts about you are more than the sand on the

seashore? Have you ever counted a handful of sand? If so, then count the handful of sand on your local seashore. Then the sand on the sea bed in your local bay. Then count the sand on the ocean bed, and then the sand of the ocean beds of the world. God's thoughts about you are more. Your way is in no way hid from the Lord. God spends two whole chapters in Genesis describing your creation and only half a verse on the creation of the stars. You matter to God and since that is true what else really matters?

MAY 6

"But thou, Israel, art my servant, Jacob whom I have chosen, the seed of Abraham my friend. Thou whom I have taken from the ends of the earth, and called thee from the chief men thereof, and said unto thee, Thou art my servant; I have chosen thee, and not cast thee away."
Isaiah 41 v 8-9

What kind of people does the Lord use? What kind of platform does the God display His glory from? His people, of course. What, then do I expect concerning His people? Are they all wonderfully talented and possessed with great intellects and be able to give brilliant answers to all the questions put to them? No. In Israel's time they were surrounded by enemies, they had no water, the valleys through which they passed were barren waste, they were powerless of themselves. It is among such people that God has always found His chosen ones. Not high and mighty but the lowly and obscure. God should always have the room to work. He needs emptiness to receive Him; weakness to be empowered by Him. The poor in spirit are His, the persecuted and tempted; do you qualify?

MAY 7

"Fear thou not; for I am with thee: be not dismayed; for I am thy God: I will strengthen thee; yea, I will help thee; yea, I will uphold thee with the right hand of my righteousness."
Isaiah 41 v 10

Gloom? 'With thee'. Enemies? 'Be not dismayed for I am thy God'. Feeling weak? 'I will strengthen thee'. Insurmountable difficulties? 'I will help thee'. Frightened out of your mind and stumbling? 'I will uphold thee with the right hand of my righteousness'. Tell me, my reader, WHAT MORE DO YOU WANT? IS HE NOT ENOUGH FOR YOU ANYMORE?

MAY 8

"Behold I will make thee a new sharp threshing instrument having teeth: thou shalt thresh the mountains, and beat them small, and shalt make the hills as chaff. Thou shalt fan them, and the wind shall carry them away, and the whirlwind shall scatter them: and thou shalt rejoice in the Lord, and shalt glory in the Holy One of Israel."
Isaiah 41 v 15-16

Do you think that I look across Northern Ireland every day and do not tremble? Hardly a day passes without a bomb somewhere or a bullet being blasted into someone's brain in this Province of trouble. Sectarianism is so marked that there are not only sects, but there are sects within sects within sects. The hatred is monumental in a land that is so naturally and breathtakingly beautiful and whose people are so kind to strangers and often so very unkind to each other. Am I going to hate the land I love? No. I must preach God's

Word and live for the Lord Jesus above all the strife, in season and out of season. And I must not deviate from this path. As God used Israel as a sharp threshing instrument and made the nation into such a formative influence on the history of the world, there is a similar experience awaiting all who will surrender themselves absolutely to the hands of God. What Christian is there that does not desire power to thresh the mountains of sin and evil until they become like heaps of chaff on the threshing floor? Let those kind of people mark well today's text and words 'I will make thee'. It applies even in Northern Ireland. Are you willing to be that instrument?

M A Y 9

"When the poor and needy seek water, and there is none, and their tongue faileth for thirst I, the Lord will hear them, I the God of Israel will not forsake them. I will open rivers in high places, and fountains in the midst of the valleys: I will make the wilderness a pool of water, and the dry land springs of water. I will plant in the wilderness the cedar, and the shittah tree, and the myrtle, and the oil tree; I will set in the desert the fir tree, and the pine, and the box tree together .. that the hand of the Lord hath done this, and the Holy One of Israel hath created it."
Isaiah 41 v 17-20

Rest your eye today upon the quote 'I wills'. I will hear. I will not forsake. I will open. I will make. I will plant. Millions have found that the promises of God are just absolutely absolute. We all know of lovers' promises. We have all heard politicians make promises. But the promises of God are different. To the ordinary eye they would not mean much but to the eye of faith they make a vast amount of difference. Faith is conscious that God is there; faith recognises that there is a loving purpose to every trial; faith knows that God is teaching lessons through all of life's experiences. Outwardly there may still be the wasting illness, the little child may still be pining, that unemployment may still raise its ugly head, those circumstances may still be very straightened, that, that hope may still be deferred; but the eye of faith still sees beauty in it all. Because of faith, rivers can flow over barren heights, fountains can come up in valleys, the wilderness can become a pool and the desert become a forest glade. May the Lord open our eyes to the dimension of faith today.

MAY 10

"But thou, Israel, art my servant .. the seed of Abraham, my friend."
Isaiah 41 v 8

Again and again in Scripture we are reminded of Abraham, God's friend. What was it about this man who occupies so many pages and verses of Scripture? It was his faith. God loves to see people actually take Him at His Word. God told Abraham that if he would leave Ur of the Chaldees he would be led to a city which God had built. And Abraham obeyed.
I once sat in Bahrain airport in sweltering heat in the middle of the night. As the jet refuelled we were given a respite from our long journey to the Far East and, as I sat there, watching the Arabs around me in their long, flowing gowns I fell to thinking about Abraham. Bahrain is not all that far from where Ur of the Chaldees stood. Education was well developed at Ur from the Persian Gulf bringing copper ore, ivory and gold. The moon god

was worshipped at the great Ziggurat temple there. It was in Abraham's time a centre of culture and sophistication. Yet, Abraham left it.

Each step of real advance in the divine life will involve an altar on which some dear fragment of the self life has been offered. God said 'Go' and Abraham went and moved the times he lived in. He did this, not by being beneath their spell, but by rising up at the call of God and stepping outside of them.

Funny, I thought as the jet winged away from the Middle East, the only thing we remember now about Ur of the Chaldees is that Abraham left it.

MAY 11

"Behold my servant .. he shall not cry, nor lift up, nor cause his voice to be heard in the street."
Isaiah 42 v 1-2

I happen to serve with a group of writers as a reviewer of Christian books and I declare that some of these days I am going to read on a publisher's blurb: 'This writer is, in fact, the greatest thing since sliced bread'! The Lord's humility was astounding. His design was not to be an idol but to break idols. He became to be despised, not to be crowned. he made a long journey across Samaria to reach just one person. Seventy five thousand angels could have wiped out the opposition at the cross but no soul destroying angel smote the men who spat in His face. There was no courting of the rich and powerful. It was the common people who heard Him gladly. He expended His energy on dying thieves, fallen men and women, peasantry of Galilee. He lived to do His Father's will. Is this the quality of your work for God?

Is it just that I want to be famous?
To have my work the common talk of men?
For if that is my secret ambition,
God save me from an awful end.

Is it just that I like adulation?
Is that why I serve the Lord?
For if that is my sole motivation,
It's one I can ill afford.

Is it just that I like success stories?
God help me if that is my aim,
For Paul seemed a virtual failure,
And his Saviour seemed exactly the same.

No! Let me just live to God's glory,
As I pass through life's every phase,
As long as the work is accomplished,
And the Lord gets all of the praise.

MAY 12

"Fear not: for I have redeemed thee, I have called thee by thy name; thou art mine. When thou passest through the waters, I will be with thee; and through the rivers, they shall not overflow thee: when thou walkest through the fire, thou shalt not be burned; neither shall the flame kindle upon thee. For I am the Lord thy God, the Holy One of Israel."
Isaiah 43 v 1-3

F Scott Fitzgerald's short stories are something else. He was both the star and spokesman for the 'Jazz age', the 1920's, 'the greatest and gaudiest spree in history' which saw 'a whole race going hedonistic,

deciding on pleasure'. But the age in which he flourished took him with it when it crashed. In 1939, a year before he died of a heart attack, worn out by alcoholism, he wrote:
'The horror has now come like a storm - what if this night pre-figured the night after death - what if all thereafter was an eternal quivering on the edge of an abyss with everything base and vicious in one's self urging one forward and the baseness and viciousness of the world just ahead. No choice, no road, no hope - only the endless repetition of the sordid and the semi tragic'. Quietly compare the words of the author of the 'Great Gatsby' with today's text. Mull them over. If you are thinking that the cost of following the Lord Jesus in this world is 'costing you too dear', then read Fitzgerald's haunting words again. The cost of following your Lord is very dear but the cost of refusing to follow Him is even dearer. Selah.

M A Y 1 3

"This people have I formed for myself, they shall show forth my praise."
Isaiah 43 v 21

There lay in a hospital ward in Belfast, two ladies. I went to have a word with one of them one day and asked how long it was since she had entered the ward. 'Eighteen years ago', she said quietly. I was shocked with the reality of what she had just said; but I was in for an even bigger shock. 'My friend over there is here longer than me', the lady added. 'Yes, that's true', her friend admitted when I asked her if it were so, 'I came in the day before she did!' Amazingly they are two of the most contented people I know!

We can show forth God's praise by suffering just as much as by active service. To lie still, day after day, without complaint, satisfied with what pleases Him may produce more praise than to write hymns which stir successive generations to praise the Lord. To accept God's Will without murmur declares God's praises more than we imagine. Let's praise Him today, no matter what.

MAY 14

"But thou hast not called upon me, O Jacob; but thou hast been weary of me, O Israel. Thou hast not brought me the small cattle of thy burnt offerings; neither hast thou honoured me with thy sacrifices .. Thou hast brought me no sweet cane with money .. thou hast wearied me with thine iniquities."
Isaiah 43 v 22-24

Prayerlessness. Neglect of little things. Lack of sweetness. These three things were all missing in Israel's service for God. Often they are missing in ours. Is there prayerlessness in your life? Remember that prayer is not an argument with God to persuade Him to move things your way but an exercise by which you are enabled by His Spirit to move yourself His way. Is there a neglect of little things in your life? Remember that small is beautiful and that small responsibilities cared for are also beautiful for God. Is there lack of sweetness in your life? Then remember that biblical orthodoxy minus compassion equals the ugliest thing in the world. Often we do things for the Lord, because we must, or because we will, not because of love to the Lord. Let's get prayer, attention to detail and sweetness together carefully in our lives so that we will be prayerful, careful and not 'sourful Christians'.

MAY 15

"He feedeth on ashes."
Isaiah 44 v 20

Jack London became the highest paid living writer in history, the world's first 'Millionaire Novelist' he wrote: 'I believe that life is a mess .. it is like yeast, a ferment, a thing that moves and may move for a minute, an hour, a year, or a hundred years, but that in the end it will cease to move. The big eat the little that they may continue to move, the strong eat the weak that they may retain their strength. The lucky eat the most and move the longest, that is all'.

Janis Joplin, the queen of rock music, became a major cult heroine. On stage, often to as many as twenty five thousand people, she was both wanted and adored. Off stage she had whiskey and heroin to comfort her.

'I can't sleep! I go to bed worrying and I wake up worrying every morning, worrying that they'll have found out I really can't sing!'.

Her record 'Cheap Thrills' sold one million dollars worth of copies; she died on the 4th October 1970 mainlined on heroin. She had written: 'Most of my biggest problems now are what colour scheme to use on my next string of beads'. Poor Janis. Poor Jack. Like millions of others they had fed on ashes. Let's worship any other god than the Lord and so will we.

Ashes, feeding on ashes,
Dry, tasteless and dead,
Are there many feeding on ashes in life?
Millions, I'm afraid.

Milk, feeding on milk,
Life giving, refreshing like dew,
Are there many drinking the milk of the Word?
Few, mighty few.

Meat, feeding on meat,
Succulent, strengthening, tough,
Are there many eating the meat of the Word?
Never, never enough.

MAY 16

*"To open before him the two leaved gates; and the gates
shall not be shut."*
Isaiah 45 v 1

It was getting time for going home, though it certainly
didn't look like it. Tens of thousands of the children of
Israel were in the city of Babylon, held captive by their
enemies and there was a siege on, outside. It had been
going on for months. A king called Cyrus was being
laughed to scorn at his attempts to get his army to scale
Babylons' massive walls and to force her mighty gates.
But when God promised through the prophet that one
day those two leaved gates would be open to Him, no
man could shut them. One night in fancied security,
Belshazzar made a feast to a thousand of his lords. The
vigilance of the guards was relaxed, the mystic hand on
the walls of the royal banqueting hall traced the decree
that the kingdom was at an end, and it passed into the
hands of the Medes and Persians that very night. Cyrus
diverted the mighty river which traversed the city into a
vast reservoir, arranged for the storage of water; and, as
it left its ancient course, his troops marched along the
oozy channel and burst into the city with wild cries that
startled the revellers, but led to their deaths. In a single
night the power of Babylon had been broken as God had
promised it would. The most outstanding man in
Babylon was Daniel and the historian Josephus says that
he took an early opportunity of aquainting Cyrus with
the history of God's people and with those wonderful

predictions that the prophet had made concerning them.
Cyrus repatriated God's people and they returned to
their homeland as those that dreamed. When God opens
gates, no man can shut them. Not even those gates that
seem to bar your way today.

MAY 17

"Bel boweth down, .. they stoop, they bow down together;
they could not deliver the burden, but themselves are gone
into captivity."
Isaiah 46 v 1-2

Bel and Nebo were gods of the Babylonians. The
Persians under Cyrus ripped these gods off their
pedestals and with rude hands pitched them into the
back of ox wagons. Time was when plagues hit Babylon
Bel and Nebo had been carried through the streets with
great pomp and ceremony. Now, they were being carried
into captivity and not a thing they could do to deliver
themselves, never to speak of anyone else.
It is a dreadful mistake to worship gods who, as Isaiah
said, cannot deliver. Voltaire, the famous French atheist,
gave most of his talent and energies to destroying the
Christian faith. He said in one hundred years there
would be no Bible. When he came to die he was heard to
scream over and over again, 'The Nazarene! The
Nazarene! The Nazarene!'. His maid said that not for all
the wealth in Europe would she ever want to watch an
infidel die. His gods could deliver no peace.
I heard recently of the death of Martyn Lloyd-Jones. His
daughter Lady Catherwood was praying at his bedside,
'Lord spare my father to your people'. He interrupted
her with this incredible sentence: 'Don't hinder me from
the glory!' That's the way to die. With such a vision
that's the way to live too, because, says Peter, 'Make

your calling and election sure; for if ye do these things
ye shall never fall: for so an entrance shall be ministered
unto you, abundantly, into the everlasting kingdom of
our Lord and Saviour Jesus Christ.' Be gone, all Bels and
Nebos.

'Oh time, why dost thou move so slowly?
Oh sin be removed out of the way,
Oh day, oh fairest of days, dawn'.

MAY 18

*"Even to your old age I am he; and even to hoar hairs will I
carry you: I have made, and I will bear; even I will carry,
and will deliver you."*
Isaiah 46 v 4

God is our burden bearer. 'Your Christianity is a
shoulder to cry on', sneer the sceptics. No. It is far
more than that. It is a shoulder to be carried on. God's
everlasting arms are both a cradle and a carriage. Cast
your burden upon the Lord and He will sustain you.
I love the story of the man who had a dream. He
dreamed he was walking along the beach with the Lord.
Across the sky flashed scenes from his life. For each
scene, he noticed two sets of footprints in the sand, one
belonged to him, and the other to the Lord. When the
last scene of his life flashed before him, he looked back
at the footprints in the sand. He noticed that many times
along the path of his life there was only one set of
footprints. He also noticed that it happened at the very
lowest and saddest times in his life.
This really bothered him and he questioned the Lord
about it. 'Lord you said that once I decided to follow

you, you'd walk with me all the way. But I have noticed
that during the most troublesome times in my life, there
is only one set of footprints. I don't understand why,
when I needed you most would you leave me?'
The Lord replied, 'My precious child, I love you and
would never leave you. During your times of trial and
suffering, when you see only one set of footprints, it was
then that I carried you.'

MAY 19

*"Remember the former things of old: for I am God, and
there is none else."*
Isaiah 46 v 9

Home thoughts. Have you ever been homesick?
Homesickness is a feeling in the pit of the stomach.
It is a longing in the eye. It is an entire disenchantment
with the things of the present. Even in a child it is a
'Come on, Dad, let's go home'. Watch people on holiday.
Sure, they enjoy it all: for about a week. Then almost
imperceptibly thoughts of home come creeping in.
Coming home is often, by far, the better part of the
holiday.
But imagine a seventy year exile from home, and it
wasn't any holiday, it was captivity. Suddenly there
comes a Prophet on the scene with the Word from God
about home. 'Remember the former things of old.', he
said. How they remembered! The power of God
amongst them! The glory of the temple! The Godliness
of the revival days with Hezekiah! The singing! The
Psalms of David and the Proverbs of Solomon which
Hezekiah had his literary guild of writers arrange in the
golden age of Israel's spiritual literary excellence!
Galilee! Nain! Nazareth! Bethlehem! Jerusalem! Home!

'For I am God and there is none else.', said the Prophet
with his message from heaven. Only God could take
them home, and no one else. And He did.
And us? If we are trusting in Christ there are only two
places we can ever be. 'In the body', or at home 'with the
Lord'. To be at home! 'Even if we were to find,', said Mr
William Purdie at a wonderful service in Glasgow a few
days before his death, 'a word or phrase, or sentence to
describe heaven, we would not be permitted to disclose
it.' What did he mean? He meant just what Paul meant
when he said 'I knew a man in Christ above fourteen
years ago, such a one caught up to the third heaven ..
how he was caught up into paradise and heard
unspeakable words, which it is not lawful for a man to
utter'. Paul actually told the Corinthians: 'We would
prefer to be away from the body and at home with the
Lord'. Heaven is the land of our desire, our land of
promise. It will be a place to explore forever, the richness
and fullness of all that God in Christ has done.
Unutterable, inexhaustible love.
The prospect of heaven for a believer is just a constant,
exciting, source of comfort and joy. If it isn't, if we have
lost our enthusiasm for going home, then we have
succumbed to the subtle pull of the earth that is causing
the pull of Heaven to be cancelled out. Let's stop giving
into the love of softening things. Remember the things of
old for soon and very soon we are going home. At last.

MAY 20

*"Thou art wearied in the multitude of thy counsels. Let now
the astrologers, the star gazers, the monthly prognosticators,
stand up and save thee from these things that shall come*

upon thee. Behold, they shall be as stubble; the fire shall
burn them; they shall not deliver themselves."
Isaiah 47 v 13-14

God hates the occult. He hates their pride in their
predictions and explicitly forbids His people
fortune telling, spiritism, and black and white magic.
Isn't it a mercy that the Lord shields us from the future?
If we knew what lay ahead for us we might not want to
go on. We know not what the future holds but we do
know who holds the future. In today's verse Isaiah was
giving God's final word to the Babylonish occult. It is a
word with relevance in our day too.
Satan is gaining support today not only in jungle tribes
and violent inner cities but among university professors
and affluent suburbanites. The French spend one million
francs a year consulting sixty thousand sorcerers. World-
wide spiritism has at least seventy million adherents.
Horoscope columns appear in over one thousand
newspapers and magazines. The Daily Telegraph
magazines reports that astrologers are consulted by
company directors wanting to know the best days for
floating shares. One Scotland Yard official says there is
presently more black magic in Britain than ever there
was in the middle ages. The Exorcist grossed one
hundred and fifty million dollars. The Bible teacher
Peter Anderson reckons that 80% of school teenagers
have experience of the spirit world through the ouija
board. The Daily Mirror reports 40,000 witches in Great
Britain alone.
Talk about the Devil? Millions are. Not only about him
but with him. A standard must be raised against him to
show the absolute victory over Satan which is available
in the Lord Jesus. Is there victory available?
A little girl was asked what she did whenever the Devil
knocked at the door of her heart. She answered smiling
'I send Jesus to answer the door!' Let's do the same.

MAY 21

"I will not give my glory unto another."
Isaiah 48 v 11

I knew an old lady once called Miss McCarthy. She was quite a lady. I used to mow her lawn for her as a lad and she would often speak to me of the things of the Lord. She had served God in China and once told my mother that the Chinese for the text 'Thou wilt keep him in perfect peace whose mind is stayed upon thee' read 'Thou wilt keep him in perfect peace whose mind stops at God'. We never forgot her explanation.
One day I talked to her about revival. 'Why did it not come? Would it come?'. Can I ever forget her answer? 'When no denomination, no group of Christians, no magazine, no official organ, no anything claims that the blessing is coming through them - then we shall have it. God must get the glory.' So it tarries.

MAY 22

"O that thou hadst hearkened to my commandments!
then had thy peace been as a river, and thy righteousness
as the waves of the sea."
Isaiah 48 v 18

Heart-rending text isn't it? Rivers that run deep are calm on the surface. So is a life that is obeying the Lord Jesus. If only we had listened to God's commandments on so many occasions in our lives, then would our peace have been as a river. And more. Our righteousness would have been as the waves of the sea. Not the waves of the shore, casting up mire and dirt. Waves of the mid ocean. How I love to water ski in the ocean! I have fallen headlong in the deep ocean water of the Atlantic and felt the waves rolling over me; exhilarating; clean; fresh. Oh that my righteousness were always like that!

But Israel would not listen. Her neck was like an iron sinew and her brow was as brass. She trusted inn the idol and the graven image and would not hear, or know, or open her ear. The Lord pleaded with her but she refused to listen. So God took his people via Babylon with all its bitter anguish until, as in a furnace, the dross of God's peoples lives was purged away. There are many of God's people at this time going through the furnace of chastisement who would not have been required to if only they had been willing and obedient to the Lord's voice. Not that the furnace always indicates unfaithfulness; but if we are unfaithful, we must expect the furnace of chastisement.

MAY 23

"The Lord hath called me from the womb."
Isaiah 49 v 1

Was there not a lot of Rachel in Joseph, Jochebed in Moses, Hanna in Samuel, Elizabeth in John the Baptist, Eunice in Timothy, Monica in Augustine, Susannah in John and Charles Wesley, and your mum in you? I remember hearing Billy Graham tell 50,000 people in Belfast how his mother got him a big galvanised tub on their farm every Saturday night and as she scrubbed him till she had him repeat the words of John 3 v 16 until he knew them by heart. He preached on John 3 v 16 that night and amongst many others, three friends of mine were gloriously converted. How they thanked God for Billy Graham's mother!
To make a man, God very often begins with his mother. When you educate a man you educate an individual but when you educate a woman you educate a whole family. 'Anyone,' said F. B. Meyer, 'that can influence women by speech or pen, education or example, has an almost unrivalled power over the destinies of our race.'

MAY 24

"In the shadow of his hand hath he hid me, and made me a polished shaft."
Isaiah 49 v 2

There is more to archery than meets the eye. Many of us assume that all you will have to do is point an arrow in the right direction, let it go, and it will land on the target. That simply isn't true. Not only is it very important how you let go, but the amount of tension of the bow, and the position of your arms and shoulders, the release, and where you fix your eyes in relation to the tip of the arrow are also important. The condition of the arrow is also absolutely vital. In archery a rusted arrow point will fail to penetrate and glance away from the target, and so in war, a sword or spear corroded by rust would not cleave its way through any helmet or shield.

Even a breath of damp will leave its corroding mark on an arrow head. Rust can best be removed by sandpaper or the file. In this beautiful verse the Prophet is speaking of how God uses His servants as a polished shaft. If we would be useful for the Lord then we must have no rust in our lives resulting from inconsistency or permitted sin. So God uses the fret of daily life, the wear and tear of irritating and vexing circumstances as his sandpaper and file to guard us from whatever would blunt the edge or diminish the effect of our work. Want to be useful for God? Don't resist God's polishing process.

MAY 25

"In his quiver hath he hid me."
Isaiah 49 v 2

God has not flung you away as a worthless thing. He has left you as a polished shaft in His quiver in the

very shadow of His hand. He is keeping you close until
the moment comes when He can send you most swiftly
and surely on some errand for Him. It is very important
to remember that the quiver is vitally bound to the
warrior, within easy reach of His hand and guarded very
jealously by Him. What were arrows made for but to be
used? Let us be content to be in the Master's quiver to be
used by Him just whenever He wishes and to be sent by
Him just to whatever target He chooses.

MAY 26

"Then I said, I have laboured in vain, I have spent my
strength for naught and in vain: yet surely my judgement is
with the Lord, and my work with my God."
Isaiah 49 v 4

I have never in all my life met any servant of God
anywhere in the world who at some stage during his
or her work for the Lord did not want to quit. I know a
mighty servant of God who one day drew me aside and
told me that while visiting one under his pastoral care
he was told that not one word that he had ever spoken
had ever meant anything to the person he was visiting.
So discouraged was this beloved man of God by this
comment that he could not preach the following Sunday.
He began to question his entire call to the ministry. That
wicked comment by someone who ought to have known
better very nearly ruined his future service for God.
We must always remember that it was as a result of
nervous overstrain after that great day of Carmel that
Elijah threw himself down beneath the Juniper tree and
wanted to die. We are so long in learning lessons that
half our life is over before we feel that we are at last
pursuing the right tract and have at last discovered our
niche for God. Even then we feel ourselves to be such
apparent failures in the Master's service.

The tremendous thing about today's text is that the prophet points out that judgement of a servant of the Lord's work is with the Lord. The Lord does not judge things as men and women judge them. He knows your heart, my friend, and knows your faithful service in that lonely place for Him. Keep on going for the Master today despite what you feel to be apparent failure and lean heavily upon the Lord. Did not your Lord before seem to die as an apparent failure? The very Disciples seemed disposed to go back to their fishing boats. The nation abhorred Him, men despised Him, rulers mocked Him. Yet the very cross of Christ which men deemed Christ's supreme disgrace has become the stepping stone to universal dominion.

You are not home yet and all that you have attempted in the Master's name will have far more repercussions than you ever dreamed. Whatever you do today, don't quit!

MAY 27

"The Lord God hath given me the tongue of the learned, that I should know how to speak a word in season to him that is weary."
Isaiah 50 v 4

Isaiah certainly had been given a word in season to a weary nation. As he had brought them the promise of their release and eventual home coming he had touched a nation. Speech. If only we could see what an encouraging word of kindness could do we would pour out thousands of them daily. Solomon realised what such words could do; 'Anxiety in the heart of man causes depression, but a good word makes it glad. He who gives the right answer kisses the lips. There is gold and a multitude of rubies but the lips of knowledge are a precious jewel. The words of a man's mouth are deep waters, the well's spring of wisdom is a flowing brook. Death and life are in the power of a tongue. Righteous lips are the delight of kings and they love him who speaks what is right.'

In any one day we meet a lot of people and those of us who are believers must constantly ask the Lord to give us the right word for the people we meet.

I always love the story my encouraging Scots friend Mr Willie McClachlan once told me. One day Willie was out trying to get his kite to lift into the air as a little boy and it was flying most erratically and then diving to earth and breaking the bow. 'What you need,' said a passer by, 'is a divot to your draigon, sonny.' A draigon is the broad Scots word for a kite. 'A what?' asked Willie. 'A divot to your draigon!' he replied. The man leaned down and took up a small clod of earth and grass and tied it to Willie's kite string. Away she soared, perfectly. The divot gave the kite weight and balance. Willie's story often reminds me of part of a poem on the power of words which says 'Boys flying kites haul in their white winged birds but you can't do that when you're flying words'. Words, once uttered, can never be retrieved. May ours ever and always be a word in season to him that is weary.

MAY 28

"Who is among you that feareth the Lord, that obeyeth the voice of his servant, that walketh in darkness, and hath no light? let him trust in the name of the Lord, and stay upon his God. Behold, all ye that kindle a fire, that compass yourselves about with sparks; walk in the light of your fire, and in the sparks that ye have kindled. This shall ye have of mine hand; ye shall lie down in sorrow."
Isaiah 50 v 10-11

Want sorrow? Who of us does? Yet we shall surely have it if we trust in our own intelligence alone. 'To thine own self be true', is a dangerous motto to live by. Very dangerous. 'Walk in the light of your fire .. ye

shall lie down in sorrow', warns the prophet.
Think of the people in Scripture who walked in their
own light. Jacob walked in his for a time and lay on a
pillow of stone. Joseph's brothers did the same and
suffered humiliation and sorrow later in life. Miriam did
and her subsequent leprosy came as a direct result. Israel
did and wandered with sorrow in the wilderness for
forty years. David did so, disastrously, one day in
Jerusalem and some of his Psalms are an eternal
comment on the sorrow that followed. What of the elder
brother in the story of the Prodigal Son? What of Judas?
What of the rich farmer? All these examples are beacons
to warn us off the rocks of self trust. The answer to it all
is to trust in the Lord with all our hearts, to not lean on
our own understanding, to, in all our ways,
acknowledge Him and He will direct our paths. The end
of those who do this is peace.

MAY 29

*"Look unto the rock whence ye are hewn, and to the hole of
the pit whence ye are digged."*
Isaiah 51 v 1

Abraham Lincoln had something. History has not
shown that the rustic rail-road lawyer never forgot
his humble roots. The man who protected small town
folks and their rights did not, as he puts it, 'Swap horses
mid-stream'. Soon he was to hold the 'Dis-United States'
together. He did not forget the rock from which he was
hewn, like some folks do.
Whether it be a great president or a nation, an individual
or a group of individuals, it is vital to remember the
smallness of our beginnings. The prophet was telling
Israel to do just that. The rock from which they were
hewn was hard and did not receive impressions easily,
the hole of the pit out of which they were dug was an
idolatrous family in Ur of the Chaldees and the

generation of slaves in Egypt. 'Don't forget it!', warns
Isaiah. Look back down the line of your life. Has the
Lord not been good to you beyond all measuring? What
do we have but what we have received? Are we
grateful? There is nothing in all this universe as
ungrateful as mankind. Even an ox knows his master,
the Scripture says, 'but Israel does not know'. Are we
any better? Let's go on a spiritual rock climb today and
let's do a bit of spiritual pot-holing into the bargain. If it
doesn't humble and refresh us, we do not know the Lord
God.

M A Y 3 0

"Shake thyself from the dust; arise, and sit down, O
Jerusalem: loose thyself from the bands of thy neck, O
captive daughter of Zion. For thus saith the Lord, Ye have
sold yourselves for nought."
Isaiah 52 v 2-3

And so, home they come! The shackles of slavery are
broken, the Babylonish dust falls from their feet to
the ground and the people of Israel are, at last, free. Was
their backsliding worth anything? God's sad moment
was 'Ye have sold yourselves for nought'. As this month
of May draws to a close do sad eyes read these words?
For years perhaps you have unfortunately been away
from the Lord. Rebellion, stubbornness, disillusionment,
or perhaps just a sad, slow, drift took you away from
joyful, busy service for the Lord Jesus. Was it worth it
all? Never, anywhere in the world will you find a truly
happy backslider. For the sake of a glass of wine, a
companion, a loss of face, a social position, people
compromise their dedication to the kingdom of God.
The result? Misery. They sell themselves for nothing,
play the fool and err exceedingly. As Israel headed
home from exile they had got nothing by it, nor did God.
Never look back unless you want to go that way.

MAY 31

"All we like sheep have gone astray; we have turned every one to his own way; and the Lord hath laid on him the iniquity of us all. He was oppressed, and he was afflicted, yet he opened not his mouth: he is brought as a lamb to the slaughter, and as a sheep before her shearers is dumb, so he openeth not his mouth."
Isaiah 53 v 6-7

We end these May readings with the greatest of all Old Testament chapters dealing with the sufferings of the Lord Jesus. Fascinating, that in the exact centre of this great fifty third chapter of Isaiah we find the words 'He is led as a lamb to the slaughter'. A coincidence? No. For twenty seven chapters Isaiah writes a great poem, divided into three groups of nine and in the middle chapter of the middle nine and in the middle couplet of that chapter, are the words 'The Lamb'. Why? God always puts the lamb at the centre! The fifty third chapter is the hub around which the whole wheel of Isaiah's message coming redemption revolves. It was at the hub of Israel's home coming. So it will be for us. In that heavenly Jerusalem 'The Lamb is the light thereof'. The only ones who enter are those whose names are written in the Lamb's book of life. 'The throne of God and of the Lamb shall be in it.' The Lamb is all the glory of Immanuel's land. As the great Bible teacher Richard Baxter put it; 'The light of the city is the face of Jesus. The music of the city is the name of Jesus. The harmony of the city is the praise of Jesus. The theme of the city is the love of Jesus. The joy of the city is the presence of Jesus. The employment of the city is the service of Jesus. The strength of the city is the omnipotence of Jesus. The magnetic centre and super glory of the city is Jesus Himself. The duration of the city is the eternity of Jesus'. Home indeed.

JUNE

'If you cannot find Pixies on your own doorstep you'll never find Fairyland', wrote F. W. Boreham. Norman Gayle put it another way:

'Why will your mind forever go
to Meads in sunny Greece?
Our songbirds have as fine a flow,
Our sheep as fair a fleece;
Among our hills the honey bee,
And in the leaning pear
I tell you there is Arcady
In leafy Warwickshire.'

How very true! If we look around at the ordinary things we suddenly find that they are not so ordinary after all. I intend to do that this month with five seemingly ordinary characters who were at the back of the great ministry of the apostle Paul. We'll take a week each with four of them, the fifth are, in fact, a pair. Without them Paul would never have done what he did. Maybe, as a result of this months readings, you will put your gifts into the service of the Master and see that little is much if God is in it.

JUNE 1

"And there was a certain disciple at Damascus, named Ananias."
Acts 9 v 10

Not your most-voted-to-succeed-man-of-the-year. Not a singer-songwriter. Not a pastor, teacher. Not an apostle even a preacher. Not a recognised leader. Just a certain disciple named Ananias. The right man, in the right place, with the right message, at the right time. Doctor Luke records for us that he was a devout man, and well spoken of by the Jews. This was no small compliment since many Jews hated believers. Yet, this man was to become God's highway to the heart of the newly converted Saul of Tarsus who was to become God's highway to Europe. God had a job for Ananias to do and he found him amongst the every day 'nitty gritty' of Damascus; faithful, ready, willing and humble enough to do as he was bidden. How about you?

JUNE 2

"To him said the Lord in a vision , Ananias. And he said, Behold, I am here, Lord."
Acts 9 v 10

Fred Lemon, Cockney, ex-burglar, Christian writer and witness, is famous all over Britain for his public prayers. A friend of mine heard Fred at a very distinguished gathering in the city of Manchester began his public prayer with these refreshing words, 'It's Fred 'ere Lord!' I dare the Dean of Saint George's Chapel in Windsor Castle to try that approach as the Royal Family

worship next Christmas morning! But Fred is more
Scriptural than many may give him credit for. Ananias
used exactly the same approach. 'Ananias?' asked the
Lord, 'I am here, Lord.', answered our friend.
Don't you think we could do with a bit more reverent
heart to heart talking with God? I listen to men talk with
me and then I hear them talk to God. It seems that they
are often two different people. Was Ananias a different
man with the Lord than with Paul? There lay no trace of
false piety with this man. The sheer, utter, down-to-earth
sincerity of Ananias in prayer would take a lot of
pompous, dry, cliche-riden nonsense out of our public
and private praying. Let's study the prayers of the Bible
and compare them to our own and set to absorbing their
approach. It will be somewhat akin to a breath of fresh
air, or a dying fire raked and re-fuelled.

JUNE 3

*"Lord, I have heard by many of this man, how much evil he
has done to thy saints at Jerusalem: And here he hath
authority from the chief priests to bind all that call on thy
name. But the Lord said unto him, Go thy way: for he is a
chosen vessel unto me, to bear my name before the Gentiles,
and kings, and the children of Israel: For I will show him
how great things he must suffer for my name's sake. And
Ananias went his way."*
Acts 9 v 13-17

The sheer obedience of Ananias is an inspiration. In
the teeth of all he had heard concerning Saul he
went to see him at the Lord's bidding. Quietly and
carefully he found a street called Straight, the house of

Judas and Saul and, as a result the Pharisee of Pharisees
was encouraged on his new found Christian way.
Millions were to be influenced as a result. The link of
Ananias in the chain of Paul's life was absolutely vital.
Did Ananias realise that he was opening a historic door
the day he opened the door on Straight Street? The Lord
had said He was and that was enough. Better to have the
whole world against you and do God's bidding than to
have the whole world for you and disobey God. Watch
the door you knock today. You could be opening one of
the most important doors in the nation.

JUNE 4

*"Brother Saul, the Lord, even Jesus, that appeared unto thee
in the way as thou camest, hath sent me."*
Acts 9 v 17

A nanias knew very well that Saul hated the very
name of the Lord Jesus. It was the Christian claim
that Jesus of Nazareth was the Lord of Lords that made
Saul of Tarsus try to extinguish the light of the Gospel.
But now things had changed. Ananias bravely calls him
'Brother Saul' and then launches into his ministry of
encouragement. But notice how he does it. 'The Lord',
he says, 'even Jesus .. hath sent me'. Ananias was
absolutely faithful to the Lordship of Christ. Not only
Jesus had sent him, he said, but the Lord Jesus.
Who knows where you and I may be before this day is
through? We shall meet many who will blaspheme that
lovely Name. Will we remain true, no matter what the
cost? As Agustine said 'He values not Christ at all who
does not value Christ above all'.

JUNE 5

"Then was Saul certain days with the disciples which were at Damascus."
Acts 9 v 19

Ananias must have got to work immediately and introduced Saul to the fellowship of the Christians at Damascus. No easy task. Can you imagine how they first felt when Saul was introduced to them as a believer? But Ananias was the bridge builder. Now, the Church of Christ from Paris to Puckets Creek thank God for the bridge that he built, never to speak of the Christians at Damascus.

What is the lesson from this? We must never complain that our circumstances are too narrow to have much influence for the Lord. We do not need to live in the limelight to do true service for our Master. Ananias proves that publicity is not essential to true success.

'If that person may be,
Stronger for the strength I bring,
Sweeter for the songs I sing,
Happier for the path I tread,
Lighter for the light I shed,
Richer for the gifts I give,
Purer for the life I live,
Nobler for the death I die,
Not in vain have I been I.

JUNE 6

"And straightway he preached Christ in the synagogues, that he is the Son of God."
Acts 9 v 20

C an there have been any greater reward for Ananias than seeing Saul preach Christ in Synagogues? He was glad he had obeyed the Lord in encouraging Saul. Never say that you are of no significance to the Lord. Perhaps you feel like the Scots woman Bob Christie of BBC Scotland told me about. She was praying and this was what she said; 'Lord some of us are vessels of silver and some of us are vessels of gold, and some of us are vessels of wood. But you know Lord that some of us are plain mugs!' Too true!

The truest service to the Lord Jesus is not what we merely do for Him but surely it is what we allow Him to do through us. Far more vital than what we do is what we are. Five simple words shot through with the love of Christ from the lips of a Christian will accomplish more than five thousand sermons delivered merely in the energy of the flesh. That is a fact. Take note of this man Ananias for he teaches us the secret of making the so called commonplace beautiful and what may seem to be very earthly, heavenly.

JUNE 7

"But all that heard him were amazed, and said; Is not this he that destroyed them which called on this name in Jerusalem, and came hither for that intent, that he might bring them bound unto the chief priests? But Saul increased the more in strength, and confounded the Jews which dwelt at Damascus, proving that this is very Christ."
Acts 9 v 21-22

W e leave our short study of the life of Ananias with that lovely little phrase in our hearts 'But Saul increaseth the more in strength'. Let us remember that the humble Ananias who went to Paul at the Lord's bidding did not start by explaining who or what he was. He was content to be the faithful anonymous messenger of the Lord Jesus. He delivered his message and was content to let God handle the results. The very exciting thing is that the work done for the Lord will, in fact, never end. The writers, film producers, business men, politicians, fashion designers, you name it, of this world, have to see their work come to an end. But God's work goes on forever. When God opens a door no man can shut it and although we may see a difficulty in every opportunity, God sees an opportunity in every difficulty. He takes all His mountains away. Let Ananias teach us that no work is insignificant for God. No messenger of the Lord is commonplace. It is the aggregate of commonplace things which constitutes the greatest of all influences in the history of mankind.

'A commonplace life', we say and we sigh;
Yet why should we sigh as we say?
A commonplace sun in the commonplace sky,
Makes lovely the commonplace day,
The moon and the stars, they are commonplace things,
The flower that blooms and the robin that sings;
Yet sad were the world and unhappy our lot,
If flowers all failed and the sunshine came not!
And God, who considers each separate soul,
From commonplace lives makes a beautiful whole'.

JUNE 8

"It seemed good to me also, having had perfect understanding of all things from the very first, to write unto thee in order, most excellent Theophilus."
Luke 1 v 3

He was the doctor who wrote it all down. Luke, the Bible's most loved Physician. Let's spend a week with him, the shy and modest friend of Paul, who never drew attention to himself. His activities are so modestly suppressed we must take care not to pass him by too lightly. As in the book of Esther, the name of God is nowhere stated, yet He is implied throughout, so in the Gospel of Luke and the Acts of the Apostles the skilful fingers, the sympathetic heart, and the cultured mind of Luke are always perceptible. He was not of the Jewish blood and we deduce that he had not known Christ personally in the flesh. What marked his writings? He had a very high opinion of womanhood. It is to Luke that we owe the life like pictures of Elizabeth, the Virgin Mary, Anna, Mary of Magdala, Martha and Mary of Bethany, Dorcas, Lydia, Joanna, the wife of Chauza, Herod's steward, Susanna, Rhoda, etc. In Luke's pages we meet more widows than in any other book of the Bible. It is Luke who records that one of the first social duties undertaken by the infant church at Jerusalem was the daily care and maintenance of the widows.

The attitude to womanhood in Western Europe in general is frightening. I consider that a person who reads newspapers which present women as something that exists particularly to gratify man's sexual appetite are guilty of supporting an industry which glorifies rampant lust. Ulster Television made a major documentary recently on the sexual harassment of woman in offices and factories where they work. This is now such a major problem that trade unions are deeply encouraging women to bring their case before tribunals, one of which was recently successful against an Ulster employer. Luke would certainly have defended such women as well. It is noteworthy that on two occasions Christ defended women's intuition against the reasoning of the twelve. we find women bravely continuing in Christ's company right through the long hours of the

Crucifixion and beyond. Again and again Luke shows us
Christ's teaching constantly defending the sacredness of
womanhood.

It is interesting to remember that since these first women
who were in the Lord's company, women have usually
comprised the majority of any Christian congregation.
Why? As a recent writer put it: 'No one who is not a
woman can appreciate the sense of hope, comfort,
understanding and inspiration a woman receives from
studying Christ in the Gospels'. His words 'take my
yoke upon you and learn of me' was every bit offered to
a woman as to a man. Luke showed that Christ has
liberated women as Gloria Steinhem or Germaine Greer
never can.

JUNE 9

*"For the Son of man is come to seek and to save
that which was lost."*
Luke 19 v 10

There are many people in this world whom society
rejects as of no importance. Luke, to his eternal
credit, wrote to his friend Theophilus to show how the
Saviour was the outcasts' champion. He tells the story of
the reclaiming of the prostitute at Simon the Pharisee's
house and the message on forgiveness that followed.
What about the redeeming of the swindler Zaccaus?
What of the conversion of the criminal known to history
as the dying thief? In Luke we read of the Lord Jesus
dealing with the victims of disease, lepers, the victims of
insanity induced by spiritism, and the victims of
religious feuds. Luke was very people-orientated and he
showed very clearly that his Saviour is the Saviour of
sinners. Lets go out to a lost world with the same
message today.

JUNE 10

"Luke, the beloved physician."
Colossians 4 v 14

There are very clear indications in Luke's writings of his medical interest. Where Matthew and Mark only speak of a fever, Luke particularises it as a 'high fever'. Luke speaks of a certain man not simply of having leprosy but as being 'full of leprosy'. It was a very human touch that he omits the statement that the woman with the haemorrhage had spent all her money on doctors! But another more marked and more significant feature is Luke's interest in death. How often in his professional work he would have had to stand by and watch a patient of his, in spite of all he had to do for him, succumb to disease or old age. There must have been occasions when he fell to wondering about the significance of death. Was it the final catastrophe? Was there something beyond? Could a person be certain about their destiny in the next world? In the Lord Jesus, Luke found answers to all of these questions so that when Luke writes he introduces us at every turn, in a way that no other writer does, to people who are on the point of going out into the next world or have just passed over. We read of Simeon. We read of Jarius's daughter. We read of the dying thief being told by the Lord: 'Today thou shalt be with me in paradise'. It is Luke who tells us of the rich farmer of the rich man and the beggar of Christ's talking with Moses and Elijah about the death He would die. Life is clearly meant to be a journey to a goal and death is not an extinction. Is it not fascinating that from cultured medical doctors to dying thieves the Lord Jesus has proved not only the answer to life but to death? Trust Him today.

JUNE 11

"And one of them, when he saw that he was healed, turned back, and with a loud voice glorified God, And fell down on his face at his feet, giving him thanks: and he was a Samaritan."
Luke 17 v 15-17

In Luke's writings we see the breadth of the great love of God and the way the Gospel reaches out across the world breaking all barriers down. Luke uses the word 'Salvation' thirteen times in his entire writings. He employs the verb 'to save' more than does any other evangelist. In fact, the truth of salvation is the key to the theology of Luke. He has a truly international view of the Gospel. The messages of the Angel concerned men in general, not especially Israel. He takes the genealogy of Jesus right back to Adam and does not stop at Abraham. He tells us a lot about Samaritans when the disciples wanted to call down fire on them, or the Good Samaritan, or the information that the grateful leper was a Samaritan, as in today's text. He refers to Gentiles in the Song of Simeon, the healing of the centurions slave, he records words about people coming from all directions of the compass to sit in God's Kingdom and he speaks of the commission that the Gospel be preached to all nations.

We must remember that God does not teach that all will be saved. Luke distinguishes between 'The sons of this world' and 'The sons of light'. The Gospel, however, is freely offered to all men but they have a responsibility to repent and believe it. The tragedy of today is that so many of us have such a narrow view of the great Gospel of Jesus Christ. Would that God would give us a vision that the message of the Gospel is to reach out to everyone everywhere, no matter what their condition or social position. I wonder who are the 'Samaritans' in your town? Do you witness to them?

JUNE 12

"And on my servants and on my handmaidens I will pour out in those days of my spirit."
Acts 2 v 18

Luke lays great emphasis on the power of the Holy Spirit. The Spirit of God is prominent in his writings right from the very beginning. There is the prophecy that John the Baptist would be filled with the Spirit. Elizabeth and Zechariah are said to have been filled with the Spirit. The same Spirit was 'upon' Simeon. The Holy Spirit was active in connection to the ministry of Jesus. To Mary, 'The Holy Spirit shall come upon you'. When the Saviour was baptised the Holy Spirit came upon Him 'In bodily form, as a dove', the very same Spirit led Him into the wilderness. When He preached in the Synagogue at Nazareth, Jesus applied to Himself the words 'The Spirit of the Lord is upon Me'. According to Luke blasphemy against the Holy Spirit is the gravest of sins. The Acts of the Apostles gives the full thrust of Luke's emphasis on the Spirit of God. Nowhere does Luke think of God as leaving us to serve Him as best we can of our own resources. Never. Christians have the might and power of the Holy Spirit behind them when their lives are clean and obedient to the Lord. The Spirit can fill them to overflowing and use them to world-wide blessing. Let us never grieve the Spirit of God in our lives. Many gifts of the Spirit can be counterfeited by Satan but there is one thing that Satan can counterfeit; it is a godly life. The Holy Spirit produces character. Let Him.

JUNE 13

"And he led them out as far as to Bethany, and he lifted up his hands, and blessed them. And it came to pass while he

blessed them, he was parted from them, and carried up into heaven. And they worshipped him, and returned to Jerusalem with great joy: And were continually in the temple, praising and blessing God. Amen."
Luke 24 v 50-53

There is joy in Luke's writings as well as in his heart. Some of the greatest hymns of the Christian faith are found on his pages. Mary's, Simeon's; the verb 'rejoice' and the noun 'joy' are often found. There is 'laughter' in the Gospel and even merry-making at the home-coming of the Prodigal Son. There was joy at Zacchaeus's reception and joy at the return of the lost sheep. The lovely thing about Luke's Gospel is that it ends in joy as it began. 'And they worshipped Him and returned to Jerusalem with great joy'. And what of the future? Joy is the serious business of heaven.

JUNE 14

"Only Luke is with me."
2 Timothy 4 v 11

Paul has been re-arrested and when that took place thousands of his Christian friends deserted him. Luke is his sole comfort to his lonely end. And yet not his sole comfort for he says 'The Lord stood with me and strengthened me'; the Good Physician and the Beloved Physician held him up. Paul's comment 'Only Luke is with me' is a beautiful epitaph to the doctor's lovely life. His hands had reached for the sick and his pen has reached the heart of millions. His feet travelled from Jerusalem to Rome for the Lord's sake. His voice comforted and encouraged. His silver and his gold were poured into God's service. His will stayed loyal to the very end, and Foxe's Book of Martyrs says he was supposed to have been hanged on an olive tree by the idolatrous priests of Greece. Luke's love was poured out for the Lord Jesus, defending the truth of Christ's miraculous virgin birth and his all atoning death, and plying his pen under God's guidance to good effect. He was responsible for the spiritual upbuilding of an unknown Roman called Theophilus and millions in the world as a result. He was indeed, ever, only, all for God. He was the quiet doctor who led an extraordinary life. We owe him an incalculable debt. Let's follow closely the Lord he exhalted.

JUNE 15

"And there accompanied him into Asia, Sopater of Berea; and of the Thessalonians, Aristarchus and Secundus; and Gaius of Derbe, and Timotheus; and of Asia, Tychicus and Trophimus."
Acts 20 v 4

It is very probable that nine out of ten lists of Paul's friends would omit Tychicus altogether. But few men served Paul better than he did, though his rank in the Church was one of the humblest. Tychicus was a letter carrier in the days when a letter was an event. Even in our day the postman tends to be 'mentally invisible' because he fills so usual a place in our daily life as to be taken for granted, a bit like fresh air and daylight. But the man who for the last seven years of Paul's ministry was the trusty messenger, first of the Ephesian Churches and then of Paul can only be ignored through lack of thought. He might have been mentally invisible, but he was spiritually indispensible.

It is hardly possible to exaggerate the importance letters had between separate Churches in moulding the development of the Church of Christ and in its correspondence flowed its very life blood. Viewed in this light, Tychicus had a place of honoured prominence. Paul wrote, Tychicus carried, but God gave the increase. Praetorian guards might hold Paul fast in his lodgings by the Tiber but the people in Philippi and Colosse and Ephesus hung upon his words. Why? Because of Tychicus.

Let us in this age of the micro chip and telecommunications not neglect the letter. I feel that our writing has greatly decreased in recent years and recent post office statistics prove that. It is a pity. Professor Marshall McLuhan once stated that television was going to outlive writing but the amazing thing is that he had to write a book to convince everybody! When God wanted to communicate with us He wrote to us. Letters of sheer encouragement have tremendous effect. The word 'Congratulations' is not hard to write. If someone has done a good job write to them today and tell them so. Let the following little poem never have to be said by any friend of ours;

'In life's dying embers I have two regrets,
When I am right no one remembers,
When I am wrong no one forgets'.

JUNE 16

"But that ye also may know my affairs, and how I do, Tychicus, a beloved brother and faithful minister in the Lord, shall make known to you all things."
Ephesians 6 v 21

He must have been a trustworthy fellow, Tychicus. There is such a thing as a gossip but there is also another thing known as the truthful passing on of news.

Paul's friends were hungry for news of him and to Tychicus the task was given of telling how things were. There is no touch of exaggeration with this man. No 'Boost Paul' memos. Few are the people who can be summed up as 'Loved' and 'Faithful' and few are those who can be trusted to tell news without exaggeration. It was, for Tychicus, a sacred trust and he executed it perfectly. I can see him with measured words and burning heart tell those far scattered and persecuted Churches how things fared with their beloved leader. He told things as they were, not as he thought they were, or should be. I am sure that he spoke of his friends' great successes for God as well as his heart-breaking problems. Let Tychicus be the Patron Saint of 'Passing-on-the-news' as we chat on the phone today or warm our feet on someone's fender tonight.

JUNE 17

"Whom I have sent unto you .. that he might comfort your hearts."
Ephesians 6 v 22

Wherever Tychicus went he brought comfort with him. Paul knew this only too well and that's why he sent him to the Ephesian Church. I always love that story of Philip Keller's who, when he lived in Africa, showed two of his friends some hospitality. Mr Keller and his friends then continued on a safari and after some time one of his friends missed his hat. They rang back to the Keller home to see if they had left it there. Mrs Keller went on a quick search through the house and then returned to the telephone. 'The only thing those two left behind them in our house,' she said quietly, 'was a blessing.' That's the way to live. Dispense a bit of comfort and blessing wherever you go today.

JUNE 18

"Put them in mind .. to speak evil of no man, to be no brawlers, but gentle, showing all meekness unto all men .. when I shall send Artemas unto thee, or Tychicus .."
Titus 3 v 1-2, 12

Titus was Paul's greatest 'trouble-shooter'. Whenever divisions occurred in churches, disorders, resentments, uncertainties, Titus was sent in and by the Spirit's power helped to mend the fracture. But the Titus' of this world need help too. Tychius is the man for the job. Paul will send him. Not only with the chief of staff, if you like, but with the subordinates, Tychicus is used of God to inspire, help, and encourage wherever he goes.

His long journeys are quickly marked on the map but the needs of imagination to picture the weariness of the road and the perils of the way. Dangers of crossing rivers, dangers from robbers, dangers from the city, dangers from the desert. It was not by easy methods or soft living that Tychicus was used of God to make a Kingdom within an Empire. The great feature of this lovely man was that he was able to communicate encouragement and comfort to people at all levels of the Church of Jesus Christ in the day in which he lived. It was the Christian traveller like Tychicus and the letters he bore which achieved the great results. Such communication was the greatest factor in the development of the Church; it kept alive the interest not only of the Christian Churches in one another and strengthened their mutual affection by giving frequent opportunity of expressing it. It must have been great to be a Titus but surely it must have been greater still to be one who was used by God to fuel the Spiritual fire of the Titus' of this world. Such was Tychicus and such a ministry is open to all of us.

JUNE 19

"Tychicus .. who is a beloved brother."
Colossians 4 v 7

L et us think again of the work of Paul's letter carrier. The main aim of Tychicus was to link up one distant point with another but his every journey was dotted with halting places for nightly shelter. In each of these he would be more than likely housed under a Christian roof while that was possible. Pagan Inns were commonly places of the worst character regarding morality. Hence Paul's charge is to Christian's to be hospitable. In many cases the little local Churches would probably be summoned to hear what the letter Tychicus carried had to say. These letters proved so inspiring, as hearts glowed and hands clasped with fresh fervour under their messages, that Church borrowed from Church those precious writings. The crisis that occurred in one congregation is likely at some period to occur in other similar bodies; the letter that spoke direct to the heart of one man or one body of men would speak direct to the body of all men due to their common human nature. Colosse would, no doubt, lend its letter to Philippi and vice versa. Each would take a copy of the other's treasure. Philemon would allow Paul's letter to him to be added to the sacred writings. So gradually the pile of letters grew until at last we had the New Testament. The man who had no small share in this work of unity is Tychicus, the King's messenger. The practical application of all this is that of course every Christian is but the King's messenger. We carry the good news of the Gospel to men and women and boys and girls everywhere and sometimes they are none too pleased at the message we carry. They scold us about it, they argue with us about it, they sometimes even despise us for it. Yet we must take no heed of their censure or praise with regard to carrying on for the Lord. If a telegram boy arrived at your door with a message you would not box his ears if you did not like the message contained in the telegram, would you? Unfortunately that is the way some people behave towards the Tychicus' of this world. Never mind. Just get all the message delivered, that's what is important. We are, after all, God's telegram boys.

JUNE 20

"Tychicus .. fellow servant in the Lord."
Colossians 4 v 7

Not to be served but to serve: this is the motto for the Christian, as it was for Tychicus. The Lord Jesus gave some great ministry in the upper room but he turned from giving divine doctrine to washing dirty feet in a very few seconds. God is committed to one major objective in all of our lives and that is to conform us to the image of His Son. What is 'the image of His Son'? What was He like? He came to serve. 'Whoever wants to be great among you shall be your servant', the Lord Jesus taught.

In the whole Evangelical scene these days the thing that seems to get emphasis is size and success and we lose sight of our primary calling to be servants. I have a friend called George Bates and he rings me up now and again with this introduction, 'I just want to wash your feet, brother'. It may sound Irish, washing feet on a telephone, but I'll tell you something, it is always refreshing! Find someone today and serve them.

JUNE 21

"That he might know your estate."
Colossians 4 v 8

As we leave our study of Paul's letter carrier, Tychicus, today's text tells us clearly that Tychicus cared for others. He was the symbol of the growth of Christian unity as he sought to bind the believers together wherever he travelled. Paul is saying 'He has won our affection, he has inspired with us trust, he has shouldered our burdens. All there is to know of us he can tell you, all that you need of help and strength he will endeavour to give you by his own personal influence and his touch with Christ'.

We need the spirit of Tychicus. I sometimes think when we say, 'How are you', to our friends, if they took half an hour to tell us we wouldn't have time to listen! Do we really mean 'How are you'? Do we really care for their estate? Tychicus had the same love for one as he had for thousands. It is important to listen to our friends as they talk and try to be sensitive to what their needs are, and then to reach out and try and meet those needs. We don't really know each other as we should. We can meet at Church services all our lives and never know one another's true state. Let Tychicus point the way to change.

JUNE 22

"A certain Jew named Aquila, born in Pontus, lately come from Italy, with his wife Priscilla."
Acts 18 v 2

Patrick Moore could tell us, as probably no other man could, that to follow a star's course through space is a very fascinating occupation. But the telescope reveals the fact that many stars are double. More than ten thousand of them have a comrade.

Around Paul there cluster many bright lights but there is a double star. Aquila is never mentioned apart from his wife, Priscilla. Their witness for Christ was dual. Their friendship for Paul is a double star friendship. It brought into his lonely life blessing of a woman's friendship and a man's comradeship. Interesting that in four out of six places where this pair is named the wife stands first. Luke calls her by her familiar name, Priscilla, and Paul, always mindful for her social standing, speaks of her by her Roman name, Prisca. It is a love match of great interest. Priscilla, probably a high born Roman married the Jewish tent maker Aquila and in Christ all divisions of social prestige, family pride and national ties are broken down.

Contractual marriage is being touted among certain groups today. Sign a marriage contract which spells out all responsibilities and decisions, splitting them equally between the man and woman. This, they say, will lead to freedom and harmony. No. Marriage is not a two headed monster. God created marriage with one head only. The husband is to be the head, the leader of his wife. This is to be a leadership of love. Leadership without love ends in tyranny, but in marriage, love without leadership leads to fanciful romanticism.

Priscilla may have been a high born Roman but her humble tentmaker husband was the leader and she followed his leadership to the inestimable blessing of many a people, as we shall see. Aquila never felt threatened by his wife's abilities. Nor should you. If your wife gets more phonecalls than you do, if your gifts overlap, so what? God did not bring you together to compete with one another but to complete one another. This double star did just that.

JUNE 23

"Because that Claudius had commanded all Jews to depart from Rome."
Acts 18 v 2

It is, in Europe, Midsummer Day. We are at the half-way stage of this year. The last half may see some very real changes in our lives. Things certainly changed dramatically for Priscilla and Aquila. Suddenly the clouds began to gather on the horizon of their happiness. There were riots in the streets of the Jewish Colony across the Tiber in Rome and the cause was that old apple of Jewish discord, the question, 'Who is the Messiah?'

Aquila and many others held unswerving loyalty to the Lord Jesus but they met with fanatical opposition. There were no rioters like the Jews, as Pilate and other Roman governors knew to their cost. It was not very difficult for Claudius to issue a short act ordering the immediate deportation of all Jews. It sounded simple but it was a serious thing for Aquila and his wife as it was for many another. For them it meant financial disaster and social exile.

Some of the Jews evaded the order and hid themselves in the slums. So wide was this practice that the policy at last proved a failure and had only a temporary effect. But these two subjects of Christ were loyal to the orders of their earthly sovereign. So Claudius was the minister of God for good and Priscilla and Aquila, moved to Corinth, the great shipping centre. This was likely to prove a good place for the purchase of their raw materials and a ready market for the disposal of their manufactures. Priscilla obviously learned her husbands craft and worked diligently with him in the chamber of their Corinthian lodging.

It is not the first time that a secular order has proved to be the furtherance of God's Kingdom. Have you been suddenly ordered to move from your present circumstances, or whatever and your heart is breaking? Remember that God overrules, always. Priscilla and Aquila moved away in God's will and the results were to be, in the end, of incalculable blessing to others. So it will be for you. You'll see.

JUNE 24

"And because he was of the same craft, he abode with them, and wrought: for by their occupation they were tentmakers. And he reasoned in the Synagogue every Sabbath, and persuaded the Jews and the Greeks."
Acts 18 v 3-4

Priscilla and Aquila settled in Corinth and after some time Paul came to the city. He was lonely and obscure, his Athenian mission has been less promising than he had hoped. He was not well supplied with funds and the finger of God's providence led him to Priscilla and Aquila's place of business. According to 2 Corinthians 11 v 9, we could say that they were all poor together because Paul says that he suffered want and we may be sure that Paul would not have gone hungry if his friends had not been equally needy. What an inspiring comradeship those three had! Wouldn't you have loved to hear what they all talked of as they made tents together?

There grew up in this trio such a loyal devotion to one another that Paul was moved to say in Romans 16 v 4, 'Priscilla and Aquila, my helpers in Christ Jesus: who have for my life laid down their own necks: unto whom not only I give thanks , but all the Churches of the

Gentiles.' Obviously persecution had knit them together in even closer ties.

Our homes may be humble and our circumstances may be strained but are not Priscilla and Aquila a tremendous encouragement to us to use what we have for God? May the Churches in Europe bless God for your home as they did for the tentmakers' home at Corinth.

JUNE 25

"A certain Jew named Apollos .. an eloquent man, and mighty in the scriptures, came to Ephesus .. being fervent in the spirit .. whom .. Aquila and Priscilla .. heard."
Acts 18 v 24-26

Aquila and Priscilla heard an amazing man preach. His name was Apollos. The North African had three rare qualities. He was eloquent. He was mighty in the Scriptures and he was fervent in the spirit.

Depth of mind and fluency of speech do not always go together. They did not go together in Moses and Paul. Moses had a stammer. Paul was not, it would seem, an eloquent preacher. His Christian critics said his bodily presence was weak and his speech contemptible. So it is obvious that we do not need all three qualities to be used of God. But to have all three qualities and use them for God's great glory, that is the lovely thing about Apollos.

I love the third quality of this great man: fervency of spirit. I have heard eloquent men and I have heard men mighty in the Scriptures but they lacked fervency. Fervency as an adjective means burning, glowing. Figuratively it means eager, intense. As a noun it means zeal, great heat. Eloquence without fervency sets nothing alight. Scriptural knowledge without eagerness is as dry as dust. It was Apollos' lovely quality of fervency that led Paul to say that he planted but Apollos watered. There must have been something tremendously refreshing about the ministry of Apollos. He was both bracing and inspiring, a tonic and a stimulant in one. It seems to me that it was his fervency, touched by the mighty power of the Holy Spirit that made all the difference. Don't let anyone, anywhere, take away your fervency as a Christian.

JUNE 26

"Whom when Aquila and Priscilla had heard, they took him unto them, and expounded unto him the way of God more perfectly."
Acts 18 v 26

Aquila and Priscilla were both struck by Apollos's capabilities but they noticed his inadequate spiritual information. For all his brilliance and fervency there was something really missing. Every returning Sabbath day they listened to him with increasing regret. With a weekly increasing distress they listened to what they heard, or rather did not hear, until at last they took Apollos and expounded unto him the way of God more perfectly. It took extraordinary wisdom, and tact and courage, and, especially love. Notice that it was not Paul's preaching that did it. Great though Paul's preaching was. It was their own experience of the way of God that enabled and authorised Aquila and Priscilla to take Apollos's lovely quality of fervency of spirit that led Paul to say experience went before Paul's preaching, accompanied it, and came after it. Tentmakers as they were, they read and well understood the Epistle to the Ephesians because they had all its deep mysteries already in their own hearts.

Instead of criticising Apollo's defects and comparing him unfavourably with their friend from Tarsus, these two quietly opened before him a new and beautiful Bible truth. Because of them Apollos started out on a wider path of divine blessing adding even greater glory than ever before in his track. How he must, in later years, have thanked God for the day this couple ever crossed his path. Maybe there is a similar young Apollos arising in your district. There are some things missing in his life which need to be filled up. Go to it my friends. Be an Aquila and Priscilla to him.

JUNE 27

"Paul .. sailed .. into Syria, and with him Priscilla and Aquila .. And he came to Ephesus, and left them there."
Acts 18 v 18-19

The call of God had led Paul eastwards and Aquila and Priscilla went too. They settled at Ephesus and here the hand of God continued with them. Business prospered, they had a large business room which they also consecrated to the use of Christian services. The Church of Christ was destined to have no public place of worship for many a long day. There the Ephesian Christians gathered. The building might have had no steeple but Aquila's needle pointed the way to heaven. No carved pulpit may have graced their room but, there, stood a weaver's bench. These two made tents for men but they erected a real tabernacle for their Lord at the same time: for their praise was in all the Churches. Here's a prayer for today: 'Lord, whoever enters this home of ours, at whatever time, in whatever state, may they find that even to be here is ease and may they feel like the Christians at Ephesus felt in Aquila and Priscilla's home, spiritually the better for being here. Amen.'

JUNE 28

"At my first answer no man stood with me, but all men forsook me: I pray God that it may not be laid to their charge. Notwithstanding the Lord stood with me, and strengthened me; that by me the preaching might be fully known, and that all the Gentiles might hear: and I was delivered out of the mouth of the lion. And the Lord shall deliver me from every evil work, and will preserve me unto his heavenly kingdom: to whom be the glory for ever and ever. Amen. Salute Prisca and Aquila."
2 Timothy 4 v 16-19

These words are amongst the last ones written by the Apostle Paul to his young friend Timothy just before his execution. He is lying in prison and Roman law would have permitted him to employ an advocate and call witnesses. But among all the Christians in Rome there was not one who would stand at his side in court either to speak on his behalf or to advise him in the conduct of his case or to support him by a demonstration of sympathy. If ever an accused man needed help it was Paul at this time. Like his Lord at Gethsemane, he had to face his greatest ordeal alone. Yet like his Master, Paul knew that he was not alone. The Lord stood by him and at no time did he even betray the slightest bit of self pity. Before one of the highest tribunals of the Empire, before his judges and the Emperor himself, no doubt with a large crowd of the general public present, Paul preached the Word. To that representative city, before that representative audience, he preached Christ. The whole civilised world then knew. The Word had spread.

With almost his last breath Paul says 'Salute Prisca and Aquila'. It is one thing to have friends, it is another thing to hold their friendship right to the end of our lives. This trio were faithful to each other and to their Lord right to the very end. May we too, like them, be faithful to each other and to our Lord to death itself.

JUNE 29

"Whose hearts God had touched."
1 Samuel 10 v 26

So Paul's friends were ordinary? I have yet to meet an ordinary person. Each one of us is unique. No matter what we do, if we do it as to the Lord, it becomes special. Paul's friends had their hearts touched by God and so have we. Our Lord is just as real and powerful as He was in their day. He can make what seems to be very ordinary, extraordinary.

'Glory amid drudgery
Myriad household cares!
Washing, cleaning, mending,
Sweeping down the stairs
Things I might well chafe at,
Dull and drab and drear,
How mid these is glory?

Where does it appear?
In His service Royal,
Could our eyes but see,
Each who serves is given,
Royal livery,
In life's humblest station,
Doing lowliest things,
Glory guilds all service,
For the King of Kings.'

JUNE 30

"A man that hath friends must shew himself friendly."
Proverbs 18 v 24

Paul's friends were special people and as we go off into holiday time, I hope many of you will make deep and real friendships which will last the rest of your lives. If you don't want to win a friendship then there are seven rules you must follow: they are sure to work!

1   Make sure your friendship is based on what the other person can do for you.
2   Be possessive. Do all you can to keep that person as your private property.
3   Cultivate jealousy. Keep a firm grasp on what is yours and protect it against all intruders.
4   Don't discuss your anger and irritation: explode!
5   Avoid the person who threatens and annoys you. Do all you can to stay out of his way.
6   Cultivate envy. Focus so much on what the other person has you will do anything toget it.
7   Believe that your feeling of contempt for his abilities or even his person is justified.

The outcome of following these will be misery and you will never, ever, win a friendship by them. Paul's friends followed the very opposite approach and millions have been blessed as a result. The choice is yours but as for me and my house we are going to be friendly!

JULY

*T*he Romans thought a lot of their Emperors and as Julius Caesar was born in this month they named it after him. They called it Julius. It is a month that can really boil in heat and the cricket, on July banks, is dumb. Even flies seem to forget to hum. It is a time of holiday, of relaxation, of exams forgotten (for one month anyway), of Meadow Brown butterflies and Red Admiral and ease from Spring fever. Through the summer days I want to take you on a cruise through the life of the greatest poet of all time: David. Monarch, shepherd, musician, military strategist, David was one of the most sensitive literary figures ever to put quill to paper. There never has been anyone like him. Millions of people identify with the man who fell so low and yet reached incredible heights. There is something about him that haunts the human heart. 'For My servant David's sake' became God's by-word with future generations. Let's find out why.

JULY 1

"And Samuel said unto Jesse, Are here all thy children? And he said, There remaineth yet the youngest, and, behold, he keepeth the sheep. And Samuel said unto Jesse, Send and fetch him: for we will not sit down till he come hither. And he sent, and brought him in. Now he was ruddy, and withal of a beautiful countenance, and goodly to look to. And the Lord said, Arise, anoint him: for this is he."
1 Samuel 16 v 11-12

'He keepeth the sheep'. Mark well those words. They underline everything David ever became. This lad was to grow to use the sceptre every bit as skilfully as the sling but he never lost his love to shepherding. The lad who was virtually dismissed by his father as a mere keeper of sheep was soon to keep a nation. His father complimented him better than he ever meant to.

That child around your feet may yet do more good than you imagine. Do not despise his or her legitimate interests for they display Wordsworth's dictum that 'the child is the father of the man'. I walked through an exhibition of famous people's toys recently and it was amazing to see the internationally famous racing driver's battered toy racing car, or the broadcaster's Hans Christian Andersen . Every child is different. 'Train up a child in the way he should go', wrote David's son, Solomon. 'Way' in Hebrew suggests the idea of 'characteristic', 'manner', 'mode'. They are wise parents who know the way God made their children and then fit their training accordingly. Each child is different. Jesse should have been sharper to see the embryo leader in the lad who slew the lion and the bear. The world was soon to see what he never saw. Let Jesse's carelessness and selfishness be a warning to all of us as parents. Love and watch that child and then gently point him to the mountains worth climbing, the treasures worth having, and the God who is worthy of his talents and trust. You will not be sorry.

JULY 2

*"Then answered one of the servants, and said, Behold I
have seen a son of Jesse the Bethlehemite, that is cunning in
playing, and a mighty valiant man, and a man of war, and
prudent in matters, and a comely person, and the Lord is
with him."*
1 Samuel 16 v 18

There was music, courage and cautiousness in David.
And he was good looking to boot! His gifts were
now being spoken of before the King and he was about
to walk on a wilder stage for 'a man's gift maketh room
for him'. David did not connive his way into the palace
nor did he scheme to be heard. The Lord was with him
and that was all he needed.
We live in an evil world. False ambition eats the very
soul out of courtesy, kindness, respect and contentment.
I always smile when the Queen's New Year's Honours
List comes out because of the inevitable rampant
jealousy and criticism it causes. Someone is genuinely
rewarded for a job well done but there are always voices
crowding the media trying to slime that person's Eden.
Watch false ambition, it can be a deadly trait. David had
the Lord with him and he did not need to feel jealous of
anyone or push himself where he was not welcome. He
played his music, put courage to good use and was
cautious in his movements. He was summoned to the
palace. The Lord promoted him. He will do the same for
you. False ambition, be slain, your rewards are worth
nothing!

JULY 3

*"With whom has thou left those few sheep in the wilderness?
.. thou art but a youth."*
1 Samuel 17 v 28,33

Eliab was sarcastic and Saul was sceptical. David had faith but then, surely, nine feet six inches of fleshy giant and two hundred weight of brass was too much for a singing shepherd lad. David carried no sword but his staff, no armour but the breastplate of righteousness and the helmet of salvation. And, of course, as they always do, the majority of folk did nothing but spectate. It is no different to any generation when, quietly, God touches a life and starts to use it for His glory.

But David was in possession of spiritual power which was difficult to define. The living God was a reality to him. He had no doubt that the Lord would vindicate His holy name. Youth had nothing to do with it, as far as the secret was concerned. Proving a living God is as open to a little child as it is to an old man. David took from God's vast supply while the majority around him talked or thought about it. Care to join him? You'll become a giant killer too. Immediately.

JULY 4

"The said David to the Philistine, Thou comest to me with a sword, and with a spear, and with a shield: but I come to thee in the name of the Lord of hosts, the God of the armies of Israel, whom thou hast defied."
1 Samuel 17 v 45

Oh, I have seen the day,
When with a single word,
God helping me to say,
'My trust is in the Lord!'
My soul hath quenched a thousand foes,
Fearless of all that could oppose.

- William Cowper

JULY 5

"And Saul eyed David from that day and forward."
1 Samuel 18 v 9

There was venom in that look. Behind it lay something as cruel as the grave. Jealousy rose when the women in their song compared David's tens of thousands to Saul's thousands of enemy slain. The women would have been wiser if they had given God the glory because they lit a flame of jealousy in the heart of Saul which was to burn him to death. He, in fact, started to fight God over it. He had been told that his kingdom was going to be given to a neighbour of his and the song of the women served to confirm it. Instead of praising God he started to match himself with God. He took matters in his own hands and the very next day tried to kill David, twice as he played his harp.

But David went on for God as you must do, my much envied friend. Just bear their spiteful attacks of malice and envy: overcome evil with good: suffering wrong: possess your life in patience: keep your tongue: pass on unruffled. And what will happen? They will be afraid of you: the Scripture tells us that Saul was afraid of David because the Lord was with him. You see, things are not always as they seem.

David looked to be the one who should be frightened out of his mind. Not so. The same peace can be yours in the teeth of jealousy for it came from the same God who has not changed in the slightest.

JULY 6

"Then the princes of the Philistines went forth: and it came to pass, after they went forth, that David behaved himself more wisely than all the servants of Saul; so that his name was much set by."
1 Samuel 18-30

'So that his name was precious', reads the margin of the Authorised Version. Ah! Do you find that sentimental as you read this book on this summer's morning at your kitchen table or by some swimming pool in Majorca or Florida!

'Precious'. The very mention of David's name did something to people's hearts in those far off days. His name, due to his behaviour, was of value, it was unique and rare. It was worth its weight in gold. And your name?

JULY 7

"And Jonathan spake good of David unto Saul his father."
1 Samuel 19 v 4

Take a cue from Jonathan. Before this day is through you will hear someone of a group of people speak evil of an individual. Never a day seems to pass but I hear somebody criticised or spoken evil of. Spike their guns and find something good to say about the one under attack - say it! Then watch the reaction. Go on, try it. You may find you will have to do it many times before the sun sets. I guarantee it will start a chain of events which will end in blessing. Ask Jonathan.

JULY 8

"And David fled .. and came and said before Jonathan, What have I done? what is mine iniquity? and what is my sin before thy father, that he seeketh my life?"
1 Samuel 20 v 1

Self-doubt. Who of us has not known it? The devil began to annoy the man of God and taunt him with

the feeling that maybe, after all, he had done something
wrong that had caused him to be persecuted by Saul.
I met a gentle pastor who told me that someone once
said to him, 'Not a single word you have ever said in the
last seven years has ever meant anything to me.' The
cruel jibe caused that man of God the next Lord's day to
question his call to the Christian ministry. But he picked
himself off the floor again and went on. Praise God.
Has the devil caused you to have self-doubt about your
work? Remember, he is a liar.

JULY 9

*"Jonathan cried after the lad, and said, Is not the arrow
beyond thee?"*
1 Samuel 20 v 37

David hid by the stone Ezel and waited. Jonathan
was to come by, soon, to shoot some arrows. The
arrangement was that if Jonathan said to his young
valet, 'The arrows are on this side of thee' all would be
well for David at the court of Saul, but, if he said, 'The
arrows are beyond thee', David was to flee. The message
came loud and clear. The arrow was beyond. It is said
there was danger, that David had to go in order to have
greater happiness than he would leave behind.
Are the establishment against you? The arrow said they
were against David. Are you being persecuted? The
arrow said the persecution would be so tough for David
that he had better flee. Are you feeling lonely? The
arrow said that the loneliness of being on the run from
Saul was his unenviable lot. The arrow told David that
the Lord had sent him away.
The promises of God seem hidden in this situation of
David's. Had God not promised David that he would be
king? Yes, of course. But have we not often seen in this
book 'For All Seasons' that God very often makes the

circumstances of a person's life seem to contradict the promises He makes to them? David was no exception and neither are we. God was saying to David, 'Trust in Me.' To believe that God is ordering every detail, to know that his love is prompting every thought of his mind is the secret of facing separation like David was to face. Meditate today on the bus, on the jet, on your bike, at your coffee break, or wherever, on what the arrow said.

JULY 10

"And the priest said, The sword of Goliath the Philistine, whom thou slewest in the valley of Elah, behold, it is here wrapped in a cloth behind the ephod: if thou wilt take that, take it: for there is no other save that here. And David said, There is none like that; give it me."
1 Samuel 21 v 9

Sadly we must look today at David's first major error. In his panic he fled to a town of priests called Nob just north of the city of Jerusalem. There he met Ahimelech, lied to him that he was on the King's business, and asked him for a sword. The tabernacle stood at Nob at this time and asking Ahimelech for a sword was something akin to going to your local preacher and asking him for a gun. 'We have no swords here but Goliath's.', answered the priest. The great symbol of David's faith had been carefully kept as a trophy at Nob. 'There is none like that,' answered David, 'give it me.' David, like Peter took his eyes of the Lord. He had never needed a sword to kill Goliath but he was now to trust in one to protect himself from Saul. There is a chilling lesson for all of us in this incident from David's life. The lesson is that actions out of the will of God have every bit as serious repercussions as actions in the will of God. David's lie and actions were to have spine-chilling repercussions. He was seen at Nob by Saul's Minister of Agriculture, Doeg. Doeg reported to Saul and Saul had every living thing in that little mountain town put to the edge of the sword. The entire priestly community was also exterminated. Only one, Abiathar, escaped and he fled to David in the cave of Adullum.

Sin is bitter in its consequences on others. Other people are inextricably involved in the consequences of our deeds. So, let's go watchfully and prayerfully into the coming day. Sadly, David had not gone watchfully and prayerfully into his.

JULY 11

"And he changed his behaviour before them, and feigned himself mad in their hands, and scrabbled on the doors of the gate, and let his spittle fall down upon his beard."
1 Samuel 21 v 13

David is away from his Lord. Where is he living? He is in Gath, Goliath's town, under the leadership of a heathen king called Achish. Compromised, lonely and depressed the greatest writer of Psalms in history sinks lower and lower in his public witness for the Lord. The people around him cannot understand: 'Is this not David the King of the land? Did they not sing one to another of him?' You would not want this incident on the blurb of a book about David. But it is written in God's book. Is this the writer of the 23rd Psalm pretending to be mad at the gates of the city of Gath, letting the spittle fall down on his beard so that he will be thrown out? It is the very man. 'You can all see,' said Achish, 'the man is mad.' Let every heart who feels a failure read these lines. Let every person who feels like giving up, because of some mistake they have made, ponder this shell of the former victor of the valley of Elah, this seemingly failed and wrecked man of God. You would not have given much for him as he drummed in feigned madness on the gates that day.

But God did. 'This poor man cried,' wrote David at a later time, 'and the Lord heard him and delivered him out of all his troubles.' The outward looked a disaster but inside beat a heart that could not stand the frown of God. This drove him back. He was eventually restored and sang again. If there was hope at the gates of Gath, there is hope for you.

JULY 12

"And every one that was in distress, and every one that was in debt, and every one that was discontented, gathered themselves unto him."
1 Samuel 22 v 2

An Ulsterman writing on the twelfth of July; surely he will write of King William of Orange? No. I write of another banner to which people rally, no matter what flag they fly; the banner of a sympathetic heart. David knew what distress and debt and discontent were. Penniless, he lived in a cave, hunted by Saul like a partridge on the mountain. Suddenly from all over the country four hundred men arrived who were feeling the pressures of life in the raw. In David they had sympathy and under David's leadership they were to know God's blessing. There is no one who can sympathise with suffering hearts like a suffering heart. They gather to it like bees to honey. Your suffering could lead to a new ministry for God. It did for David.

JULY 13

"And Jonathan Saul's son arose, and went to David into the wood, and strengthened his hand in God."
1 Samuel 23 v 16

No jealousy raked Jonathan's heart. No envy drove him to cut off the brilliantly gifted David. The nation who had acclaimed the son of Jesse left him, alone: they didn't seem to want to know. How fickle is public opinion! How foolish to trust in it! But Jonathan found David in the wood and strengthened his hand in God.

The staggering thing in today's text is that the man who strengthened a nation's hand in God needed his own strengthened. We often do not realise that leaders who are great men and women of faith are just as human as the rest of us. They need to be strengthened and encouraged in their faith. The ones we think are getting the most encouragement are often the ones who are getting it least. A preacher once told me that he had thanked the great Dr. Martyn Lloyd Jones for his helpful ministry. 'Thank you', said the one time assistant to the King's physician, 'Thank you for your word of encouragement. Very few people say such things to me.'

JULY 14

"The Lord forbid that I should do this thing unto my master, the Lord's anointed, to stretch forth my hand against him, seeing he is the anointed of the Lord."
1 Samuel 24 v 6

It seemed such a golden opportunity to put an end to all the misery: David's men were hiding in a cave when Saul walked right in! They whispered murder in

David's ear. It seemed as if all their problems could now
end so easily.
But David was now walking in close fellowship with the
Lord and he had no instructions to kill Saul. God had
promised David the kingdom, but not by David's hand.
So David spared Saul.
Circumstances in our lives often seem so right. The
captain was friendly, the boat was ready to sail, the
money was in the prophet's pocket, but Jonah was
running away from the will of God. Circumstances alone
must not be the criterion for our actions. David was
learning fast. Circumstances must be backed by the
agreement of God's Word and the peace of God in our
hearts about what we are doing.

JULY 15

*"And Samuel died; and all the Israelites were gathered
together, and lamented him, and buried him in his
house at Ramah. And David arose, and went
down to the wilderness of Paran."*
1 Samuel 25 v 1

Forgive me if I should sound sarcastic but I
sometimes feel that if I carried a dead body around
with me everybody would unite! Everybody seems to
drink tea at a funeral. You would think divisions never
existed. Why, it's all buns and cake and 'How are you?'
and 'No. Do sit here.' Death unites us as nothing else
does. Life, however, is a much different matter.
If our text says all the Israelites were gathered together
at Samuel's funeral then we must take it that Saul was
there as well as David. Death halted the jealousy
inspired, murderous Saul for the funeral time. Then,
sadly, poor David had to flee. Let's try, by God's grace,
to make sure that it is not just at funerals we stop our
fighting and squabbles.

JULY 16

"And there was a man in Maon, whose possessions were in Carmel; and the man was very great, and he had three thousand sheep, and a thousand goats .. the name of the man was Nabal .. but the man was churlish and evil in his doings."
1 Samuel 25 v 2-3

Nabal was great as far as his possessions went but he was not great as far as God was concerned. He was very mean to David and refused him provisions even though David had been kind to Nabal's shepherds. Bigness and true greatness are not synonymous. Often they are opposed. When the poor widow gave all that she had to the temple treasury she was the great one. The others were just big givers. When some people work their way up in the world from small jobs into great projects and from caring for individuals to dealing with masses they become too big for details and lose touch with those they once knew. The Lord who created the stars could arrange Peter's angling to coincide with the arrival of one fish that had, in its mouth, a coin that would pay the temple tribute. Our God is a great God. May we never get too big for Him to use.

JULY 17

"Now the name of the man was Nabal; and the name of his wife Abigail: and she was a woman of good understanding, and of a beautiful countenance."
1 Samuel 25 v 3

Beauty and brains: what a combination! They do not always go together but it is great when they do!

Abigail was to play a very vital role in David's life. She gave greater attention to those imperishable qualities of the inner person than she did to her own physical attractiveness, and, in the long run, they were to win her an honoured place in history.

'Look for the deep, rich, opulent fabrics,' I read in a fashion advertisement recently, 'with glitter, glimmer and shine. Glowing jewel colours: deep amethyst, rich blues, black swept with gold or accented with shocking pink. Look for the Oriental and Turkish influence, look for your own individual style.' Wow! 'a meek and gentle spirit' seems mild in comparison. But not with God. A woman, according to Scripture, does not need to be good looking to be beautiful.

JULY 18

"Abigail .. fell before David on her face .. and said .. A man is risen to pursue thee, and to seek thy soul: but the soul of my lord shall be bound in the bundle of life with the Lord thy God; and the souls of thine enemies, them shall he sling out, as out the middle of a sling .. when the Lord .. shall have appointed thee ruler over Israel .. this shall be no grief unto thee."
1 Samuel 25 v 23, 29-31

Wise men can be very unwise and good men can be bad. David, in a fit of sheer frustration and anger, took four hundred men and swore, with very vulgar language, vengeance on Nabal and everybody associated with him. As he came rampaging down by the covert of the hill there was this beautiful woman on her knees before him with animals laden with food for him and his men.

'Don't do it, David.' she pleaded, 'Remember Goliath?
God will protect you. Then, when you become King, you
will not grieve over shedding careless blood.' Abigail
could have shrugged her shoulders and said, 'What
business is it of mine? If that hot-head David, wants to
behave stupidly, so what?' But Abigail did something in
the crisis and diverted a man of God from tragedy.
Unfortunately today a large number of wives know
more, much more, than they put into circulation for God.
Shyness or whatever prevents them doing greater good.
Right? Then let Abigail show you the way.

JULY 19

*"And it came to pass about ten days after, that the Lord
smote Nabal, that he died."*
1 Samuel 25 v 38

'Preserved by Jesus when my feet made haste to
Hell', says the old evangelical hymn. Exactly. David
had been preserved and kept. Abigail's cool hand on
David's hot-head had saved him from a disaster. The
Lord handled the churlish Nabal.
Look back down your past history. Can you not see the
preserving hand of God at every turn in your life? You
would not have gone this way or that but God would
not allow it. What disasters God has diverted! Satan had
traps for your feet set and primed but God, like He did
over the wise men and Herod, took you another way.
Did David deserve God's preservation? Do we? Do not
moan at your situation. The tight corner you are in is to
preserve you from a wide corner which will lead you to
a precipice or a cul-de-sac. Paul would go to Asia but the
Spirit suffered him not.

JULY 20

"And David said in his heart, I shall now perish one day by the hand of Saul: there is nothing better for me than that I should speedily escape into the land of the Philistines; and Saul shall despair of me, to seek me any more in any coast of Israel: so I shall escape out of his hand."
1 Samuel 27 v 1

For a long time now David had suffered at Saul's hand. Nowhere seemed to be safe from Saul's murderous hate. Suddenly David thought of a plan of action: he would go and live amongst the Philistines. Saul would never think of him being there. But the plan of action based upon panic took him away out of the will of God. Away out. In fact he very nearly joined them in battle against his own people. It was a fit of mistrust. It was very dishonouring to God.

We must never say in our heart what we will do or not do. We must wait upon God until He makes the way known. As long as the way is hidden there is no need for action. David rushed out of the will of God and his plan of action led him to deceit and into one of the most spiritually barren times of his life. No Psalm is attributed to this period. He lost his song. Study his time with the Philistines and there is a harshness in it all. Never barter God's freedom for expediency.

JULY 21

"And Saul disguised himself .. and they came to the women by night: and he said .. divine unto me by the familiar spirit .. And the woman said unto him, Behold thou knowest what Saul hath done, how he hath cut off those that have familiar spirits, and the wizards, out of the land: wherefore then layest thou a snare for my life, to cause me to die?"
1 Samuel 28 v 8-9

I f David was away from God at this time, what shall we say of Saul? He who had banned practice of the occult in Israel was now dabbling in the occult himself. He was to be a sorry man he ever went near the accursed thing. We must be warned.

Satan is gaining support today not only to jungle tribes and violent inner cities but among university professors and affluent suburbanites. The French spend one million francs a year consulting 60,000 sorcerers. World-wide spiritism has, at least 70 million adherents. Horoscope columns appear in over 1,000 newspapers and magazines. One Scotland Yard official says there is presently more Black Magic in Britain than there ever was in the Middle Ages. Eighty percent of school teenagers in some areas have experience of the ouija board. Talk about the Devil? Millions are. Not only about him but to him.

The warning from today's text is clear. God knows the future and we must leave it with Him. Resist the Devil through the Lord Jesus and he will flee from you. Dabble with him and he will sift you like wheat.

JULY 22

"And David enquired at the Lord, saying, Shall I
pursue after this troop? shall I overtake them?
And he answered him, Pursue."
1 Samuel 30 v 8

W hy do millions of people identify with David? It is because he was like all of us: sometimes he was up and sometimes he was down. We identify with him because we see ourselves in him.

The spiritually barren David, after his wanderings in Philista, is in Zicklag which has just been burned with fire. Abigail has been taken captive and David's own people are talking about stoning him. Suddenly, in his distress, David turns for the first time in months to the Lord. He found Him there and waiting. God had not moved, David had. From that moment David is himself again, his old strong, glad, noble self. The sunshine of fellowship with God is his once more. He arises and goes on to victory. Why do you think God wrote this story for us? It was written for our instruction, that we, through the comfort and instruction of the Scripture, might have hope. Why not, whether you feel like it or not, enquire of the Lord today? You'll find Him unchanged.

JULY 23

"As his part is that goeth down to the battle, so shall his part be that tarrieth by the stuff: they shall part alike. And it was so from that day forward, that he made it a statute and an ordinance for Israel unto this day."
1 Samuel 30 v 24-25

The one who looks after what is at home is every bit as important as the one who goes to the battle: that was David's belief. And he made it law. This important line needs to be drawn again.
The whole economic structure here in the West is forcing many married women to go out to work but the ones who opt to stay at home to look after their children must not be frowned upon. They must not be made to feel inferior. They are doing a very important work.
In the world I live in, the world of preaching and teaching God's Word, those of us who give all of our time to this work are sometimes called 'full time Christian workers'. I can understand people using the term but it is not a Bible term. Hanna bringing up Samuel was every bit as much involved in serving the

Lord as her husband, Elkanah, worshipping the Lord at Shiloh. Some suffering patient in hospital quietly witnessing for the Lord today is every bit as much a 'full time Christian worker' as the mightiest evangelist in the world. the humble secretary in a firm, 'holding down' the office while 'the boss' is in Los Angeles getting custom is as vital a part of the operation as 'the boss' and ought to be made to realise it. Let's obey David's law in spirit as well as in letter.

JULY 24

"And the battle went sore against Saul and the archers hit him; and he was sore wounded of the archers .. Therefore Saul took a sword, and fell upon it."
1 Samuel 31 v 3-4

The death of Saul has got to be one of the saddest in the Bible. It proves conclusively that it is not a gift or the opportunity to use that gift, alone, that brings spiritual success. Saul had both and failed miserably. It is rather the steady, quiet daily dedication of the gift, and the opportunities that come to use it to the glory of God, that counts.
David had said, 'The Lord shall smite him or his day shall come to die; or he shall descend into battle, and perish. The Lord forbid that I should stretch forth mine hand against the Lord's anointed'. He was right. With long clear sight David took what I would call the 'eagle eye' view. An eagle, because of her solitary position can survey an area of some 4 1/2 square miles and dive at a speed of up to 200 mph. David had been waiting on the Lord and could see that Saul would die anyway, why should he take vengeance on him? Take an eagle eye view of your problems today. See what happens to them.

JULY 25

"And David lamented .. over Saul and over Jonathan his son .. Tell it not in Gath, publish it not in the streets of Askelon; lest the daughters of the Philistines rejoice."
2 Samuel 1 v 17,20

Magnanimity to his enemy Saul was one of David's greatest of actions. Suicide is a dreadful thing yet David did not want Saul's great failure to be the glee of the Philistines. 'Do not talk about it in Gath', he said. Gath indeed! In Gath David had done a lot of compromised talk. He had lived there and knew Gath only too well. He knew what they would say. David's recovery from backsliding was amazing but when he could have basked in the fall of his greatest enemy Saul he rather praised him. There was no 'I-told-you-so' with David.

When a great man or woman of God makes a disastrous mistake we must watch what we say about it. The dirty linen of the Church is not for the world to gloat over. We admit failure. We do not whitewash sin. But we must never give occasion for the enemies of the Gospel to dance on the grave of some believer's error by our talk. We draw a curtain of silence around it. David did.

JULY 26

"I am distressed for thee, my brother Jonathan: very pleasant hast thou been unto me."
2 Samuel 1 v 26

The essential basis of friendship is not who we know, but who we are. Friendship does not depend on meeting the right people but it depends on being the right person. Jonathan's friendship with David proves that.

Jonathan had a home background of bitterness. His father had no heart for God. Your father might be the same. His environment was weak leadership on the part of his disobedient father. His mother seems to have been no better. Yet, with all those liabilities, Jonathan entered into one of the Scriptures' great friendships. The courage of this one man re-directed a nation. Jonathan had a dynamic faith in God and he acted on the basis of who God is and tremendous things happened in his own life and in the lives of others. His potential was realised and he became the kind of person others wanted to know. His life made an impact.

The Christian has a far greater revelation of God's grace and power than Jonathan did and far more reason to trust God. This is a definite place for every believer in the body of Christ and a unique ministry for each one that only they can fill. But remember, it is not who you know, it is who you are that makes the difference.

JULY 27

"Died Abner as a fool dieth?"
2 Samuel 3 v 33

There was a civil war. Of all the wars there is none so bitter as a civil war because it divides brother from brother, father from son. David reigned over the house of Judah but Abner, captain of Saul's army, backed Ishbosheth, Saul's son. And there was a long war. The day came when Abner wanted to make peace. He went to see David and the peace conference was very successful.

But Joab was not for peace. One day he met Abner and pretended to draw him aside for a quiet chat. It was a mere pretence, for, Joab knifed Abner under his fifth rib. David distanced himself from Joab's dreadful action: at Abner's grave he wept sore and made his famous comment which is today's text. The message is that if we parley with our enemy we can be lost. Never trust the enemy on any occasion. Keep your guard. Abner was not bound hand or foot but he parleyed with his foe and died. He died as a fool. Don't you do the same.

JULY 28

"Then came all the tribes of Israel to David unto Hebron .. and they anointed David king over Israel."
2 Samuel 5 v 1,3

David's movements at this time are marked by great caution and wisdom. It would seem to have been the natural thing for the king designate to take Israel's empty throne. But David waited for 7 1/2 years in Hebron. He was in the prime of his life at 30 years of age and had plenty of opportunity to assert himself. He rather asserted himself to wait on God. Notice again and again in our studies of David's life that when he preserved that same spirit of waiting expectantly on God, he was blessed. It was for God to give him Israel's throne and he did not lift a finger to take it for himself. King over Israel at last! God kept His word and the long years since David cared for his father's sheep had passed with their tears and breathtaking joys. Patient waiting is often the highest way of doing God's will and as George Summock put it 'To lengthen my patience is the best way to shorten my troubles'. David proved it. Have we?

JULY 29

"And David perceived that the Lord had established him king over Israel, and that he had exalted his kingdom for his people Israel's sake."
2 Samuel 5 v 12

It was plain to David that God was at work. God has His own ways of revealing to us that 'in everything

both great and small we see the hand of God in all'. Let
me ask if you know this experience? Just today, twice, as
I was out and about God showed me clearly that writing
this little book was His will for me at this time. Such
things make life so meaningful and exciting, whether
you push a pen for the Lord or reign over a nation.
David recognised the hand of God even in his social
position.

Are you sure that what you are doing is the will of God
for you? Are there dreadful nagging doubts? Turn to the
searchlight of the quiet place today and talk to the Lord
about it. If you cannot perceive the hand of God in the
nitty-gritty of your life there is something dreadfully
amiss.

JULY 30

*"But when the Philistines heard that they had anointed
David king over Israel, all the Philistines came up to seek
David .. and David inquired of the Lord, saying, Shall I go
up to the Philistines? .. And the Lord said unto David, Go
up .. and the Philistines came up yet again, and when
David inquired of the Lord, he said, Thou shalt not go up."*
2 Samuel 5 v 17,19, 22-23

So, yesterday the Lord blessed you in that piece of
service for Him? Good. But today is a different day
and the same approach will not work. So many people
get trapped into thinking that God always works the
same way. A great revival came in that district, will it
come the same way again? Not necessarily. God is
always moving on. When He sends us into the world's
great waters to fish for men we must know how fish act.
We must not let our shadow get in the way. A fisherman
always keeps his face toward the light and that handles
his shadow. He is above all a patient man. We might not
catch that fish today but we may tomorrow afternoon.

Got it? David did.

'Keep yourself well out of sight,
Know the fishes' curious ways,
Keep your face towards the light,
And study patience all your days'.

JULY 31

"And David was afraid of the Lord that day."
2 Samuel 6 v 9

For a month, throughout these summer days, we have
traced David in his progress through God's school.
Sometimes he has done badly but, all in all, there ran a
thread of gold through his life. It was the fear of the
Lord. On this occasion Uzzah had touched the Ark of the
Lord when the oxen pulling it, stumbled. The Lord
smote him for his error and he died. Only priests were
allowed to touch the Ark. Again in his life David paused
and reflected on the fear of the Lord as he stood by. The
fear of man brings a snare but the fear of the Lord is the
beginning of wisdom. It is a great thing to have in your
heart.

Do we fear the Lord, enough? I'm afraid not. We rush
here and there never bothering to ask the Lord how He
feels about it. We talk but the fear of the Lord does not
guard our lips. If we feared the Lord more we would
stand less in wonder at what the microchip can do and
more at the God of the microchip who can also create a
baby's hand. Have we lost our sense of wonder because
we have lost the fear of the Lord? We have made God in
our hearts and minds too much like ourselves. Is it any
wonder, then, that we are not lost in wonder, love and
praise? Let's truly fear the Lord whatever we do and
wherever we go, today.

AUGUST

It is the hey-day of the year. In Scotland the blooming heather is like a purple carpet on the highlands. Burns wrote of 'the rustling corn; the fruited thorn, and every happy creature.' The red poppy is so silken and cheerful. It seems to draw the eye everywhere and gladdens the heart. The English schoolchildren are on holiday at last and many another, from postman to candlestick maker.

David, in our studies together, is also in his hey-day. Peace begins to break out and the Lord has prospered him above all that he could have asked or thought. How did he fare in his hey-day? Let's see.

AUGUST 1

"And Michal the daughter of Saul came out to meet David, and said, How glorious was the king of Israel today, who uncovered himself today in the eyes of the handmaids of his servants .. And David said unto Michal, It was before the Lord."
2 Samuel 6 v 20-21

David's heart was overflowing with unspeakable joy. The Ark, the great symbol of Israel and her God, was back in Jerusalem. The man was beside himself with the thrill of it all; so much so that he danced and leaped before the Lord in the streets with the rejoicing people. What an insight this gives to the heart of this man of God: the things of God excited him, thrilled him. Too many of God's people today could weep or get excited over a Hollywood epic, which is fantasy, and not a tear is shed of either sorrow for the lost or joy over sinners repenting. Their faith does not even excite them to say, 'Hallelujah', indeed if they did, they would be looked on sarcastically by many another believer!
Just like David was, Michal despised David in her heart for his behaviour. As the exulting leader of God's people returned home, she poured scorn on his dancing. 'It was before the Lord,' answered her husband 'and if you think I have been bad, next time I'll be ten times worse!' (v 22 D.B.V.). Watch that you do not try to dampen another's enthusiasm for the things of God, especially a younger believer. If you do, it were better that a milestone were hung about your neck and you were drowned. Enthusiasm for spiritual things is all too rare these days. If you are not enthusiastic then make sure you do not dampen another's enthusiasm. Because of it Michal had no child to the day of her death. Blandness in God's things is childless.

AUGUST 2

"And it came to pass, when the king sat in his house, and the Lord had given him rest .. that the king said, See now, I dwell in an house of cedar, but the ark of God dwelleth within curtains."
2 Samuel 7 v 1-2

As a man thinks in his heart, so is he. What a heart David had! As he looked around his lovely cedar home he began to think of how the Ark of God was kept in a tent with curtains around it. The work of God was miserly in its public image while he, David, lived in sophistication. David felt he must do something about it. He would build a great house for God's Ark to be placed.

It was not to be, but the Lord greatly honoured David's intention. And so it has been through the years: men and women from all walks of life see the work of the Lord cry out for help and reinforcements. From Eric Liddell who gave his life to China to my own father who on being offered a directorship in a firm, said, 'Compared to preaching the Gospel it is as a withered leaf in my hand', talents and time, money and affection have been poured out for the Lord's glory. David cared about God's things, he really cared. It was not, excuse the term, a Sunday-going-to-meeting thing with him. Is it that for us?

AUGUST 3

"What is thy servant, that thou shouldest look upon such a dead dog as I am?"
2 Samuel 9 v 8

Mephibosheth was, no doubt, brought up to fear David. Even as a little chap of five, when the news of Saul and Jonathan's death reached his home his nurse had been desperately frightened of reprisals and had run so fast out of the palace, with Mephibosheth in her arms, that he fell and was lame on both feet for the rest of his life. He had been raised far from David's presence and when summoned to the palace had to be calmed by David. 'Fear not for I will surely show thee kindness for Jonathan thy father's sake.' And the kindness shown has become almost legendary.

Is this not our experience of God? We were afraid of Him. We believed the lies of those who did not know Him. We kept as far from Him as we could. When the Gospel came to us, summoning us to the King's banquet we could hardly credit the invitation. We were received with open arms, for the Lord Jesus' sake. We were accepted in the beloved. Let's eat at His table today. The table is prepared in the very presence of our enemies. At any time we can eat meat that this world knows nothing of.

AUGUST 4

"Tarry at Jericho until your beards be grown, and then return."
2 Samuel 10 v 5

In the year 1853 a young man was asked to speak at the annual meeting of the Cambridge Sunday School Union. He spoke brilliantly but was totally unprepared for the verbal attack that a minister made upon him. The minister specially derided him for his youth and, in what he seemed to regard as a climax, said that it was a pity that boys did not adopt the Scriptural practice of tarrying at Jericho till their beards were grown before they tried to instruct their seniors.

The young man, having obtained the chairman's permission, reminded his audience that those who were bidden by King David to tarry at Jericho were not boys, but full grown men whose beards had been shaved off by their enemies as the greatest indignity they could be made to suffer. He added that the true parallel of their case could be found in a minister who, through falling into open sin, had disgraced his sacred calling and needed to go into seclusion for a while until his character had been to some extent restored. As it happened he had given an exact description of the man who had attacked him. A man in the audience felt so sorry for the young chap that he recommended him as a supply for a vacant pulpit as no other. He was nineteen years old. His name was Charles Hadden Spurgeon.

AUGUST 5

"And David sent to comfort him by the hand of his servants .. And the princes of the children of Ammon said .. hath not David rather sent his servants unto thee to search the city, and to spy it out, and to overthrow it?"
2 Samuel 10 v 2-3

Misunderstood! How often in life do we have to confess that we misunderstood someone? We did not take all the facts into consideration, we did not realise that what the person meant for good we thought was meant for evil. More marriages are on the rocks, more Churches are in trouble, more families are at war with their relations through misunderstanding than can ever be imagined.

David wanted to send comfort to Hanun, Prince of Ammon, but Hanun's men said he was only spying! It seems to me that most misunderstanding comes because of our inbuilt suspicion of people's motives. There is nothing so well meant but that it may be ill interpreted. We cannot, naturally, help this sad fact of life, but, when the Holy Spirit enters our life, on conversion, let us lean on the fact that He is the Spirit of truth. He will keep us sensitive to motivation in ourselves and others. He will give us discernment of who comes for comfort or who comes to spy. He will lead us into all truth.

AUGUST 6

"At the time when kings go forth to battle."
2 Samuel 11 v 1

Maybe he was tired. Maybe he thought he wasn't needed. Joab would do as good a job. I don't know why David stayed back from his responsibilities and relaxed on a Jerusalem rooftop when his army were in the trenches. What I do know is that when David relaxed the Devil went for him: he set a trap for David which was to plunge him into adultery, murder, civil war and endless heartache to his dying day.
Satan goes about as a roaring lion seeking whom he may devour. A lion never reveals his presence until he is about to pounce. He never roars until he has made a kill. What a roar he made through David's sin. Countless millions have said 'Great man, David, but how could he sink so low?' Let those who criticise him take heed to themselves. It is my experience that when we are relaxing and at leisure is the time Satan often attacks; it is his favourite hunting ground. On holiday? Watch it.

AUGUST 7
"And from the roof he saw a woman washing herself."
2 Samuel 11 v 2

There used to live in the UK a Godly Bible teacher called Glynn Owen. He had a great ministry in the country which reached many people. I shall always remember talking to a lady who had been to hear Glynn Owen speak on today's text. She had picked up something significant he had said and passed it on to me. 'I do not believe that David may have entirely been at fault,' Glynn Owen had said, 'if only Bathsheba had pulled the curtain a little closer things might have been very different.'

Femininity and sexuality are gifts from God. Anyone who teaches anything else is not teaching what the Bible teaches. But they must be carefully guarded. Modesty will guard them and a constant realisation of their power over men. David must never be condoned for what he did but had Bathsheba been more careful it may never have happened.

AUGUST 8

"And he made him drunk."
2 Samuel 11 v 13

Is this the great leader of Israel in his hey-day? Unfortunately it is. David tries to force Bathsheba's husband Uriah to go home to her, having already recalled him from the battle. David was desperately seeking to cover up his sin. How bad, will someone tell me, can a good man be? He made Uriah drunk. 'Woe unto him that giveth his neighbour drink,' wrote Habakkuk, 'and makest him drunken also .. the cup of the Lord's right hand shall be turned unto thee and shameful spewing shall be on thy glory .. for violence .. shall cover thee.' David made Uriah drunk and the violence in Israel that followed was frightening. What about the fury of heartbreaking violence in the famous American Kennedy family? The fact that Joseph Kennedy, when he was Ambassador to Britain, shipped boatloads of Whisky to America and capped the prohibition - alcohol-dry market - and thus making America drunk, makes one wonder if his actions did not bring the violence in his family Habakkuk speaks of? A young lad came home recently very drunk. His Christian father remonstrated with him. 'What are you talking about?' he shouted. 'You are the one who started me off: you bought me a shandy.' Selah.

AUGUST 9

"David wrote a letter to Joab .. saying Set ye Uriah in the forefront of the hottest battle .. that he may .. die."
2 Samuel 11 v 14-15

The psalmist, the keeper of sheep, the lover of God, the man, the King, wrecked and ruined for a moment of pleasure. Incredible. And then he stooped to the filthy act of having Uriah killed. Bathsheba probably never guessed the price of her protection. David thought that only he and Joab knew of his plan. It was a great relief. The child would now be born in seemingly lawful wedlock.

But there was one fatal flaw in the whole arrangement. 'The thing that David had done displeased the Lord'. No matter how we connive, or plan, or judge things if the Lord is displeased with it we are in trouble. Day and night God's hand lay heavily on David. How did he feel at this time? Read Psalm 32. Whoever, my friend, you please today, do not, please, do not, do anything to displease your Lord.

AUGUST 10

"And the Lord sent Nathan to David."
2 Samuel 12 v 1

We all know too well the 'bunglers' who walk all over a problem with their big feet and who know nothing about sensitivity. But, have we ever experienced the powerful touch of a man or woman sent from God into our lives with the encouragement that hurts to help?

Nathan was sent by God but notice God's timing. It was at least a year since David's dreadful acts. But Nathan's timing was right. He did not begin to admonish David with 'This is probably not the time nor the place but ..'And, of course, it is not always what you say, but the way you say it. There are few men in the world who could approach the chief executive of a country and accurately accuse him of adultery without ever using the word. Nathan did. Nathan knew his man. He was used to bring the King to repentance and still held him as his friend. If you find someone overtaken by a fault today, be a Nathan to them.

AUGUST 11

"But now he is dead, wherefore should I fast? can I bring him back again? I shall go to him, but he shall not return to me."
2 Samuel 12 v 23

Bathsheba's baby died. For one week it was very sick. David pleaded with God for the child's life and fasted and lay all night upon the earth. He could not be persuaded otherwise. Then David saw his servants whisper and realised that the child was dead. David washed, changed and ate bread to the consternation of his servants who thought he would be worse on the news of the baby's death. They questioned him about it and his answer has been a comfort to many a bereaved parent since: 'Should I fast? Can I bring him back again? I shall go to him but he shall not return to me.'
What does this teach us? It teaches us that those that are dead are out of the reach of prayer and that our tears cannot profit them. It also teaches that babies who die go to be with the Lord. They, are better provided for than ever they could be on earth. By the way, the consideration of our own death will greatly ease our sorrow at the death of loved ones: we shall be with them, shortly. In that single statement the repentant David said a lot.

AUGUST 1 2

"Absalom said .. Oh that I were made judge in the land,
that every man which hath any suit or cause might come
unto me, and I would do him justice!"
2 Samuel 15 v 4

There is nothing in Absalom to praise. He was a shy, cunning, selfish, dangerous man. No love for the Lord ever ruled his heart at any time I ever read of. In the text we see him courting the favour of any man who came to his father for justice. Absalom looked good . He talked smooth. He became the talk of the land but he was all talk.

It was old Matthew Henry who said, 'Those are good indeed that are in their own place, not that pretend how good they would be in other peoples places.' It is like the man a friend of mine told me about. He said he wanted to be (emphasis his!) a speaker at big 'con-fri-ences' and to preach to large 'and-i-ences'. My friend thought he had better improve his English first! Watch the all-talk Absaloms of this world. They destroy all they touch.

AUGUST 1 3

"And one told David saying, Ahithophel is among the
conspirators with Absalom."
2 Samuel 15 v 31

The tide had turned away from the once beloved hero of the valley Elah. The girls sang no more songs about him. The reverence of the children of Israel for David had gone. A few were faithful, though, but they had to climb Mt. Olivet with their barefoot King as he fled Jerusalem in a panic, was cursed by Shimei and endured a majority of the population defecting to his son.

When a friend turns traitor it hurts. But when that friend is your trusted counsellor whose very advice is an oracle of God then you feel you have been stabbed in the back. No sooner had Absalom raised his standard than Ahithophel, David's beloved advisor, defected. What made him do it? He was Bathsheba's grandfather and his son Eliam was Uriah's friend and fellow soldier. It is the law of echos. What we put out comes back, and back and back. Not even great leaders like David are exempt from it. What will you and I put into the echo bank today?

AUGUST 14

"Then said Abishai .. Why should this dead dog curse the lord the king? let me go over, I pray thee, and take off his head. And the king said, .. so let him curse .."
2 Samuel 16 v 9-10

'Sticks and stones may break my bones but names will never hurt me' may be a proverb but names can hurt in my experience. As David travelled in the civil war, Shimei, the son of Gerar, threw stones at him and shouted 'You man of Belial.' Belial means, 'Fool! Good for nothing! Vain fellow! Lawless man!' 'The Lord has given Absalom your Kingdom.' he taunted. 'There's blood on your hands!' he jeered.
From the deep darkness comes a flash of light, a journey back in David's life. It is the younger David coming through again. Shimei was a relation of Saul's and he was a chip of the old block. And David let him go. 'Let him alone and let him curse .. it may be the Lord will look on mine affliction.' said David. And the Lord did. We will forget Shimei's curse but we will never forget David's psalms, even in the 20th century. It is easier to curse the dark than to light a lamp. Which do you do?

AUGUST 15

"And the king said, And where is thy master's son? And Ziba said unto the king, Behold he abided at Jerusalem: for he said, Today shall the house of Israel restore me the kingdom of my father."
2 Samuel 16 v 3

We are back with our old friend Mephibosheth again. He is being slandered by the man David set up to look after him. David wanted to know where his best friend's son was and Ziba said he was on Absalom's side. David convinced Mephibosheth was guilty of treason, seized his lands and granted them to the liar, Ziba.

But Ziba had brought food for David and his men, and flattery, and food were his 'poisoned' recipe. David was fooled and a good man was condemned. There is a proverb Solomon wrote that says if you ever go to a rich man's table and the rich man is trying to buy you, eat with a knife at your throat. it is an excellent proverb. Anybody been trying the old flattery-and-food line with you, recently? You have been warned.

AUGUST 16

"For the Lord had appointed to defeat the good counsel of Ahithophel, to the intent that the Lord might bring evil upon Absalom."
2 Samuel 17 v 14

Things are not always as they seem. You wouldn't have given David much of a chance for survival if you had heard Ahithophel's plan in Absalom's war cabinet. David was to be hunted down with 12,000 men

that very night and killed instantly. But suddenly
Absalom asked a man called Hushai for advice and he
advised that they proceed later, with caution. Absalom
accepted his plan. Hushai secretly passed the news on to
David and the thwarted Ahithophel went and hanged
himself.

Does a traitor lurk in your life and associations? He or
she was once your trusted friend. The traitor may not
send an army of 12,000 after you but they have put great
fear into your heart by what they threaten. Remember
this story of David and Ahithophel, hurting one. If God
be for you who can be against you? God will turn your
turn-coats friend's work into confusion. Leave the
problem in God's hands. Now, go to sleep.

AUGUST 17

*"O my son Absalom! my son, my son Absalom! would God I
had died for thee, O Absalom, my son, my son!"*
2 Samuel 18 v 33

The traitor Absalom came to a miserable end. His
forces were routed. The news at last reaches David,
and, he might be a King but he forgets all that in being a
father. How many a bereaved father has sobbed David's
words? Is it a true father's cry even though it was for a
son who did not love in return.

Ever thought of God's love? Have we any notion of
what it cost the Father to see His Son torn and crucified
for our sins? And the Lord Jesus was no Absalom. He
always did those things which pleased his Father. Yet,
God so loved the world that He gave His only begotten
Son that whosoever believeth in Him should not perish
but have everlasting life. That's why He understands
when we grieve at the loss of a loved one. Nobody
understands it better.

AUGUST 18

"And Mephibosheth the son of Saul, came down to meet the king, and had neither dressed his feet, nor trimmed his beard, nor washed his clothes, from the day the king departed until the day he came again in peace .. and .. said .. Yea let him take all , forasmuch as my lord the king is come again in peace unto his own house."
2 Samuel 19 v 24,30

Y ou will have gathered that I am a fan of Mephibosheth's! To me he is a great character. Maligned and lied about he had in fact remained faithful to David all through the civil war. When David discovered this he wanted to give him back the land he had taken away from him. But Jonathan's son would have none of it: 'I don't want the land: all I want is to see you King!'
Is that not how we feel about our Lord Jesus? What does it matter who, on earth, gets praised for it as long as His work is done? If He is glorified in all, that is reward enough.

AUGUST 19

"So David slept with his fathers, and was buried in the city of David."
1 Kings 2 v 10

I n Greenland an Eskimo once gave Lord Shackelton a piece of advice: 'If in walking over ice you look back and see your footprints are damp, it means you are on very thin ice.'

David had many a damp footprint but one thing is very
discernible from his walk through life: he could not bear
the frown of God. David through most of his days kept
very short accounts with God. He kept the Lord always
before him. Perhaps the best epitaph ever written of
David was Paul's. He said, 'David, after he had served
his own generation according to the will of God, fell on
sleep.' Let's get out today and serve our generation with
the same Spirit of God to empower us. But look out for
damp footprints.

AUGUST 20

"Bless the Lord, O my soul, and forget not all his benefits:
Who forgiveth all thine iniquities; who healeth all thy
diseases; Who redeemeth thy life from destruction, who
crowneth thee with lovingkindness and tender mercies; Who
satisfieth thy mouth with good things."
Psalm 103 v 2-5

For this final phase of August I want to take a few of
David's most famous words to give us a spiritual
flavour in our hearts as we take our leave of this
amazing man of God.
What could be more indicative of David than his
constant appreciation of God's goodness to him? Dr.
Alexander Whyte loved this Psalm and his
interpretation is wonderful. In these verses, he said, we
have the Law Court - forgiveth all thine iniquities: the
Hospital - healeth all thy diseases: the Slave Market -
redeemeth thy life from destruction: the Throne Room -
crowneth thee with loving kindness: and the Banquet
Hall - satisfieth thy mouth with good things. Is that
enough for today? The Lord is enough.

AUGUST 21

"O taste and see that the Lord is good: blessed is the man that trusteth in him."
Psalm 34 v 8

If you would see, then you must taste, and, if you taste, you will see. Put God to the test of experience. I know many a young person who is doing a University thesis and giving their heart, and sometimes their very soul, to research it. Why do they not do this with God's promises in the area of every day experience? Look at tennis stars, football players, Olympic athletes. They fast and train and work to perfect their sport. Why do so few of them go in for the promises of God in the same way?
Dr. Graham Scroggie said, 'Formerly the process was to reason from principles to facts, but since Bacon's time men have reasoned from facts to principles. But David was in advance of Bacon, he followed the inductive method over 3,000 years ago.' Taste and see! Inductive it is. Disappointing it is not.

AUGUST 22

"Lord, my heart is not haughty nor mine eyes lofty: neither do I exercise myself in great matters, or in things too high for me. Surely I have behaved and quieted myself as a child that is weaned of his mother: my soul is even as a weaned child. Let Israel hope in the Lord from henceforth and for ever."
Psalm 131

Here is a Psalm for the fast lane folk if ever there was one. Deadlines! Headlines! Beelines! White lines! Rushing on! Slow down, Christian, wise up. Quiet yourself for a moment. The writer of this poem of exquisite beauty and surpassing beauty had a nation to run. He deliberately quieted himself as a contented, just fed baby. His hope was in the Lord from now on, he emphasised.

Look at your white, ashen face in the mirror. What is that heart of yours pounding for? Dry those sweaty palms. Stop aiming for things which lie beyond your powers. Know your limitations and keep within them, for, in wising to be great you may fail to be good. David didn't get into Saul's armour. Christ didn't say, 'Feed my giraffes' but 'Feed my sheep', something within our reach. Be like that contented little baby.

'I would not have the restless will,
That hurries to and fro,
Seeking for some great things to do,
Or secret thing to know,
I would be treated as a child,
And guided where I go'.

AUGUST 23

"O Lord, thou hast searched me, and known me. Thou knowest my downsitting and mine uprising, thou understandest my thought afar off. Thou compassest my path and my lying down, and art acquainted with all my ways .. such knowledge is too wonderful for me."
Psalm 139 v 1-3,6

Thoughts are heard in heaven. God knows our thoughts even before they have taken definite shape. He knows our public and our private lives. He knows our life by day and our life by night. He knows our social and secret life. He is thoroughly familiar with everything we do.

That heart of yours could go on for 100 years and it beats at the rate of 100,000 strokes every 24 hours. There is not a breath you breath that he does not know about.

Amazing that the shepherd boy of Israel's hillsides could write such a Psalm: but write it he did. As he surveyed himself and the universe, he said it was all just too wonderful for him. Let's not lose our sense of wonder either and let's follow the truth which Linnaeus, the Swedish naturalist, inscribed over the door of his lecture room: 'Live innocently: God is here'.

AUGUST 24

"Fret not thyself because of evildoers, neither be thou envious against the workers of iniquity. For they shall be cut down like the grass, and wither as the green herb."
Psalm 37 v 1-2

I remember learning this Psalm as a lad and being give ten shillings for reciting it by my Godly Sunday school teacher Mrs. Bond Walker. The ten shillings was spent long ago but the wealth she gave me in putting that Psalm into my mind will never pass.
Is there someone reading today's text and you envy the prosperity of the wicked? Indeed it seems in our society as though the evil doer is on the street and the law abiding citizens are in their homes behind bars! Often in his writings David speaks of the theme of the evil doer prospering while the Godly suffer. Obviously Saul's behaviour is very much in David's mind.
Just remember this. There is at work in the world a principle of retribution to which long history gives moral significance. Evil comes boomeranging back upon the head of the evil doer. Every sinner shall sup of his own brew. The Saul who tried to pin David to the wall was eventually pinned to the wall himself. Why should the Christian be eaten up by envy? Why should he fret? Rest and rejoice. Wait and see.

AUGUST 25

"O magnify the Lord with me, and let us exalt his name together."
Psalm 34 v 3

It is a fact that a lot of people imagine great writing is done in some exotic spot in the South of France or some tranquil mountain retreat. In fact the opposite is true. I remember standing in the Bronte Parsonage in Yorkshire and in the room where Charlotte Bronte did most of her great writing. It was no Hilton! Most of Paul's writing was done in a prison cell and this Psalm of David was written when he feigned madness to get thrown out of Gath. He seemed to be finished at that stage in his career but he found forgiveness in God and learned to sing again. He asks us to join him.

There is always a reason to be thankful in every situation. Matthew Henry said when he was robbed by a highwayman that he was grateful that it had never happened to him before! This always praising minister puzzled his congregation as to what on earth he could be grateful for in the pulpit one wild, stormy, rain soaked morning. 'Lord.' he said, 'We are grateful that every day is not like today.'

PS Have a good day and, as they say in the US, 'Have an even better day tomorrow!'

AUGUST 26

"Lord, make me to know mine end, and the measure of my days, what it is."
Psalm 39 v 4

'A breath'. 'A shadow'. 'A measure'. 'A vapour'. 'A weaver's shuttle'. Life is a very brief business. I've read those words in Chester Cathedral where they first found underneath a clock:

'When as a child I laughed and wept,
Time crept,
When as a youth I grew more bold,
Time strolled,
When I became a full grown man,
Time ran,
Soon I shall find as I journey on,
Time gone'.

But though our lives are as a breath they need not to be nothing but a breath. Our relationship with the Lord determines whether they are or not. David knew this and constantly reminds himself of it. The Methodist preacher at the grave of the multi-billionaire, Howard Hughes preached on the text 'We brought nothing into this world and it is certain we can take nothing out.' Too right. Only what's done for the Lord will last.

AUGUST 27

*"O Lord God of my salvation, I have cried day and night
before thee .. For my soul is full of troubles .. I am as
a man that hath no strength .. Lover and friend
hast thou put far from me."*
Psalm 88 v 1,3-4,18

Don't ever think that men and women of faith do not have their dark moments of despair. From those fresh faced, foot stamping, teenage young folk singing 'I will enter His gates with thanksgiving in my heart, I will enter His courts with praise', to the very man who wrote the Psalm they are singing, everyone, at some stage in their life plunges into despair. Our minds at times seem to have no understanding, no heart and no joy in God's promises.

If we study this Psalm we will see that David had a real sense of guilt in his despair. But this sense of guilt was, as always in his life, the very gem that brought him back to blessing! The last thing in the world Satan wants us to realise is our true condition before God because that casts us on God for forgiveness and salvation. That's what I love about the million seller book 'Joni' by Joni Earekson Tada. She admits morally she was not all that she should have been in her teenage years and tells where, as a believer (note) she found forgiveness in the despair of her circumstances. That's being real. There is only one Psalm like today's but thank God there is one. it assures even the most desperate that in turning to God there is hope. It teaches us to remember in the dark what God has taught us in the light.

AUGUST 28

"I will sing of the mercies of the Lord for ever."
Psalm 89 v 1

God's mercies are as sure as the sunrise. Behind the bread, the flour. Behind the flour, the mill. Behind the mill, the corn. Behind the corn, the wind. Behind the wind, the sun. Behind them all, God.

This August morning God has been feeding a multitude of the little animals of the forest. In the paths of the great oceans he has fed a multitude of sea creatures. Our own table was spread this morning with His goodness. Yet, tell me, was there a word for Him in it all. Did He blow any trumpets? Did He leave any footprints? Oh! the divine modesty of God's mercies.

I saw a cartoon in a magazine recently of a father and a
son looking at a fabulous rainbow arched over the
countryside around them. 'No!', the father was saying
indignantly, 'the rainbow is not advertising anything!'
Watching the Chelsea Flower Show on television with
my wife recently we marvelled at the riot of colour and
beauty of flowers. The commentator greatly interested
me, though. 'The nurserymen cloned this with that...' he
said, 'The nurserymen brought this from there...', he
marvelled, as we took an international trip of the flower
world. There was not a word in all of it in honour of the
One who made it all. No one could ever accuse David of
such a bias. Will you join him?

AUGUST 2 9

*"Blessed be the Lord, because he hath heard the voice of my
supplications."*
Psalm 28 v 6

Answered prayer is something to bless God for.
David's prayer life was obviously indispensable to
him. But we must always remember that although our
prayers are heard it may be some time before they are
answered.
Friends of mine were involved in working for Christ
amongst young folk in an Austrian Castle they had
bought. Their work was greatly blessed of God. Often
they wondered why until they discovered an old Bible in
the castle. On the flyleaf a prayer had been written by
the owner asking God to use his castle for God's glory.
Most of his life the castle owner had been greatly
persecuted for his faith. But now his prayers had been
answered. The interesting thing was that his prayer had
been written on that flyleaf seven hundred years
beforehand.

AUGUST 30

"The Lord is my shepherd."
Psalm 23 v 1

Here must be David's epitaph. here in five short words is the fountain head for all the historic and Godly actions that so often characterised the under-rated son of Jesse. Here was the secret of the Psalm writer who has touched Catholic and Protestant, general and private, business executive and tea lady, Queen and subject, pilot and passenger, mother and child, people of all nations for centuries. How many a person will die in some hospital ward today with today's text on their lips? If someone came to me today and said that a child I knew in another town had had an accident I would be very sorry indeed. But if someone told me that one of my own three girls had had an accident I would be sorry in a different way. Why? Because it would be my child. Watch a man show someone land he works on for someone else and then watch the land owner show someone the same ground. Would there be a difference in their attitude? There would be all the difference. Millions talk merely of 'The Shepherd.' 'The Saviour.' The Lord.', but it raises your head in a crowded room when you overhear someone say 'My Shepherd.' 'My Saviour.' 'My Lord.' There is an eternal destiny of difference between the two.

AUGUST 31

"Yea, though I walk through the valley of the shadow of death, I will fear no evil: for thou art with me; thy rod and thy staff they comfort me."
Psalm 23 v 4

In my last daily reading book we made a mistake in leaving out August 31st. I was amazed at the number of people who missed it. They had a birthday today, or whatever, and they made me promise to rectify my mistake next time around! Now my promise is discharged!

In fact as I write for you today the night has come and I have had a long busy day travelling and working since 5.20 a.m. I am glad to see the night come for soon I shall rest, at last. On my study desk the light falls on my writing paper and my pen is casting a shadow. No light: no shadow. It would just be complete darkness. It is as simple as that.

'The valley of the shadow of death' is obviously a place where there is a light. No light: no shadow. This is no Alice in Wonderland fantasy. The light in the valley is caught from the glory dwelling in Emmanuel's land where the Lamb is the light thereof. The believer need not fear death. There is a light to guide him as he walks up the valley.

When one of my children is sick I can lift her and carry her to my own bed even as she sleeps. She goes to sleep in her room and wakes up in her father's room. That's what death is for the believer. They go to sleep in this world and waken up in Heaven. And remember, as we leave David who has taught us so much of what the Lord can mean to us in this fast lane of life, it has not yet crossed man's mind the things that God has prepared for them that love Him.

SEPTEMBER

Now comes my time of year, the thoughtful days. 'More than Spring's bright unconrtol suits the Autumn of my soul.' Boys throw their sticks high in the horse-chestnut tree, the reaper is busy, the fruit will soon all be in the loft. The old is passing away. Every year I wander in the Autumn but wonder. It gets to me. Like Robert Frost said:

'I have been treading
on leaves all day
until I am Autumn-tired,
God knows all the colour
and the form of leave I have
trodden on and mired.
Perhaps I have put forth
too much strength
and been too fierce from fear.
I have safely trodden
underfoot the leaves
of another year'.

The old was passing for sure when an amazing letter was written; it said the old had passed for good. It pointed to something Autumn could never touch. Let's read it together. It's called the Epistle to the Hebrews.

SEPTEMBER 1

"God who at sundry times and in divers manners spake in time past unto the fathers by the prophets, Hath in these last days spoken unto us by his Son."
Hebrews 1 v 1-2

In Autumn there are billions of leaves that fall. Are any two of them alike? if you can find them, let me know. Yet is there a unity in those carpets of leaves you will see today from that woodland path? There is a marvellous unity. Every part of the universe interlocks and if we disturb the balance it sends a shock through the whole system.

God has a great unity in the variety of ways in which He speaks. here the shepherd, David, there the fishermen Peter, here Ruth, there Queen Esther, all kinds of men and women from all walks of life. But those sixty six books of the Bible have one great unity; they all point to God's Son. Disintegrate one and you loose them all. Notice the Lord Jesus is God's last word to this world. Anything that claims to be prophetic but tells of a revelation outside of the Word of God is false. Don't major in your life on so called spiritual experiences, major on God's declared, written word. It will save you from false cults and will preserve your peace.

'Reach my blest Saviour first,
Take Him from God's esteem,
Prove Jesus bears one spot of sin,
Then tell me I'm unclean'.

SEPTEMBER 2

"They shall perish; but thou remainest; and they shall all wax old as doth a garment; And as a vesture shalt thou fold them up, and they shall be changed: but thou art the same and thy years shall not fail."
Hebrews 1 v 11-12

As Autumn creeps on these verses are greatly highlighted. Here is something to take the sadness out of Autumn days. Everybody is getting back to the office or their place of work, the children are getting back to school, the older ones are heading for University or higher education institutions and local church activities are on the increase: there is a satisfaction in feeling the old routine return. But the truth is Autumn reminds us that life is passing. The rivers and seas, the woods, the flowers, the birds, the stars, will all get old like your best coat. They will, according to today's texts, be put away like an old garment. It is refreshing to read in these texts that Autumn days will never touch our wonderful Lord.

A North African called Augustine had run away from home. He led a very immoral life but could find no satisfaction in it. He then turned to the academic life and he became a brilliant professor of philosophy in Italy. He could still find no satisfaction. Turning to religion he gave himself to the life of a monk and to his amazement could still find no peace. Advised by a friend to read the Epistle to the Romans he sat under a tree one day in a garden and read Paul's word which says that we should make no provision for the flesh but that we should 'put on the Lord Jesus Christ'. Augustine did just that and was gloriously converted. He found that the righteousness with which Christ clothed him never grew old. Have you put it on?

SEPTEMBER 3

"Therefore God, even thy God, hath anointed thee with the oil of gladness above thy fellows."
Hebrews 1 v 9

He was unequalled in His birth. He was unequalled in His life. He was unequalled in His resurrection. He was unequalled in the things He did. Again and again men and women have tried to destroy what He taught and those that follow Him. It will just not work. Our Lord Jesus has been exalted far above all. 'I, if I be lifted up,' He said, 'will draw all men unto me.' His cross lifted Him up and there is a power in it which nothing can match. His enemies thought it was the end of any glory He ever had, in fact it was the path to greater glory. Millions glory in that cross.

'Lord,' wrote the hymnwriter, 'make me your prisoner and I shall be free.' It is true that all who trust the exalted One are truly free. 'I discovered,' wrote Alexander Solzhenitsyn, the survivor of Stalin's prison camps, 'that the only people who were free in those prisons were the believers.'

SEPTEMBER 4

"Therefore we ought to give the more earnest heed to the things we have heard, lest at any time we should let them slip."
Hebrews 2 v 1

People trifle with what God says. If God's word spoken through angels is not to be trifled with how much less should we trifle when God has spoken through His Son? People let the word of the Gospel slip and start drifting and drift into perdition. Here is a young person who does not deliberately say 'I renounce my mother's God.', but the crowd he runs with have no care for these things and he begins to let them slip. He never repents and trusts the Saviour. It's so easy. He just lies back from it all and drifts into disaster.

We must watch that fearful current of habits and associations and our evil nature. We must watch the deadly current of the pressure of temptation. Better to trust Christ as Saviour and live for Him and spread His Gospel across the waters of life and see it return to you after many days.

A few hours ago I sat at a table listening to my six year old child recount the story of Moses to a young man in her own inimitable style. He kept her 'on track' much to everybody's amusement! But as they talked my mind drifted back many years to the night when that young man as a little boy had sat listening amongst many other little children as we communicated the greatest message on earth. he had trusted the Saviour and there after many days before my very eyes he was talking of the same word to my child. Oh! the sheer romance of spreading the Gospel of Jesus Christ. Don't let the word of the Gospel slip from you, my reader. Inattentive viewers will soon be forgetful hearers. All is lost to you if the Gospel be lost. Much better to believe its message and spread it far and wide.

SEPTEMBER 5

"How shall we escape, if we neglect so great salvation; which at the first began to be spoken by the Lord, and was confirmed unto us by them that heard him."
Hebrews 2 v 3

I notice that the secular press always puts the Bible word saved in inverted commas. I noticed it the other day concerning the story of a man who they say had claimed to have been 'saved' while in prison. When they put inverted commas around a word they are wary of it, they are unsure of it, they mean it is open to a question. There are no inverted commas around the word in Scripture, but there are three tenses. There is the past tense: 'By grace,' said Paul, 'you have been saved through faith.' (R.V. Romans 2 v 8) When someone receives Christ as Saviour they are placed beyond the fear of the judgement of God. That's the past dealt with. There is the present tense: 'Unto us which are being saved the word of the cross is the power of God.' (R.V. 1 Corinthians 1 v 18) The Lord is rooting evil out of the Christian's life constantly, and saving them from the snare of the Devil.

There is the future: 'Now is our salvation nearer than when we believed. The night is far spent: the day is at hand.' (Romans 13 v 11-12)

Could any political party give you a manifesto like that? Don't neglect it.

SEPTEMBER 6

"For it became him, for whom are all things, and by whom are all things, in bringing many sons unto glory, to make the captain of their salvation perfect through sufferings."
Hebrews 2 v 10

Does today's text mean that our Lord Jesus was not always perfect? No. It means that our Lord (perfect though He always was and is), had never tasted death, could not have truly allayed our fears when we have to face it. If our Lord Jesus had never been in the wilderness facing Satan in temptation how could he help us who face temptation every day of our lives? If the Lord had never wept at the grave of Lazarus how could He ever staunch our tears? Moses was never a high priest in the wilderness because he had been brought up in the palace. Aaron was the high priest because he had suffered with the people in Egyptian slavery.

Because our Lord was weary and thirsty and hungry

and suffered more than tongue or pen could ever describe, He can be our perfect captain to take us across life's journey to our final destination.

'What is your final destination, young man?' said an airline hostess to the evangelist Arthur Blessitt as he flew out of Atlanta one day. 'Heaven!' replied the exhausted evangelist wrapped in an airline blanket! And he had a greater captain than the one on the flight deck above Atlanta. So have we. Onward!

SEPTEMBER 7

"Forasmuch then as the children are partakers of flesh and blood, he also himself likewise took part of the same; that through death he might destroy him that had the power of death, that is, the devil .. subject to bondage."
Hebrews 2 v 14-15

Until you are free to die, you are not free to live. You are a madman if you have no preparation made to die. Death haunts the human like none other. People accelerate down the fast lane even faster, take on even more responsibilities, crowd their lives out with noise and bustle, anything, as long as they don't have time to think about death. People dread the mystery of death, they dread the 'leave taking' of death, they dread what comes after death.

But there is good news. At Calvary Christ destroyed Satan's power and he was the one who had brought sin unto the world and death by sin. The power of death is broken. Christ, when trusted, delivers from the bondage of the fear of death and sets people free to live. And, by the way, have you ever known a Christian to recant on his death bed?

SEPTEMBER 8

"But with whom was he grieved forty years? was it not with them that had sinned, whose carcases fell in the wilderness?"
Hebrews 3 v 17

Unbelief. It is at the root of all kinds of sin. The children of Israel; did not believe God's promises and the results were unrest, aimlessness, unsatisfied longings, the monotony of failure, always striking and pitching their camp, and always being fed on the same food until their very soul loathed it. It was all fret and disappointment and weariness of existence. It was a life of chasing a mirage and enduring sandstorms and they had forty years of it all. Unbelief raised a barrier that shut out blessing. 'They believed not His word but murmured in their tents and hearkened not unto the voice of the Lord'.

Of what use are Christian conferences, attendance's to break the bread and drink the wine of remembrance, summer Bible conventions, in depth Bible study and seminars on this and that and the other, reading Christian books and periodicals, if all the time we have never learned to trust the Lord and to believe His word in the real world of our minds and heart and feet? Why, the whole thing is nothing better than a social club if we have not learned to trust Him. Daniel believed in his God. It shut the lions' mouths, it turned difficult days into unforgettable history. I tell you some of these days some lad or lass will stand up and say 'Well, I'm going to believe in God and trust Him.', and they'll set to work and the rest of us will burn with shame when we see what will be accomplished. Are you that lad or lass?

SEPTEMBER 9

"There remaineth therefore a rest to the people of God."
Hebrews 4 v 9

I wonder what your view of Heaven is? A kind of
'guitars-and-endless-supplies-of-Coca-Cola and
drifting-around-aimlessly-on-clouds' kind of place? The
Bible knows nothing of such sentimental nonsense. It is
clear in this letter to the Hebrews that as Canaan was the
original goal of the people of God so Heaven is the land
of desire for the Church. It's their land of promise. The
word rest in our text means a 'Sabbath rest'. It has the
idea of fulfilment, of completion. God rested on the
Sabbath. It does not mean that God did nothing on the
Sabbath, indeed it is clear that He explored His creation
saying 'It is very good.' That's what Heaven will be for
the Christian: A 'Sabbath rest' when they can explore the
richness and fullness of all that God is in Christ. A place
of open vision. It will mean the glory of revelation and
the revelation of glory.
It will be like the little boy who was always looking at
the toy soldiers in the toy shop window. Eventually they
became his and he cried, 'Look mum! I've got them at
last and there is no glass between.'

SEPTEMBER 10

*"For the Word of God is quick, and powerful, and sharper
than any twoedged sword, piercing even to the dividing
asunder of soul and spirit, and the joints and marrow, and
is a discerner of the thoughts and intents of the heart."*
Hebrews 4 v 12

L iving! Energetic! Sharp! The more I teach the
Scriptures the more I see it: wherever the word falls
it begins to breed life. Take my friend Duncan
Donaldson the 'Wild man of Airdrie'. Six policemen

could not take him. Whenever he came home at night drunk he usually kicked the door open. The night he was converted he went home and quietly opened the door and his own dog bit him! The word of God is living, for sure! The lonely woman at the well rushes to tell a city of the Christ. The dying thief blesses instead of blasphemes. The word is alive.

The word is energetic too. When it enters a believing heart the whole motivation of a life is changed. How many times in your life have you been in some corner, perhaps making a telephone call, or whatever, when the word of God flashes into your mind and changed your day? And it is sharp. Peter preached it and three thousand cried out 'What shall we do?' It is sharp to define, to criticise, to judge. What you intend you very often become. Let the word of God sift your intentions today. We may not know ourselves but the word does. Trust it.

SEPTEMBER 11

'For every high priest taken from among men is ordained for men."
Hebrews 5 v 1

'Oh no!' people say, 'Not Leviticus again!' When the subject of our Lord's High Priesthood is written or spoken about, people seem to fear a diatribe of typology. They reject typology as bad theology. 'In an age of inflation, unemployment, high interest rates, ungodly standards, we need encouragement not obscure Judaism versus Christianity material, Not teaching on the High Priesthood of Christ.' they say.

This attitude is dangerous because it makes people speak of Christ as though we would be saved anyway, even if the Lord Jesus did not minister as a High Priest for us now. This is simply not true. Israel's High Priest was appointed. He could not take honour to himself. So it is important to remember that God has appointed Christ to His task. It is a task he undertakes to the full. A high priest must bear gently with the ignorant and the erring. Our Lord Jesus does that, constantly. Remember how the Lord cleared away the ignorance of Apollos, using Aquila and Priscilla? That was His high priestly work in action. Remember the woman taken in adultery, the two on the way to Emmaus, John the Baptist's doubts? You can rest today, Christian, in the knowledge that your High Priest intercedes on your behalf. It is no obscure teaching.

'Before the throne of God above,
I have a strong, a perfect plea,
A great High Priest whose name is love,
Who ever lives to plead for me'.

SEPTEMBER 12

"For when for the time ye ought to be teachers, ye have need of that one teach you again which be the first principles of the oracles of God; and are become such as have need of milk .. is unskilful in the word of righteousness: for he is a babe. But strong meat belongeth to them that are of fullage."
Hebrews 5 v 12-14

Christian basics are very important. Indeed they are as important at the end of a Christian's life as at the beginning: but the point is the beginning is not a stopping place. To remain a spiritual baby all our days would be a very sad state of affairs. Obviously the writer to the Hebrews had a real problem trying to teach these Christians the deeper things of God. We all need to grow deeper, as we grow older, in spiritual matters. Watch Christians who don't and everything goes well for a while until the storms and crises of life begin to blow up. The very things they need to know to keep them in the storm, they don't know, and so they fail to be a bright witness for God in the crises. Be sure that when the sun shines and things go easily, when local church affairs prosper and you feel like singing all the day, that you take care to store your mind and heart with the riches of God's word that in an evil day you will be able, having done all, to stand. Babies are great on days when the sun shines but on their own in a snowstorm or in a rainstorm they are in another category. Let's please learn to grow up because a great spiritual storm in our land is brewing.

SEPTEMBER 13

"Surely blessing I will bless thee, and multiplying I will multiply thee."
Hebrews 6 v 14

It is interesting that this lovely promise was not spoken to Abraham when he first believed God. It was spoken when he offered Isaac on the altar. 'Now I know,' said God, 'that thou fearest me.' God knew before, didn't He? Yes, at the level of His foreknowledge. But God must always know at the level of experience. He tested his friend, Abraham.

A test will come to all of us. It will test us to see if we are all theory and talk. God had bound up a lot of promises in Isaac but he was testing Abraham by saying, 'Who do you trust? Isaac or Me?'

I was recently tested. I said in the pulpit one evening that the media were not interested in the subject of the judgement of God and a message on the judgement of God would not be broadcast. Months later the phone rang and a BBC voice asked if I would go on a phone-in radio programme on the subject of the judgement of God. I had no choice, I had to go and take part! Watch what you say for you will be tested. Often, as Abraham, you will be tested at your tenderest point: the point of your love. Let's be genuine.

SEPTEMBER **14**

"Which hope we have as an anchor of the soul, both sure and stedfast, and which entereth into that within the vail; Whither the forerunner is for us entered, even Jesus."
Hebrews 6 v 19-20

I'm told that in olden times, when there was not enough water to float a ship into a harbour, the anchor would be carried over the shoals and fixed in the calm water of the inner basin. In the Jewish Tabernacle the high priest would pass through the blue veil that hid the Holy of Holies from the people and he took their hope with him that he would be accepted on their behalf before God.

Our great High Priest died on a cross and that veil was rent from the top to the bottom. The Lord Jesus rose from the grave and is gone into that celestial world before us. But he hasn't gone alone. He has taken our hope with Him and it is fixed there. It is called an anchor of the soul. Poor is the person whose hope is anchored in this world alone. As sure as night comes they will perish on the rocks.

SEPTEMBER **15**

"It is impossible for those who were once enlightened, and have tasted of the heavenly gift, and were made partakers of the Holy Ghost, and have tasted the good word of God and the powers of the world to come, If they shall fall away, to renew them again unto repentance; seeing they crucify to themselves the Son of God afresh, and put him to an open shame."
Hebrews 6 v 4-6

How many a fierce argument has raged around these verses. How many a soul has got into fierce mental anguish over them? Is this verse saying it is possible for a Christian to fall away and never be renewed? No. I do not believe that the people spoken of in today's text were true believers in the first place. Let me quote Professor David Gooding:

'Please observe what God actually says. He does not say that it is impossible to forgive those people's sin. He does not say He is not prepared to forgive them. That is not the point at all. He says it is impossible to get them to change their minds after this. He will never get them to repent or have anything to do with Christ.'

'But,' you say, 'that is saying a lot isn't it? How do you know?' Well, for this simple reason. The only thing that could possibly bring them to repentance is the Holy Spirit's power. Once they have felt that and deliberately rejected it, there is no other power in God's universe that could possibly reach them. Think about it.

SEPTEMBER 16

"For this Melchisedec .."
Hebrews 7 v 1

Who? Christ, 'A priest after the order of Melchisedec?' People's brows furrow and they turn to the News at Ten as soon as they get home, or the nearest newspaper. 'Let's go into the real world, preacher,' they'll say, 'who was this obscure Melchisedec anyway?'

In Hebrew his name means 'King of Righteousness'. He was the head of a large clan gathered round a place called Salem. Note the order. Righteousness first, then peace. No peace until there is righteousness first. Got it? But he was more. He embodied a striking picture of our Lord Jesus. He came into the world in an amazing way. As far as the record goes he was without father, without mother and without genealogy. Is he a myth? No, he undoubtedly did have parents but the fact that we are not told of them brings a lesson. We hear nothing of his death. In Scripture he has been made like unto the Son of God. He had no beginning and shall have no end of life. He was not only a king, he was a priest. Why is Christ after his order? Because Jewish high priests from Aaron on, died. It was not a permanent priesthood, not a perfect priesthood either. But the Lord Jesus lives in the power of an endless life. What a pen portrait of our Lord Melchisedec was!

As Autumn days fall upon us and the old order passes let us pause and learn that the Jewish priesthood is obsolete, cancelled, unperfect, useless, done with forever. 'Melchisedec' is a great word for Autumn days for it tells us that Christians have a high priest whose priesthood does not have to be handed on to somebody else. It will never change hands. Autumn can never touch it.

SEPTEMBER 17

"He is able also to save them to the uttermost that come unto God by him seeing he ever liveth to make intercession for them."
Hebrews 7 v 25

Now, can you see the vital teaching regarding Christ's priesthood? No doctrine is more important as you travel the lanes of life today. It will save you from those who teach that a Christian can reach a state of sinlessness in this life. Your experience tells you how the flesh desperately tries to get the upper hand in your life: we need the perpetual cleansing through the blood of our Lord Jesus Christ. That is what His cross accomplished. Thank God for a finished work and an ever interceding High Priest.

This teaching will also preserve to us what I judge to be a fast receding truth in our day: the truth of Priesthood of all believers. I heard Tony Benn, the M.P., on the BBC programme 'Any Questions', whose mother is an outstanding Christian, remind Lord Hailsham of this great doctrine recently! We could all do with a reminder. It is vital that all believers understand that they can act as priests before God and offer sacrifice of praise and prayer and to love God. There are others who persist in saying that they are called as a priesthood to offer the perpetual sacrifice of Calvary in the elements of the Lord's Supper. What do these sincere people do with the Lord's word that he made 'one great sacrifice for sin forever' and sat down at the right hand of God? Calvary is over, we remember it and God will make sure we will never forget it, but the continual priesthood of our Saviour will continue not only to save us from our sins but from doctrinal error too.

SEPTEMBER 18

"I will make a new covenant .. Now that which decayeth and waxed old is ready to vanish away."
Hebrews 8 v 8,13

A covenant is a promise and God made a promise with His people, Israel. It was called the Old Covenant. Under this promise if you kept your part of it, God kept His. The people had only to fail in their part and the whole Covenant was ruined. But what of the new?
'I will put my laws into their minds.' says God. They will naturally think upon them. And when you become a Christian that's exactly what happens, God's law put you on what I would call a constant 'automatic pilot'. 'I will write it on their hearts.' It is not just intellectual but

emotional. They will obey because they love to obey, God is saying, 'And their iniquities will I remember no more.'
Does this mean we can do as we like? No, but it does set us free to do as God likes. What if we fail? We have an advocate with the Father, Jesus Christ the Righteous and it is being hid from Him that gives us acceptance before God. Are we enjoying the terms of this Covenant in our daily lives or are we hanging on to the Old still thinking, 'If I make a mistake there is no hope for me?' If we are, no wonder we feel like Autumn in our souls.

SEPTEMBER 19

"But by his own blood he entered in once into the holy place, having obtained eternal redemption for us."
Hebrews 9 v 12

I was visiting Edinburgh one day with my friend Robert McClukey. He took me to the Castle and there was Scotland's Crown in a glass case. Innocently I asked a tall man standing by with a lot of brass buttons on his coat, 'How much is it worth?' He erupted ! 'Worth?', he exploded 'Three thousand men died in one day to put that crown on the head of Robert the Bruce. If you can put a price on human blood you are welcome to try - the crown is priceless!'
'You've got a sermon there.', smiled Robert as we retreated! Indeed I had. If human blood is priceless what will we say of Divine life that became human life and poured out precious blood at Calvary to give us everlasting life? 'By His own blood' says Hebrews 9 v 14. It was Royal blood. 'Without spot' says our text; it was innocent blood. Above all, it was priceless. Is it precious to you?

SEPTEMBER 20

*"Hath he appeared to put away sin .. now to appear in the
presence of God for us .. and then unto them that look for
him shall he appear the second time without sin unto
salvation."*
Hebrews 9 v 26-28

That first appearance was so incredibly moving. He
lay in Mary's arms and there was no room for them
in the inn. The shadow of a cross fell on Him
immediately and the next thirty three years saw Him go
unflinchingly to the cross. He arose from the grave and
now appears in the presence of God for us. That is the
second appearance. Then, as far as earth is concerned He
shall appear again not to save us from sins pitfalls but to
save us from the very presence of sin and to effect the
redemption of our bodies. We shall go to be with Him.
There are three appearances: are we looking for the last?
Notice the implication of the text. The mark of true
believers is that they are looking for Him. As Bill Freel
put it: 'As Christians we should not be exitists looking
for our going but adventists looking for His coming.'

SEPTEMBER 21

"To do thy will, O God."
Hebrews 10 v 9

There had been a series of bad harvests. An Israelite
had fallen into deep arrears to a rich neighbouring
creditor. He owed him more than ever his land could
raise. What should he do? He would sell his service and
so work out his debt. For six years he worked and the
Israelite was then called by his master for a discharge.
'No,' said the Israelite, 'I do not want to go out free. I
love working for you and I love you. I will serve you for

the rest of my life.' It happened often and was ratified by the master piercing his servant's ear with an aul to the doorpost, leaving a permanent and indelible impression of his servants new relationship.

I stood in a little shop by Yorkminster introducing two friends of mine to a lady who had run that little Christian book shop for many years. 'I was converted, girls,' she said, 'when I was eighteen. And I can tell you this. If I had a thousand lives He could have them every one.'

SEPTEMBER 22

"Having therefore, brethren, boldness to enter into the holiest by the blood of Jesus."
Hebrews 10 v 19

If we begin to imagine that our day to day progress in the Christian life is a measure of our acceptance before God, we would immediately be in despair. We would not draw near to God in prayer and enjoy His presence. The Devil wants us to think in such a way. He wants the Christian to live like a spiritual pauper every day instead of like a son or daughter of the King. Wake up, guilt ridden one, have you ever heard of justification? Because of Calvary's work the believer is justified: he is absolved of sin, released from its penalty, and restored as righteous!

Now, go to it and enjoy your position. Enter God's presence boldly. Don't be afraid to speak up. The Spirit of God urges you to do so. You have a right to be there. He is subtle but you are not stupid. Come on, spend time with God today in His presence. Wait there until you get an impression from God and later on today when someone is in need He will give you the strength to give that impression, expression. Let today be a day of holy boldness!

SEPTEMBER **23**

"Now faith is the substance of things hoped for, the evidence of things not seen."
Hebrews 11 v 1

What is faith? Somebody has to make a promise. Second, there must be a good reason for believing in the integrity of the promiser. Third, there must be an assurance that it will be as promised. 'Seeing is believing', for the shrewd person of the world but 'believing is seeing' for the shrewd Christian. That is faith.

Do you want to be a great person of faith? As I write I see from my window a little bird feeding on berries. What a feast it is having! The promises of God are faith's native food. Are you having a feast? Read what God has done in the past. Read and inwardly digest His promises. Then believe them and see your faith lift you from mediocrity, watch it make the nitty-gritty become the ground of true greatness. It applied to Moses in the palace, and Gideon on his farm, David as a shepherd and Samuel as a prophet. No class can buy it. It can master insuperable difficulties. And, by the way, you cannot please God without it. Have faith in God.

SEPTEMBER **24**

"By faith Enoch..."
Hebrews 11 v 5

I was in Tokyo on a train. My mum always taught me not to shove, but, my mum would have been no good on Japanese trains! People are so jam packed at times you can hardly get your hand into your pocket to get your ticket out! You've got to shove to get out yourself!

This train was travelling, if I remember, at night and was not so crowded. I was chatting to my university days friend, Tom Hill. With great secular prospects at home, Tom, at the call of God, had left them all and gone to Japan to serve the Lord in the spreading of the Gospel. 'Japan is the evangelist's graveyard,' said my friend, 'the people are, by and large, indifferent to the Gospel and so hard.' I could see that. What kept him there? 'I only ask one thing,' said my friend, 'I only ask that through it all I will be allowed to walk with God.'

Those words are alive in me even now. Enoch and Tom lived by the same guiding star.

SEPTEMBER 25

"By faith Noah..."
Hebrews 11 v 7

The Christians by their very stance are saying, 'There is something better than this present society.' That is why the world often hates them.

Take Noah. By his mere act of building an Ark he condemned the society in which he lived, even if he had never opened his mouth. We're not asked to build an Ark but we are asked to declare that judgement is coming. We are not naturally hostile to the world but when we profess to be saved we are declaring that there is a better one coming. It is not spiritual snobbishness, or holier-than-thou-ism. It is a fact. We may be called 'Noahs' and be jeered and laughed at and heckled but, no matter. When our Saviour said His Church was the light of the world, He implied that the world was in spiritual darkness. When He said His people were the salt of the earth He implied society was rotten and needed a preservative. Take it or leave it: Christians are 'agin things as they are. By faith.

SEPTEMBER 26

"By faith Abraham..."
Hebrews 11 v 8

Recently I read the Scripture Union's 'Family Pilgrims Progress' to my children. I recommend it to all families: it did me as much good as it did my children. Christians are losing their pilgrim character in the fast lane these days and it is time they touched the brake pedal and pulled over for a while to think about what it is costing them.

Abraham, like Noah, was saying 'This world is no longer any place for me, I'm getting out!' It didn't make him a lazy, no good business man. I can tell you he was in big business. It didn't make him a dismal moaner either, crowing about what he had given up back at Ur of the Chaldees to become a pilgrim. He used the world to make himself friends of 'the mammon of righteousness'. Read Luke 16 v 9 and learn it until you can almost say it backwards. It is saying that people of faith use their tents (houses), and camels (cars), servants (employees), and wealth (money) or whatever they possess to win people for the Lord. Then, as I heard the Bible teacher Mr. George Harpur put it, on a snowy night in Ulster, 'When you get to heaven people will come running to you shouting 'Hey you, do you remember me? The Lord used your kindness and wiseness to get me here!'.' I'm telling you, it is a ministry worth thinking about and putting into practise. By faith.

SEPTEMBER 27

"God is not ashamed to be called their God."
Hebrews 11 v 16

If Enoch, or Noah, or Sarah, or Isaac, or Joseph, or Gideon, or any other of the great heroes of faith, had given up all for the Lord and found the life of faith disappointing, their God would have every right to be ashamed of them. But God has no cause, never had, never will have, any cause to be ashamed of them. God knew what it would cost them all just as he knows what a life of faith will cost you. 'But,' you add, 'there are disappointments along the way.' True, heartbreaking ones, at that. But was anyone ever bitterly disappointed with God who had true faith in Him?

I've heard the story told in pulpits all my life but it will not suffer for the repeating. 'The great personality' was travelling on a liner along with a person who had given many years abroad in Christian service. The band played, the press called, the crowd welcomed 'the personality' home. The servant of God felt disappointed. There was no one to greet him. He slipped quietly down the gangplank feeling sick at heart until he heard the voice of God whisper in his ear, 'But you're not home, yet.' Selah.

SEPTEMBER 28

"Who through faith subdued kingdoms, wrought righteousness, obtained promises, stopped the mouths of lions .. And others had trial of cruel mockings and scourgings .. They were stoned, they were sawn asunder, were tempted, were slain with the sword."
Hebrews 11 v 33, 36-37

There is one very clear message from these very moving texts for us today. Some of these heroes were delivered from their foes and some of them were

delivered to their foes. David for example escaped
Goliath, but others were 'slain with the sword'. For the
latter it may have seemed that the heavens were as brass
and the promises of God mocked them. 'That's where
your faith gets you.' the world still mocks. Gets you?
A Bible teacher once told 'If you go preaching you will
never get on in this world.' 'Which world are you
talking about?', he replied. Sometimes faith is asked to
go to its limit and face complete disaster here in this
world. But what of the next? If we are allowed to be
delivered from our foes in this world according to the
will of God, good. If we are not, good. Either way when
death strikes us down we shall fall into heaven.

SEPTEMBER 29

*"Wherefore seeing we also are compassed with so great a
cloud of witnesses, let us lay aside every weight, and the sin
which doth so easily beset us, and let us run with patience
the race that is set before us, Looking unto Jesus the author
and finisher of our faith."*
Hebrews 12 v 1-2

We all know our own particular weight which
hinders us in the Christian race. The Holy Spirit
pin-points it. We must throw it off. Sebastian Coe
certainly didn't have any extra weight as he won the
Olympic 1500 metres, twice. Neither should Christians
in the race set before them. An athlete gladly forgoes
much that other men value and what is pleasant to
himself because his mind is intent on the prize. Let's get
everything out of our way that would hinder attainment
in spiritual matters. What is Olympic Gold in
comparison to the Master's 'Well done'? The incentive

and the strategy in the race is for us to look unto the face of Jesus.

To change the metaphor I love the story of the old mariner who was asked on the beach one day if the fishing pot he was working on with a large hole at the top were not useless in fishing. 'Surely,' said the questioner, 'the fish will swim out of the hole.' 'You don't know much about fish, son.' the old mariner replied. 'The fish swim in and through the hole and get so taken up with the fact that they seem to be caught that they forget to look up.' That's it. Look up and see Him there who made an end of all your sin. And you will escape every net Satan throws around you to hinder you in the Christian race.

SEPTEMBER 30

"Jesus Christ the same yesterday, and to day and for ever."
Hebrews 13 v 8

So Autumn is now really upon us since we first began September days, you and I. Change and decay in all around we see very clearly. Not only in the trees and hedgerows and fields, either. People change. Options change. Attitudes change. Moods change. Temperaments change. Leaders change. But Jesus Christ remains the same. 'The same,' said a friend of mine, 'is a Divine title.' Time is foiled in the Lord Jesus. Watch the person getting promoted in his job. Unfortunately sometimes he wants to know his old friends no more. Now that our Lord Jesus has been exalted far above all, has He altered? He is just the same Jesus, He still feeds on the backslidden Peters of this world, He still tells them the right side of the ship to let their net down on, He still bears the griefs of the bereaved families of this world, He still graces on our tables as the unseen guest with His face uplifted in blessing. The Gospels are not a record of the past but a record of what He is always doing. The Old Covenant has gone but the New Covenant remains because its instigator and Lord remains. There is never an Autumn in Him.

OCTOBER

'*O all wide places, far from feverous towns!
Great shining seas! Pine forests!
Mountains wild!
Rock bosomed shores! Rough heaths and sheep
cropt downs!
Vast pallid clouds! Blue spaces undefiled!
Room! Give me room! Give loneliness and air!
Free things and plenteous in your regions fair!'*

We all identify with George McDonald's poem. The
crowded lanes of the motorways of life look
different from the air. We all love to fly above
them, up, up and away. But it is the eagle's
domain not just the airlines.

Mr. Bill Gothard of the Institute in Basic Youth
Conflicts in Oak Brook, Illinois, whose Bible
teaching has been of blessing to hundreds of
thousands of people, has published a fascinating
book called 'The Eagle Story'. I am assured that I
can take some of Mr. Gothard's fascinating
material and apply it to my own situation. So, this
October, let's do some eagle spotting. October is the
month of fruits, not blossoms, and may these
studies produce much spiritual fruit.

OCTOBER 1

*"Bless the Lord, O my soul .. Who satisfieth thy mouth with
good things; so that thy youth is renewed like the eagle's."*
Psalm 103 v 1, 5

Eagles have been soaring almost motionless in near
hurricane force winds; moving only the tips of their
feathers to adjust for the varying wind speeds. It seems
almost as if the eagle is nailed to the sky in a storm. It is
not nailed. An eagle's amazing ability to manoeuvre has
to do with those all important feathers. One eagle was
found to have 7,182 feathers!
Each year the eagle is renewed, replacing every single
feather in its entire body over a period of several
months. The eagle, unlike other birds, is not severely
handicapped because no two adjacent wing feathers fall
out or moult at the same time. This enables the eagle to
continue flying throughout the entire renewal process!
So it is that God's people are constantly renewed while
serving Him. I preached for a week once, with my friend
Dr. Alan Redpath who was then 75 years of age. I shall
never forget praying with him in that Co. Wicklow
town. One evening before we went out to preach: 'Lord,'
he said, 'we want to serve you to our very last ounce of
strength and to our very last drop of blood.' Amen, to
that!

OCTOBER 2

"As an eagle stirreth up her nest .. so the Lord."
Deuteronomy 32 v 11

Eagles mate for life and return to the same nest every
year, making necessary repairs and additions. One
pair of eagles was observed for 25 years in the same
location. Their nest grew to be 20 feet deep and 9 1/2

feet across! Support trees often give way under the ever increasing weight of such nests!

But staying in such a nest for all of its life will not get the young eaglet into the sky. The care of the parent is phenomenal, even to replacing its body shade with a layer of sticks and debris to shade the young from the sun's heat while it goes hunting. But the time must come for progress from the nest so the parents begin to stir the nest. It is time to move on.

We usually don't like it when the Lord stirs our nest. We are often very stubborn about it. But it is a call to a great adventure. You may think it cruel that you must lose your job, or change your job, or move house or that you do not get what you desire. Don't resist God's stirrings. He wants you to soar.

OCTOBER 3

"As an eagle .. fluttereth over her young."
Deuteronomy 32 v 11

In the brood of an eagle there is keen competition between eaglets. The first eaglet to hatch is usually the largest and demands the most food. The nestlings are fed by the mother eagle. The father does the hunting and the meal comes to be broken into bite-size portions for the eaglet. That breaking up of the food for the eaglets is vital to their survival.

A preacher once arrived to find only one man in his congregation to listen to his preaching: 'I will give him what I would have given a packed congregation.' he thought. When the service was over he asked his patient listener what he thought. 'I am a farmer,' said the man, 'if I went out with a full load of hay to feed my cattle and only one lonely critter showed up, I tell you one thing, I sure wouldn't dump the whole load on him!' Wise words.

Let's break the bread of God's word carefully to meet the needs of those we are feeding. He is a fool who gives a steak to a little baby and he is equally a fool who only feeds a grown person on milk.

OCTOBER 4

"I bear you on eagles' wings."
Exodus 19 v 4

A fter spending two or three months in the security of the nest the young eaglet is ready to learn to fly: the 'stirring up' process is over. The first flight is usually from the nest to a rock but on subsequent flights the adult eagle may actually accompany the eaglet using its primary feathers to create an air current which lifts the eaglet.
I was always of the impression that eagles actually carry their young on their wings, dropping them into the abyss and then diving to catch them, taking them higher each time. I always thought that by the principle of 'must do' being a good master eaglets learned to fly! Research with those who know of these things tell me that it aerodynamically impossible; the eaglets by the time they are ready to fly are too heavy for their parents to physically carry them on their 'pinions'. Rather, the eaglet flies himself and the parent creates the conditions for flight.
The primary meaning of the Hebrew word 'bare' in today's text means 'to lift'. When God puts someone out to serve Him or sends a Christian on an errand for Him He 'bares' them, He creates the 'air currents' to lift them to the task. No matter how difficult the day, God will bare His own on eagles' wings.

OCTOBER 5

"As the eagle ..."
Deuteronomy 28 v 49

The eagle's vision is exceptionally sharp: each eye has two areas of acute vision as compared with the human eye which has only one. The eyes are placed forward on the eagle's head giving him acute depth perception and this is very important as the eagle must know precisely when to pull out of a dive. The forward placement of its eyes also enables the eagle to see to each side, peripheral vision. The eagle's area of vision covers almost 270∞ which is much more than a man's and this enables it to spot an object as small as a rabbit from a distance of almost 2 miles.

Another fascinating fact is that an eagle can see with its eyes shut. In addition to its normal pair of eyelids the eagle has a set of clear eyelids called 'nicitating membranes'. These eyelids can be closed for protection from the wind, hungry eaglets or the violence of the kill without affecting the eagle's vision.

Double vision is a great asset to the eagle but it is also of great asset to the Christian. Human eyes are wonderful but it is much better to have eyes as well. The young man with Elisha saw a huge army of Syrians but Elisha saw the mountains around him filled with chariots of fire as well. Use your double vision, Christian, as you live out your life today.

OCTOBER 6

"Riches .. fly away as an eagle toward heaven."
Proverbs 23 v 5

In the ancient world nothing was safe: moths went for clothes, rats went for poison, worms went for buried treasure, thieves broke into homes. Now, of course, modern man would argue all is changed, treasures can be protected, we have insecticides, rat poison, mouse traps, rust proof paints, burglar alarms, insurance, and lasers. Let us not be fooled because with all of man's devices his riches can still fly away as swiftly as an eagle toward heaven.

An eagle flies in storms when other birds seek shelter. So it is with riches when the storm of an economic slump comes, or inflation, or devaluation: man's riches fly away in a storm like an eagle toward heaven.

One great irreversible fact is that treasure in heaven can never fly away. It is incorruptible. What is it? It is the development of Christlike character. It is active endeavour to introduce others to Christ. It is investing money in causes whose dividends are everlasting. It is the only gilt edged security whose gilt will never tarnish. Let's set our heart on it.

OCTOBER 7

"The forth beast was like a flying eagle."
Revelation 4 v 7

From Napoleon to the Romans, from Charlemagne to the United States the eagle has been the official symbol of nations and armies. There is something about the bird, its grace in flight, its royal pose, its size, its spread, its awesome power. An eagle gives people a feeling of fear and wonder at the same time.

If the head of an eagle is studied carefully, just above each eye is a bone protrusion which extends over the eye much like a furrowed eyebrow. These protrusions lend to the eagle's face the human expression of decisiveness. If it were not there the eyes would look much like a chicken's, and with all due respect to the chicken, no nation or army on earth has a chicken as its symbol!

It is good to be decisive in life. We must not 'chicken out' of making important decisions and sticking by the consequences. How often the Church seems to take no

position on any issue and therefore loses its
effectiveness.
Got a decision to make today? Have it, today. And again,
don't forget that old motto: 'Always gently refuse that
which you intend to ultimately deny.'

OCTOBER 8

"Too wonderful for me .. The way of an eagle in the air."
Proverbs 30 v 18-19

Tack. It is a little word with great importance,
especially in relation to wind direction. It applies to
the eagle in the air just as much as a yacht at sea. God
has built into the eagle's wings aerodynamic possibilities
that give it the ability to change its tack when the wind
changes direction. The eagle's wings are characterised
by primary feathers which are separated at the tips like
the fingers of a hand. The separations play a major role
in the power and stability of the eagle in flight.
Whirlpools of air are formed by each primary feather.
These collide and cancel the drag effect on the wing,
allowing the eagle to fly almost effortlessly.
Tack is so vital in the Christian life. The winds of change
can come hurtling down from one direction this week
and come hurtling up from another next week. God has
made the Christian's body the temple of the Holy Spirit
and because of the Spirit's power He can give the
Christian the exact 'tack' needed to meet oncoming
winds.
It was the same Spirit who guided Philip into the desert
as guided Philip into Samaria. The Spirit said to Philip,
'Go near and join thyself to this chariot.' Philip ran and
got up into the chariot the Ethiopian was riding in to
discover he was reading a verse about Jesus! If Philip
had not run he would have arrived at the wrong verse!
The tack used was perfect. The Spirit behind such tack
makes no mistakes.

OCTOBER 9

"As the eagle .. so with the Lord."
Deuteronomy 28 v 49

A soaring eagle, gliding effortlessly at altitudes of over 2,000 feet, can give the illusion that an eagle moves almost at a snail's pace. To the casual observer 'the monarch of the sky' appears sluggish. He is a fool who is so deceived by his eyes. When an eagle spots its prey it will turn sharply, fold its wings into a tight, aerodynamic formation and dive at speeds of up to 200 m.p.h. that's faster than a Porsche in the fast lane! 'As with the eagle .. so with the Lord', says our text: it was the last address to the children of Israel ever given by Moses and he knew what he was talking about. God's ways to the casual observer appear slow. People demand instant action from God and then say He is not there when He does not give it. When God does act the speed of light appears sluggish in comparison. Do not be deceived, God is not passive at any time. God demands all men, everywhere, to repent and trust the Saviour. If they do not, He will act. The judgement of God when it falls is swift and he who hardens his neck will suddenly, says the Scripture, be destroyed and that without remedy. Again and again the swiftness of the eagle is emphasised in the Bible, and Moses in today's text knew God's judgement at first hand and so compared its swiftness to the eagle's. Let's keep it in mind: whether in judgement on the unbeliever or in the chastisement on the believer, God can move very swiftly.

OCTOBER 10

"Believe not every spirit, but try the spirits whether they are of God."
1 John 4 v 1

An eagle is a majestic bird but it can be brought down. A trapper can lay out some fish on a daily basis to lure an eagle in. Once the daily habit of eating the fish is established a trap can be sprung. The most deadly traps are hidden but if an eagle follows its instincts it will be able to see visible evidences of their presence. Why would fish be lying in grass day after day? It is not their natural habitat.

The Devil's incognito is one of his cleverest tricks and he can appear to us as an Angel of Light. So we must test every sermon we hear, every book we read, all the teaching we come across with the word of God. Things that are unfamiliar should be very suspect and very weighed up before being accepted. The wiles of the Devil are set to stop us soaring and to trap us and cage us for the rest of our lives. It is a sad thing to have a saved soul and a wasted life. Let's just remember: hidden dangers have visible evidences. Make sure you look for them.

OCTOBER 11

"For we wrestle not against flesh and blood, but against principalities, against powers, against the rulers of the darkness of this world, against spiritual wickedness in high places."
Ephesians 6 v 12

We want to continue on yesterday's theme today: the most dangerous enemies are unseen. The eagle who ignores this can be trapped and so can the Christian. There are unseen principalities and powers operating in the sphere of invisible reality against the Church of Jesus Christ. They have no moral principles, no code of honour, no higher feelings. They are utterly unscrupulous, ruthless and cunning. Darkness is their

habitat, the darkness of falsehood and sin.
Unfortunately, today, the fact of the existence of these
hierarchies of evil is being forgotten by the Church.
Everything is being attributed to the psychological. Was
the attack of Satan on the lovely child of Bethlehem,
through Herod's selfish ambition, psychological? Were
the fiendish insinuations of the Devil on the Saviour in
the wilderness just mere imagination? Why did that
bloodlike sweat pour down that sacred face in
Gethsemane? Satan was sorely tempting the sinless
Saviour. Why did the Lord Jesus say to Peter 'Get thee
behind me Satan', when Peter had protested against the
Lord's determination to go to Calvary? Satan can attack
you through your very best friends. Let's never forget
that Satan is a master at covering his tracks.

OCTOBER 12

*"And when the woman saw the tree was good for food .. she
took of the fruit thereof."*
Genesis 3 v 6

D eadly traps always appeal to basic needs. What
works in trapping an eagle also worked in trapping
Eve. Satan attacked Eve along the line of her appetite.
He did the very same when he tempted the hungry Lord
Jesus in the wilderness; 'If thou be the Son of God make
these stones bread.' When Demas left the path of serving
God, Paul, his colleague, said 'Demas hath forsaken me
having loved this present world!' Satan had tempted
Demas with present comforts as Demas wrestled with
the persecution, loneliness and imprisonment afforded
to a keen servant of God in the early days of the Roman

Empire. Demas left the track for the comforts of by-path meadow.

Let's watch for the attack of Satan through our basic needs. From Eve to David, from Adam to Peter, we can be trapped and led to deny the life of faith and to deny the Lord His rightful place in our hearts and lives.

OCTOBER 13

"Obey them that have the rule over you, and submit yourselves: for they watch for your souls."
Hebrews 13 v 17

A trapper, once he has lured an eagle in by fish, then sets up a net over the fish. It is a strong hoop net with a long handle dug into the ground. Fish are set under the net. The eagle swoops down for his fish and is, at first, very suspicious of the net. He flies around it, eyes it carefully and approaches with caution. With beak and claw he pulls the fish from under the net and hops quickly back. The eagle has senses to detect danger but ignores them to get food. The next day he goes under the net without apprehension.

Again and again God uses not only the Holy Spirit to warn us but wise parents, Godly friends, Spiritual pastors, wise elders. Often Satan tempts us to throw aside their cautions and to go our own way. We ignore their advice, if it is Bible based, at our peril. I remember a warning coming from a preacher in a pulpit, once, and unknown to him, it was so relevant to the person sitting beside me that the person gripped my arm with fear. Don't ignore such messages. They are warnings of hidden danger.

OCTOBER 14

"Be not deceived; God is not mocked: for whatsoever a man soweth, that shall he also reap."
Galatians 6 v 7

We all love something for nothing but everything has its price. An eagle soon discovers that free fish leads to the trapper's net and often the Zoo's cage. I stood one summer's day and gazed at a golden eagle in Edinburgh Zoo and I must admit his misery caused me long, long thoughts. The caged eagle looks the saddest of birds.

In life adultery appears to be as soft as down but, in the end, it is a screaming vulture. Compromise seems to be an easy option but in the end undermines the very principles of living and brings collapse. Laziness in the form of a little folding of the hands and a little more sleep seems the thing but poverty is soon knocking on the door. Everything has its price. The wages of sin seems easy money at the time but the actual wages of sin is death. Watch free provisions for they have hidden costs. Whatsoever a man soweth, that shall he also reap.

OCTOBER 15

"He that soweth to his flesh, shall of the flesh reap corruption; but he that soweth to the Spirit shall of the Spirit reap life everlasting."
Galatians 6 v 8

There are two root causes behind the circumstances which affect our lives: God or Satan. These things that come are not mere coincidences or accidents. We must discern the source. I often feel today's text perfectly sums up success or failure in the Christian life.

In the Christian life there are definitely two powers struggling, the one against the other. The law of the Spirit of life in Christ is greater than the law of sin and death because Satan was defeated at the cross. Christ faced Satan where he exercised power and broke that power. The Lord made a public example of Satan and overcame him and if we submit to the Lord Jesus we will overcome Satan too.

An eagle is also subject to a law which would drag it down. If an eagle in flight folded his wings he would plummet by the law of gravity. Despite the power of gravity, he overcomes it. We cannot overcome the law of sin and death, but in the Christ who bears us on eagle's wings we can overcome.

OCTOBER 16

"I will say to my soul .. take thine ease."
Luke 12 v 19

Our aim should never be to work for a life of ease. Easy fish costs the eagle freedom. The rich man of the Bible thought he had a long time to enjoy ease. He forgot about his soul and the reality of death and God called him a fool. He died that night.

Soberly I write it, my reader: what if this were your last day on earth? It could be. How do you plan to spend it? Are you dreaming of ease and rest and merriment? Don't let such dreams dull you alertness to impending danger. The Bible says that it is better to go to the House of Mourning than the House of Feasting. It makes us wise up. We get our priorities right. Easy meat and a life of ease does not prepare us for eternity. Just as there is no Utopia of easy fish for an eagle on this earth so there is no Utopia of rest and ease on this earth. Anyway, what would it profit anyone if they were to gain the whole world and lose their soul?

OCTOBER 17

"Sir, we would see Jesus."
John 12 v 21

Some Greeks expressed the desire to see Jesus. Through Philip and Andrew they sought an introduction. At the very moment those Greeks came Israel had decisively turned against the Lord Jesus. What a sore temptation it must have been to welcome this approach from out beyond Israel in the wider world He had come to win. But he immediately said 'Except a corn of wheat fall into the ground and die it abideth alone: but if it die, it bringeth forth much fruit .. now is my soul troubled.'
Why was His soul troubled? The answer is that He was being tempted to by-pass the cross and turn to the Gentiles. It was only if he were 'lifted up from the earth' He would draw all men unto Him. Satan was using a lovely request to halt Calvary. deadly traps look harmless until they are sprung. The eagle accepts the presence of the trap when he comes to eat the trapper's fish. It becomes part of his world. The Lord Jesus knew the deadly destruction of Satan's harmless looking traps and avoided them. So by His grace, must we.

OCTOBER 18

"Can a man take fire in his bosom and his clothes not be burned?"
Proverbs 6 v 27

The trapper now moves to catch the eagle. At the dead of night he ties a strong cord to the rim of the hoop. Then he runs the cord down to the ground, under a shallow root and into a nearby thicket. He pulls the cord. The net bends down until it covers the rock. When he releases the cord the net rebounds to its former position. He loosens the dirt at the base of the handle and after satisfying himself that all is in readiness, he baits the trap and creeps into the thicket to await the growing dawn.

Mighty wings are soon heard above him. This time there is no hesitation, the bird has been lured into accepting the structure as part of the established order. He starts to eat the fish. Suddenly there is a movement and, despite a last moment attempt by the eagle to spring free into the safety of the air, the trap is sprung and closes too swiftly for escape.

'Can a man take fire in his bosom and his clothes not be burned?', asks Scripture. No. Only pride and false confidence tell us we can enjoy the pleasures of sin and not get caught in sin's consequences. No more powerful figure than Samson strode across Israel. But he took fire in his bosom and his testimony for God was burnt alive. The eagle is no match for a trap once sprung and neither are we.

OCTOBER 19

"Know ye not, that to whom ye yield yourselves servants to obey, his servants ye are to whom ye obey; whether of sin unto death, or of obedience unto righteousness?"
Romans 6 v 16

Two possibilities face a trapped eagle: captivity or death. No matter how furiously he beats his wings, tears with his beak, clutches with his talons, he will find any effort to free himself only results in greater destruction and bondage. Unless the victim is freed the azure blue will know him no more.

So it is when Satan's trap of sin is sprung in our lives. Unless someone gets us out we've had it. Praise God there is a way out. It has to do with yielding to the Lord Jesus and this brings incredible freedom from the bondage Satan brings. For the next few days we shall study how the Saviour faced Satan's attacks and how he overcame them. Meanwhile watch to whom you yield for:

'He breaks the power of cancelled sin,
He sets the prisoner free,
His blood can make the foulest clean,
His blood avails for me'.

OCTOBER 20

"There hath no temptation taken you but such as is common to man: but God is faithful, who will not suffer you to be tempted above that ye are able; but will with the temptation also make a way to escape, that ye may be able to bear it."
1 Corinthians 10 v 13

Recently I was suddenly tempted to do wrong. The temptation was strong but the Lord gave the victory and the temptation passed. Suddenly I felt guilty, unclean. I shouldn't have. There is no sin in being tempted, the sin is yielding to temptation. It is important to remember that sin does not necessitate sinning. With every temptation God will provide a way of escape. When the Lord was tempted in the wilderness He was alone. Solitude does not prevent temptation, in fact it often greatly increases it. But for Him, as for us, on the basis of His victory, there was a way of escape. Learn this principle and learn it well for even to the very brink of Jordan you will find Satan nibbling at your heels. When tempted pray 'Lord Jesus come close to me now and shew me the way of escape.' He always will, if you ask Him.

OCTOBER 21

"Then was Jesus led up of the spirit into the wilderness to be tempted of the devil. And when he had fasted forty days and forty nights, he was afterward an hungered. And when the tempter came to him, he said, If thou be the Son of God, command that these stones be made bread."
Matthew 4 v1-3

Notice the setting of this great onslaught of Satan against the Lord Jesus. It was in the wilderness. It was shimmering, solitary, burning wilderness. The Bible has a lot to say about the wilderness because the nation of Israel had failed there so miserably. Now Satan attacks in the wilderness again. The timing of his attack was also very significant. The Lord Jesus had just been baptised and the voice from the heavens had said, 'This is my beloved Son in whom I am well pleased.' Satan's favourite time for attack is following a time when God has been honoured. Elijah after Carmel, David after Goliath, even Paul after his great writing is struck with 'a thorn in the flesh, the messenger of Satan to buffet me.' After blessing comes buffeting.

Notice that he does not give a point blank denial, he just casts a doubt, 'If thou be the Son of God.' The Lord had proved for 30 years that He was just that but the Devil casts doubt over it. And he will do the same with you. Recently, maybe, you enjoyed a special time of blessing from God. You would never doubt again, you said. But the Devil has come and cast doubt by saying 'It was just excitement, there was nothing in it!' Remember those times at the Lord's table when the Lord drew near? The Devil calls it 'just imagination'. Don't let Satan rob you of past blessings or past experiences of God.

Notice that the Lord Jesus often used His power to meet human need: Cana of Galilee and the 5,000 on the mountainside knew that. But Jesus was not going to be pushed into making stones bread at the Devil's instigation. The lesson is clear, trounce, by God's power, Satan's 'If's' and don't be pushed into the good to miss the better.

OCTOBER 22

"He answered and said, It is written, Man shall not live by bread alone, but by every word that proceedeth out of the mouth of God."
Matthew 4 v 4

I f the Lord needed to have recourse to the Scriptures as 'The sword of the spirit which is the Word of God' it is certain that we do. The Lord could have used angelic force against Satan, or, He could have unveiled His glory, or, He could have used devastating logic and reason, but He used the best weapon, and, so must we. His adversary shifted his point of attack constantly, because error can have many forms, but the Lord continually used His one defence: the word of God. The Lord also displayed a most marvellous trust in His Heavenly Father. He was willing to do without food if necessary in order to do His Father's will. Where Eve fell, He overcame. Two more lessons for every Christian are clear from our text: use God's word as a defence against every attack of the evil one and trust in God even if it means going without to do so.

OCTOBER 23

"The devil taketh him up into the holy city and setteth him on a pinnacle of the temple. And saith unto him, If thou be the Son of God, cast thyself down: for it is written, He shall give his angels charge concerning thee: and in their hands they shall bear thee up, lest at any time thou dash thy foot against a stone."
Matthew 4 v 5-6

S atan is an excellent theologian: he is good at quoting Scripture. So, the Lord Jesus trusts in His father, does he? Right: there is a promise in a marvellous Psalm of

safety for those who do that, is there not? Satan quotes it
while tempting the Saviour to do the very opposite. He
was wanting Him to either get killed or make a public
exhibition of Himself. He would have been 'a King for a
day' had it come off. But those who would have
marvelled would have remained firmly in Satan's camp
at the same time.

It was in a high and Holy place the saviour was
tempted. High and Holy places are a favourite hunting
ground for Satan. If your cup is full of spiritual blessing,
watch out. Satan would just love to spill it all out. It will
take a steady hand to carry it. Walk humbly and
carefully and do not tempt the Lord your God by trying
to force His hand to do anything. No jumps to fame,
please. Trust Him and all will be well.

OCTOBER 24

"Again, the devil taketh him up into an exceeding high
mountain and sheweth him all the kingdoms of the world,
and the glory of them; And saith unto him, All these things
will I give thee, if thou wilt fall down and worship me."
Matthew 4 v 8-9

Ambition is a very powerful force in a person's life.
Obviously the Lord's main ambition was to do His
Father's will but Satan, the grasper, assaults the Lord
Jesus with the offer of the Kingdoms of this world if He
will worship him. Here is the very heart of the tempter.
Satan wants world dominion by disobedience: the Lord
Jesus was going to have world dominion by obedience
by taking on Himself the form of a servant. Satan just
could not break down the Saviour's single-mindedness:
no compromise or inducement could make Him turn
back.

How did the Lord harrow Satan on this temptation? He had no discussion on the matter, He harrowed him by not asking him to go but by telling him. Does it work? I was staying with a family recently and after the evening service was over I sat down to an excellent meal with my friends. My hostess had had a difficult day. 'Do you know what I did?', she smiled, 'I was so tired of Satan's attacks all day, I simply opened the door and told him to get out!' I was glad Satan had got that treatment and not me! My hostess was right in line with Scripture. 'Get thee hence, Satan.'

OCTOBER 25

"There is therefore now no condemnation to them which are in Christ Jesus."
Romans 8 v 1

Calvary has inflicted on Satan a fatal blow. At Calvary the Lord Jesus stooped to conquer. Satan means 'accuser', and, as a result of Calvary every man, woman and child who hides in His completed work cannot be condemned. The occult and all other cults, the whole world of demonic activity has been robbed of its power by Calvary. Death and sin, disobedience and rebellion were overcome at Calvary and such was the size of the victory that whenever Christ's name is named in faith, Satan is bound to flee. Where the first man failed the second man from heaven won. Lift up your heart today and thank God for Jesus. As October nears its end let this word ring in your heart in your afternoon walk amidst falling leaves. No condemnation! No condemnation! Calvary is the greatest barrier to hell and the very door to heaven.

OCTOBER 26

"That I may know him and the power of his resurrection and the fellowship of his sufferings."
Philippians 3 v 10

We have, in a spiritual sense, seen the eagle released over the last few days. What now? The answer is that turbulent winds will batter us constantly until our 'soaring' days are over. We must expect it. As October days draw to a close let's think of what benefits turbulent winds will bring.

The happy truth is that turbulent winds cause the eagle to fly higher! There is tremendous lifting power in the thermal updrafts of turbulent winds. These updrafts cause the eagle to reach great heights as he soars with them. The turbulent winds of persecution that came against the early Church only caused the Church to grow as they soared spiritually with the situation, going everywhere preaching the word. Make sure you use every turbulence that comes your way today to soar for God. Rejoice when the turbulence comes. The power of Christ's resurrection will carry you far, the fellowship of His sufferings will bring you joy unspeakable.

OCTOBER 27

"Ye are the salt of the earth."
Matthew 5 v 13

Turbulent winds give the eagle a larger view. I remember an eagle, from a height of half a mile, can survey an area some four and a half square miles! As the winds of life cause you to wait on the Lord and you soar as a result you will be able to see things that no one else can see. Is it true that Peter and Andrew knew more than Aristotle and Plato did? Is it true that those disciples of

Christ described by some onlookers as 'without grammar and idiots' had knowledge the philosophies of men could not match? Jesus said so: 'You are the salt of the earth.' he said, 'You are the light of the world.' A fisherman, the light of the world? Why? Because he knew the Lord.

So it is, in your office, or school, or factory, or shop, if you know the Lord you can shed more light than Einstein on the real issues back of this universe. God says He has hidden things from the wise and the prudent and revealed them unto babes. So shine, brothers, shine.

OCTOBER 28

"Notwithstanding ..."
2 Timothy 4 v 17

Turbulent winds lift the eagle above harassment. At lower elevations the eagle is often harassed by suspicious crows, disgruntled hawks and other smaller birds. As the eagle soars higher, he leaves behind all these distractions.

So it is when we live by the law of life in Christ. Listen to Paul, again in prison in Rome: 'All they which are in Asia be turned away from me,', 'Demas hath forsaken me,', 'The cloak that I left in Troas .. bring,', 'Alexander the coppersmith did me much harm,', 'At my first answer no man stood with me, but all men forsook me.' The list is frightening, the winds of loneliness and desertion were certainly fiercely against him. Suddenly up comes this mighty word: 'Notwithstanding the Lord stood with me and strengthened me; that by me the preaching might be fully known and that all the Gentiles might hear; and I was delivered out of the mouth of the lion and the Lord shall deliver me from every evil work and will preserve me unto His heavenly Kingdom: to whom be the glory forever and ever. Amen.' Some soaring!

OCTOBER 29

"... and not be weary."
Isaiah 40 v 31

Turbulent winds allow the eagle to use less effort. The wings of the eagle are designed for gliding in the winds. The feathers' structure prevents stalling, reduces the turbulence, and produces a relatively smooth ride with minimum effort, even in rough winds. The rougher it gets the smoother the ride.

How many an unbeliever has gazed in disbelief at the strength a believer gets in the face of great odds. A lady once told me that the first great influence to touch her life regarding the reality of the Gospel was to watch the believers and unbelievers die in a hospital where she worked. The believers' faith had stirred her to faith in Christ. may God give us incorrigible faith: a faith that burns like a fire that cannot be put out. The greater the storm, the more we can lean on what God has provided for us to combat the turbulence. We can do all things through Christ who strengthens us.

OCTOBER 30

"The joy of the Lord is your strength."
Nehemiah 8 v 10

Turbulent winds allow the eagle to stay up longer. The eagle uses the winds to soar and glide for long periods of time. In the winds the eagle first glides in long shallow circles downward and then spirals upward with a thermal draft. The eagle must feed and care for its young, it must fight off enemies and come down to earth often but long soaring, despite the nitty-gritty, is a tremendous part of its life and universal appeal.

I know a man who was imprisoned in Africa for his faith in Christ. He told me of the dreadful conditions he was put in. 'I was sorry when I was set free!', he said. Sorry? 'Yes I was in there for the cause of Christ and the joy I got over that time of imprisonment was greater than I have ever known before. I was sorry when I had to leave.' The same joy can be yours today and you don't need to be in prison for the Lord's sake to experience it.

OCTOBER 31

"We glory in tribulations also: knowing that tribulation worketh patience; And patience experience; and experience, hope."
Romans 5 v 3-4

It has been good to walk through October days with you. It is my prayer that many of these insights into the world of the eagle which I first learned from Bill Gothard and have tried to apply in my own life will be a help to you.

One final thought for today before November winds come upon us: 'The wings that lift us out of despair, are made by God from the weight of care.' Again and again we have touched the truth in this book that we should let the storms and trials, heartaches and pressures, troubles and cares all drive us to God. If we do we will go much further in less time. Normally the eagle flies at a speed of 50 m.p.h. however when he glides in turbulent winds, speeds of over 100 m.p.h. are not uncommon. Despite all I have written about the fast lane I have to admit that we all need to pull out into it now and again to get folk in need. Go with God in the turbulent winds of your life: safe journey and keep soaring!

NOVEMBER

November seems to be a month of negatives. 'No shade. No shine. No butterflies. No bees. No fruits. No flowers. No leaves. No birds.' Negatives, maybe, but Shelley caught the essence of November when he wrote, 'Wild Spirit, which art moving everywhere, destroyer and preserver.' In a sense it is like the mushrooms and toadstools to be found all over the wood in November days: some are edible and very nutritious and others are poisonous. There are good things and bad things in November, the destroyer and preserver.

This month I want to devote two weeks' meditations to things I would like to see destroyed in modern life and two weeks to what I would love to see preserved. May November be a truly memorable month for you and your family.

NOVEMBER 1

"And the driving is like the driving of Jehu the son of
Nimshi; for he driveth furiously."
2 Kings 9 v 20

L et's destroy rushing. The pace of life in the West is
getting much too hectic. Ever see a scramble for
coats and hats and papers as soon as a pilot cuts his
engines on an aircraft? You would think the aircraft was
on fire and the passengers were never going to get out.
Have you joined the local Jehus as they wait at your
local traffic lights? Why, it is like the start of the
Indianapolis 500! Sit back, let them all rush off the
aircraft. You'll find that the tortoise will often pass the
hare at the baggage claim area. Ease the accelerator, let
them roar away from the lights. You'll live to see another
day.
Let's buy our Christmas cards in January next year and
some Christmas presents too. Destroy the rush. Let's set
off twenty minutes earlier to the Church service and sit
quietly reading a hymn or spending a little time in silent
prayer before it all starts. Destroy the rush that comes
through the door when the quartz watches 'bleep' at the
hour the service begins and for ten minutes after!
Heart attacks could be halved if we took the quieter road
to the seaside, the slower lane on the motorway to work,
the hour other than the rush hour to get that vital
assignment done. Learn it, friend, it took ulcerative
colitis to teach it to me. Destroy rushing before it
destroys you.

NOVEMBER 2

"Peter seeing him saith to Jesus, Lord, and what shall this
man do? Jesus saith .. What is that to thee?"
John 21 v 21-22

L et's destroy interrupting. I know there is a time for interrupting even the most important conversation but are we not all interrupting each other too much? Here is a chap who is suffering the most awful toothache or neuralgia or stomach-ache. He begins to describe what he is going through when over here someone interrupts him by telling him how back last year they had this toothache, or stomach-ache or neuralgia which their doctor said was the worst case he had come across in twenty years!

The is an unquestionable relief in being able to talk about someone about a problem whether it be a roof leaking or a teenager rebelling or whatever: a problem shared is a problem halved. The problem is that we are all so quick to tell what we went through with a similar problem that the person sharing his problem finds that it hasn't been halved but doubled - by us!

Television is the culprit because no decent discussion programme is any good, as far as the producer is concerned, unless there are a lot of lively interruptions! I can't help but admire Sir Robin Day but I would not want to go to him about a problem because he would be sure to interrupt by saying half way through, 'Thank you but now I would like to bring in Mr. Brown who has a similar problem and ..!'

NOVEMBER 3

"Go ye and tell that fox ..."
Luke 13 v 32

L et's destroy 'Nosey Parkerism'. I don't know who the original Nosey Parker was but he has a lot of relations. A word of witness, of advice, of help and counsel is much needed in these days but unwarranted intrusion into folks' lives and plans is not on.

'Where are you going on holiday this year?', can in fact mean according to the answer, all kinds of reactions. The questioner is often not interested in whether you have a good holiday: he is just being a Nosey Parker. 'The Alps?' (we're jealous), 'The Costa Brava?' (we're going there too), 'Disney World?' (where did you get the money), 'Portavogie?', 'Port Talbot?' (you're broke!). Let's trim that little phrase, 'If I were you', and let's destroy the phrase 'Did you know that the Jones'...' The book of Proverbs bids drink from our own well, not another's. Let's do just that. Let Nosey Parker drink from as many as he likes.

NOVEMBER 4

"If a fox go up, he shall even break down their stone wall."
Nehemiah 4 v 3

Let's destroy the vindictive 'put down' phrase. It is so easy in life to knock things down. I have heard the most spiritual of men and women derisively abused by what may appear to be a humorous phrase but which is, in fact, a 'put down' phrase.

Nehemiah was doing excellent work for God rebuilding the great wall of Jerusalem. There was a great spiritual revival going on amongst God's people. Gates burned down by terrorists were remade and hung in place. The great wall of the City of Zion rose proudly once more. Was everybody delighted? Don't you believe it. Sanballat the Horonite jeered. 'What do these feeble Jews? Will they revive the stones out of the heaps of the rubbish which are burned?' Tobiah the Ammonite threw one of the most sarcastic 'put down' phrases in all of Scripture at the good work. 'Even,' he said, 'if a fox go up, he shall even break down their stone wall.'

The Dean Swifts and Cassandras and the Nigel Dempsters of this world have millions of readers but did ever one of their phrases build anyone up in the things

that really matter? Popular? Yes. A blessing? No.
If you are smarting under a 'put down' phrase then the
best way to get rid of it is to say something today to help
encourage the people you meet. They will be delighted
too meet you for they will have met any amount whose
delight is to put them down.

N O V E M B E R 5

*"He that speaketh flattery to his friends, even the eyes of his
children shall fail."*
Job 17 v 5

L et's destroy flattery. As Robert Browning said in 'The
Lost Leader', 'Just for a handful of silver He left us,
just for a riband to stock in his coat.' How many a gift is
destroyed by flattery? How many a ministry which has
had the hand of God upon it and under which people
are getting help and encouragement, been wrecked
because the one being used was flattered by what
seemed to be a work more suited to his gifts. 'The grass
is always greener on the other side of the fence, and,
although we always know it we're sometimes hard to
convince.' Flattery can draw us to the other side of the
fence, and, as the man said, 'Too far East is West.'
A great playwrite was asked what he thought of the
great queues waiting to get in to see his play. 'The same
crowd,' he said, 'would come to see me hung.'

N O V E M B E R 6

"She shall be praised."
Proverbs 31 v 30

L et's destroy the new attitude to the sacredness of
womanhood. By and large they have to now stand
in buses while men sit. No longer are doors opened for

them as frequently as in yesteryear. To see a man stand when a woman enters a room is becoming a rare thing. A lot of women are now equal with men. They curse equally, they drink equally, they smoke equally. Is it for the better?

Let me ask a very simple question. Would you like the memory of your child to be of a woman smelling of nicotine, a cocktail in her hand, pushing you and your childhood needs away, or giving that responsibility to someone else, while she entertains 'the world and his wife'. Or, would you like your child to find you, unawares, on your knees in prayer, now and again, and to smell lavender and to feel love and faith and hope coming from you?

Old fashioned? Give it to me any day in comparison with the clever, slick, women of the T.V. soap operas and the advertising hoarding. I have written it in this book before and I do so again: let's destroy all that seeks to destroy the sacredness of womanhood.

NOVEMBER 7

"To every thing there is a season ..."
Ecclesiastes 3 v 1

Let's destroy superficiality. If there is one thing about many Christians it is the feeling that they have to be 'trendy' to make any impact on their generation. They are always saying that they have to show the unbelievers that 'Christians can have fun too, you know.' So they are forever frivolous, forever joking, forever on-the-surface when out and about.

It is because of this superficial approach that many people cannot get Christians to give them help just when they need it most. The very people who should be acting as a light set on a hill are actually hiding that light by superficial conversation and behaviour. The Bible says there is a time for laughter, indeed if there wasn't we would die for lack of it. There is a reason for it. Nevertheless lets not be forever laughing. There is a time to reach for the stars, too.

NOVEMBER 8

"A time to rend ..."
Ecclesiastes 3 v 7

Let's destroy clichés. The first person I'd need to start with is myself. I'm sure in this book could count dozens of clichés ('could count dozens' is a cliché!). It is very difficult to work to get fresh language into our communication. I once heard a man preach and he said, 'Sinner friend in the meeting tonight ...', eighty one times during the service! I know, because I counted them!

Phrases like 'The sun is splitting the trees' and 'We will leave no stone unturned' will probably never be destroyed in the English Language but does this fact have to apply to phrases like 'Shall we bow our hearts together' or 'the announcements for the incoming week are ...'? When Mark Twain said that a cauliflower was a cabbage with a college education he was getting there! Yet, for me, the best example of cliché destruction was the man who defined committee work. He said that 'A camel is a horse designed by a committee!' Fresh, accurate language indeed. Try some cliché destruction as you talk today.

"He .. began to wash the disciples' feet."
John 13 v 5

L et's destroy meetingitis. It is often in organised
Church meetings that the local Church, designed to
show us the better use of our time, gets into a fast lane
that is almost the 'Dizzy Lane'! Such a flurry of activity
can be caused that there is no time to reflect. Let me,
once again, repeat one of my favourite stories about a
chap I heard of.
This chap was always going to the local Church services.
Monday night he was at this service, Tuesday night he
was at that service. One evening his exasperated wife
challenged him as to where he was going. 'Oh,' he
replied, 'tonight is missionary night. There's a
missionary showing a set of slides entitled 'Going
through Africa with a camel.' I'm looking forward to it.'
'You're not going.' said his wife, emphatically. 'And why
not?', questioned her husband. 'Because you are going
into the kitchen to go through china with a dishcloth!'
she replied.
Witness is vital, fellowship and worship together must
not be forgotten or forsaken. But let's go through china,
too!

*"So Saul died for his transgression which he committed
against the Lord, even against the word of the Lord, which
he kept not and also for asking counsel of one that had a
familiar spirit, to inquire of it; And enquired not the Lord."*
1 Chronicles 10 v 13-14

L et's destroy prayerlessness. Do you remember the
story of Saul and the witch at Endor? Impatience led

Israel's King to enquire of a sorceress about his future. She called up her usual 'familiar spirit' but the sudden unexpected appearance of the spirit of Samuel struck her with terror. It was God who sent Samuel up. The medium's complete lack of composure at the appearance of a real spirit is a complete and irrefutable demonstration that the real spirit of a deceased person does not appear at a mediumistic seance, even though it would claim to do so. Today's text is a very clear warning of God's anger rising against prayerlessness. God was extremely angry with Saul for not enquiring of him in prayer. Let's take serious note of this.

The best way to learn how to pray is to pray. You could read a book on health and waste away. You could read many books on driving a car and never drive one an inch. You could read hundreds of books on prayer, hear many messages on prayer and never enjoy five minutes in it. Selfishness hinders prayer. Sin hinders prayer. Idols in our hearts hinder prayer. Doubting hinders prayer. But remember, God answers prayer. So let's destroy prayerlessness.

NOVEMBER 11

"The fear of man bringeth a snare."
Proverbs 29 v 25

Let's destroy the fear of critics. let me illustrate the stupidity of such a fear with a story from yesteryear. An old man and his son were driving a horse before them to market to sell.

'Why have you no more wit,', said a critic to the man on the road, 'than your son to trudge it afoot and let the horse go light?' So the old man set his son upon the horse and walked.

'Why, Sir,' said another to the boy, 'you lazy rogue, must you ride and let your old father go afoot?' The old man then took his son down and got up himself.

'Do you see,', said a third, 'how the lazy old knave rides himself and the poor young fellow has much ado to keep after him?' The father then took up his son behind him. The next person they met asked the old man whether or not the horse were his. 'Yes.', he replied. 'Truth, there's little sign of it!', said the other, 'By the way you load him!'

'Well,', said the old man to himself, 'and what am I to do now? I'm laughed at if the horse is empty, or, if one of us rides, or both of us.' So he came to the conclusion that he would carry the horse to the market. When he got there everybody fell about laughing so much that the old man in anger threw the horse into a river and went home. The good man was willing to please everybody but had the ill fortune to please nobody and lost his horse into the bargain.

NOVEMBER 12

"Go to now ..."
James 4 v 13

Let's destroy procrastination. Never did there exist a more professional thief. Beat him to the ground. Jump on him. Refuse to let him into any part of your life. If you do he'll strip you of everything worth doing or planning. And do it now! How? Try this.

'If with pleasure you are viewing,
Any work a man is doing,
If you like him or love him tell him now,
Don't withhold your approbation,
Till the parson makes oration,
And he lies with snow white lilies on his brow,
For no matter how you shout it,
He won't really care about it,
He won't really know how many teardrops you have shed,

If you think some praise is due him,
Now's the time to slip it to him,
For he cannot read his tombstone when he's dead.

More than fame and more than money,
Is the comment kind and sunny,
And the hearty warm approval of a friend,
For it gives to life a savour,
And makes you stronger, braver,
And it gives you heart and spirit to the end,
If he earns your praise - bestow it,
If you like him, let him know it,
Let the words of true encouragement be said,
Do not wait till his life is over,
And he's underneath the clover,
For he cannot read his tombstone when he's dead.'

The little word 'now' scares the life out of
procrastination. Use it!

NOVEMBER 13

*"A man's life consisteth not in the abundance of the things
which he possesseth."*
Luke 12 v 15

Let's destroy the grip of materialism. Here is some
writing of Luci Shaw which she calls 'The View from
the Country Club'. Tomorrow we shall look at 'The View
from the Cross' as seen by Peter, James and Paul.
'God forbid that I should ever have the inconvenience of
unprepared food or clothes that need ironing. God
forbid that I should suffer from the lack of a colour T.V.,
Polaroid cameras, or a stereo tape deck. Please see to it
that I am not deprived of good coffee, my IBM
typewriter and a telephone in every room. God forbid
that I should ever spend my valuable time in chit-chat
with my new neighbour no matter how lonely he is. God

forbid that I should ever have to push past the velvet
curtains of suburban living and come to grips with real
life that I should seek goals beyond my own satisfaction,
comfort, fulfilment, security and social success. God
forbid that tragedy should ever strike through to me in
my luxurious habitat, so carefully planned. God forbid
that death or disillusionment should happen; that I
should need the contrast of darkness to know what light
is: of sorrow to discover joy; of guilt to find forgiveness.
Oh! God forbid that I should suffer!'
Is this your prayer?

NOVEMBER 14

"The sufferings of this present time."
Romans 8 v 18

Let's destroy our negative attitude to suffering. Here
is J.B. Philips translation of several passages from
the writings of James, Peter and Paul. It is a view from
the cross.
'When all kinds of trial and temptations crowd into your
lives, my brothers, don't resist them as intruders, but
welcome them as friends. Realise that they come to test
your faith and to produce in you the quality of
endurance.' (James 1 v 2-4)
'Experience shows that the more we share Christ's
sufferings, the more we are able to give of His
encouragement.' (2 Corinthians 1 v 6-7)
'Since Christ had to suffer for us, you must fortify
yourselves with the same inner attitude that He must
have had. You must realise that to be dead to sin
inevitably means pain, and you should not therefore
spend the rest of you time here on earth indulging your
physical nature, but in the doing the will of God.' (1
Peter 4 v 1-2)

'I beg you not to be unduly alarmed at the fiery ordeals
which come to test your faith, as though this were some
abnormal experience. You should be glad because it
means that you are called to share Christ's sufferings.
One day, when He shows Himself in full splendour, to
men, you will be filled with the most tremendous joy.' (1
Peter 4 v 12-13)
'After you have borne these sufferings a very little while,
the God of all grace, who has called you to share His
eternal splendour through Christ, will Himself make
you whole and secure and strong.' (1 Peter 5 v 10)

N O V E M B E R **1 5**

"Sound speech .. cannot be condemned."
Titus 2 v 8

Preserving is often a lot more difficult than
destroying. In the work of preserving something we
sometimes have to clean it, or bolster it, or protect it, or
bring in professional help to advise on it. All in all if it is
worth preserving it is worth spending time on both in
thought and action. Here is my two week preservation
order!
Let's first preserve the fading art of good and helpful
conversation. Ever been in a lift with strangers, or a
dentist's or doctor's surgery or at a funeral? Over each
seems to be a sign which says 'Thou shalt not dare open
thy mouth to even say that it's a nice day!' I am too well
aware that if you get some people talking it can rain for
forty days or forty nights but that's not the
conversationalist I want to preserve. The gem I'm after is
the helpful person who 'breaks the ice' with a helpful
comment which brings folks together.
Honestly some people just don't try. They are amazing.
If there was £50,000 to be gained by talking for half an

hour they would never give over but if it is a lonely
heart, a lost soul, a foot-sore pilgrim, a confused
teenager, a disillusioned student or whatever, they
haven't a word of kindness for them. 'Anxiety in the
heart of a man causes depression but a good word
makes it glad.' 'He who gives the right answer kisses the
lips.' 'There is gold and a multitude of rubies but the lips
of knowledge are a precious jewel.' So says God's word,
so let's try to preserve words like that in our
conversation. They will do more than we can ever
calculate. Let a few slip out, today.

NOVEMBER 16

"I have .. quieted myself."
Psalm 131 v 2

L et's preserve that quiet place. You know what I
mean, don't you? That coffee shop with the hot
scones where you suddenly feel relaxed. That garden
corner where you breath again and can dig your hands
into the soil. That corner of the factory or shop where
you disappear with your newspaper crossword and
forget the mortgage and interest rates and grocery bills
and the value of the pound and your next-door
neighbours' midnight parties and quiet yourself with
'Ex-schoolfellow disturbed, yes, but does as he's told' or
'Being stingy managed the reverse around the East'. (No
answers on a postcard please!) It is your quiet place! It
may be a favourite book, a quiet stroll, a doughnut or a
cup of tea, but find that quiet place, find it.
The Lord Jesus found it in the mountains, you might
find it in Toronto's Eaton Centre or Ballyjamesduff's '
country road but as sure as daylight if you do not come
apart and rest awhile, you will come apart.

NOVEMBER 17

"And one of you say .. Depart in peace, be ye warmed and filled; notwithstanding ye give them not those things which are needful to the body; what doth it profit?"
James 2 v 16

Let's preserve compassion. When we think of the horrors of the disaster in Africa just now; of the heart-rendering moans of starving men, women and children in refugee camps without any water, sanitation or food, of little ones so weary they cannot even swat away the flies that swarm around them, the huge mountains of food in EEC countries which are dumped or destroyed which could go a long way to alleviating the situation let's not lie back with a 'What is it to me? I can do nothing.' We can all do something.
Compassion is what makes a person feel pain when somebody else hurts. Millions are hurting, desperately, through no fault of their own and people will not care what we know until they know that we care. Homer said, 'There is no exercise better for the heart than reaching down and lifting people up.' Let's never become individuals without compassion. Faith without works is dead.
A lady once turned to a Christian leader for help and he promised to pray for her. She later wrote this poem.

I was hungry,
And you formed humanities groups to discuss my hunger,
I was imprisoned,
And you crept off quietly to your Chapel and prayed for my release,
I was naked,
And in your mind you debated the morality of my appearance,
I was sick,

And you knelt and thanked God for your health,
I was homeless,
And you preached to me of the Spiritual shelter of the
love of God,
I was lonely,
And you left me alone to pray for me.
You seem so holy, so close to God,
But I am still very hungry - and lonely - and cold.

NOVEMBER 18

"For we brought nothing into this world, and it is certain we can carry nothing out."
1 Timothy 6 v 7

Let's preserve simplicity. How often have we seen intelligent people when faced with something complex baulk at being humble enough to say, 'I don't know the answer to this.' 'I don't know' seem to be three very difficult little words to get out. I always chuckle at the difference between these two verses, both saying the same thing!

'Scintillate, scintillate, globule vivific,
How I consider thy nature specific,
Loftily poised in the either capacious,
Strongly resembling a gem carbonaceous.'

'Twinkle , twinkle, little star,
How I wonder what you are,
Up above the world so high,
Like a diamond in the sky.'

Let's preserve simplicity and that includes simplicity in our personal lifestyle. Let's renounce waste and let's oppose extravagance.

We must recognise, as Dr. Ronald Sider put it, the 'Distinction between necessities and luxuries, creative hobbies and empty status symbols, modesty and vanity, occasional celebrations and normal routine, and between the service of God and slavery to fashion!'
Let's always remember that simplicity's first cousin is contentment. Our battle cry is not 'Nothing!' but 'Enough!' Godliness with contentment is great gain. It is a combination which preserves simplicity.

NOVEMBER 19

"Where there is no vision, the people perish."
Proverbs 29 v 18

L et's preserve visionaries. Visionaries may seem out of fashion at the moment but they are desperately needed. Visionaries are people who have a deep dissatisfaction with what is and a clear grasp of what could be. Look at Scripture. Moses was appalled at the way the Israelites were treated in Egypt and with a clear vision of the 'Promised Land' he led them out. Nehemiah brought incredible blessing to God's people when he called on them to work together and rebuild the wall of Jerusalem. But notice that he had first inspected the wreck of a wall at the dead of night himself and realised what could be done. What of the Pharisee of Pharisees, Saul of Tarsus, who bridged the gap between Jew and Gentile with his mighty preaching of the Gospel? He died because of it.
Karl Marx was a visionary, and Mao Tse Tung and Hitler: but visionaries for what? They cared not who they killed in order to change things. There are plenty who have visions and their visions are wrong but the vision of 3,000 million people unevangelised and of getting the Gospel to them is not a false vision. The vision of broken hearts and wrecked people in our hectic

society who need tender loving care and the hope the
Gospel brings is not a false vision. Behind every great
achievement is a dreamer of great dreams. Would you
rather be a Joseph or one of his brothers? With
discipline, perseverance and humble service this world
can be a better place because of you. Be a visionary for
the Lord Jesus and may you be preserved to us for a
long time.

N O V E M B E R 2 0

"For with the same measure."
Luke 6 v 38

L et's preserve a realisation of cause and effect. We
often forget this great principle in life. You can't do a
kindness without a reward. You can't light a candle
without feeling the warmth. You can't throw a stone in
water without causing ripples. You can't pluck a rose
without part of its fragrance remaining with you. You
can't throw mud without losing ground.
Peter denied his Lord but went out and repented and
became mighty for God. Judas betrayed his Lord and
went out and hanged himself and became mighty for the
Devil. Joshua and Caleb had faith in God and got into
the 'Promised Land', millions of the children of Israel
did not have faith in God and their carcasses littered the
desert. Ruth said to Naomi, 'Where thou goest I will go.'
and walked into Bible history, Orpah said, in effect,
'Where thou goest I cannot go.' and walked out of Bible
history. The little lad said to God, 'Here is my lunch.'
and he was rewarded with seeing 5,000 fed: Nabal said,
'David will get no lunch from me.' and did not realise
that he would not live to eat many more himself.
Cause and effect are written into every move we make in
life. Thomas Mart gave himself three years to solve the
problems of refrigeration in order to ship meat from

Australia to Britain. It took him twenty six years. He lived to see the first shipment off but died before learning it had landed safely: millions have benefited by the effects of the motto he had painted twenty times around the cornice of his study ceiling which reads, 'To persevere is to succeed.'

Let's not refrigerate our realisation of the power of cause and effect, though! Let's thaw it and by God's grace, keep it in mind.

NOVEMBER 21

"Even so, come, Lord Jesus."
Revelation 22 v 20

Let's preserve an anticipation of our Lord's return. Take this hope away from our lives and it will affect every decision and every move we make.

A story is told of a tourist who was travelling along the shores of Lake Como in North Italy. When he arrived at Castle Villa Asconti a friendly old gardener opened the gate and showed him the grounds which the old man kept in perfect order. The tourist asked him when the owner had last been there:

'Twelve years ago.'

'Does he ever write to you?'

'No.'

'From whom do you receive your instructions?'

'From his agent in Milan.'

'Does he come?'

'Never.'

'Who then comes here?'

'I am almost always alone, except once in a while for a tourist.'

'But you keep the garden in such fine condition, just as though you expect your master to come tomorrow.'

And the gardener replied, 'Today sir, today.'

NOVEMBER 22

"Then Eli called Samuel .. And he said, What is the thing the Lord hath said unto thee? .. And Samuel told him every whit."
1 Samuel 3 v 16-18

Let's preserve the capacity as adults to learn from children. Often God speaks to me through my children in the things they do and say. They are a foolish people who do not learn from the children around them.

'I watched God work today: amazing thing,
Holding a sparrow small, in manner mild,
He knelt beside a brook to bathe its wing,
I watched God work today, within a child.

I saw God smile today! He smiled at me,
While tenderly His fingers soothed the place,
The tiny bird nestled contentedly,
I saw God smile today in that child's face.

I heard God talk today! He told me there,
In tones sincere that made my heart rejoice,
His home with this frail bird He longed to share,
I heard God talk today, with child-like voice.

I felt God's love tonight! T'was while he blessed,
The little creature, sheltered from harm,
He whispered of all things He loved me best,
I felt God's love tonight in my child's arms.'

NOVEMBER 23

"Others .. were slain."
Hebrews 11 v 36-37

Let's preserve today, a memorial in this little book to my friend, John McConville. The troubles of Ulster affect all who live on this island but when they come close they not only affect, they positively break your heart. Let me tell you about John.

He was a young man who was living for one thing above all others; for John, to live was Christ. There was no doubt about that. From evangelism amongst children to giving out evangelistic literature with us on huge housing estates, to his plan to give his life to overseas work for God. John was someone very special.

Yet he never got to his planned overseas work for the Lord. He rang me up on the phone often under deep conviction of the Spirit as to the will of God for his life. His great burden was to carry the good news to those that did not know it. He never got there. Why? One evening whilst travelling home with nine friends from his work, the van in which he was travelling was flagged down. It was an ambush. The men were taken out of the van, asked their religion (according to the one who was allowed to go) and machine-gunned into eternity.

As I stood by John's coffin a few days later an uncle of his said quietly, 'You know when John was asked his religion he never said he was a Protestant, he always said that he was a Christian.' They tell me a Gospel tract was found near where he lay. One wonders how the word 'martyr' is defined? Martyrs do not only die at burning stakes or in steaming jungles. They can die on a roadside in the hills of South Armagh.

Do not, please, ask me to explain it. John's death will puzzle me to the day my call comes. Whoever or wherever you are today spare a thought for the aching hearts who, through acts of terrorism, never get over losing their loved ones but who have to get used to the fact that they are no longer with us. Pray for those aching hearts today. I cannot explain why John died but I know that surely a great young man fell that day. Of his memory we say 'He is still near us pointing upward.'

NOVEMBER 24

"He must increase, but I must decrease."
John 3 v 30

L et's preserve a spiritual check-up list in our lives. It
is tough questioning, but truly effective. Are you
sitting comfortably? You won't be for long! Here it
comes:

1   Can I work with other people? Can other people
work with me?

2   Do I tend to dominate? Can I leave the real work to
others?

3   Do I love the people I am called to work with? Do I
know them intimately and at depth? Do I clear up
misunderstandings with them quickly and never
criticise them to others?

4   Have I a secret longing always to be first?

5   Do I want God's cause to advance, or is it my chief
desire that I should advance it?

6   Can I hear my colleagues praised and sincerely
enjoy it?

7   Can I hear others praised for what I have done for
God and still be gladder that it was done than
grieved to be neglected?

8   Am I willing to take my wages in Christian service
from God, alone?

9   Am I after anything for myself?

NOVEMBER 25

*"Seek ye first the kingdom of God and His righteousness;
and all these things shall be added unto you."*
Matthew 6 v 33

L et's preserve one great overriding principle in our lives, about everything and everybody else: to seek first the Kingdom of God. It's not easy.

'You see, I have an education to get. And after all you can't get very far in this world without one. And besides, just think what a B.A., or an M.A., or a Ph.D. can do for your cause.'
'But seek ye first ...'
'Yes Lord, but ...'
'Well, you're only young once and if I don't take in the world now, I'll never be in the condition to later on. And didn't Paul say that you have given us 'all things richly to enjoy? I just want to revel in your beautiful creation - that's all, Lord.'
'But seek ye first ...'
'Yes Lord, but ...'
'Well there's this girl, Lord. And if I don't move now, I might lose her. Didn't you yourself say that 'It is not good that a man should be alone?' I agree with thy word, Lord.'
'But seek ye first ...'
'Yes Lord, but ...'
'Well thou art asking a lot. I mean there's a big world out there and precious few seem to be aware of my existence, let alone live by faith in thee. And just look at Thy people, Lord. How many of them live as to the world as Thou art telling me to? One in a hundred maybe? I mean, it's scary to step out like that. Couldn't I have one of those ninety nine other jobs?'
'But made Himself of no reputation, and took upon Him the form of a servant, and was made in the likeness of men: and being found in fashion as a man, He humbled Himself, and became obedient unto death, even the death of the cross.'
'But ... Yes, Lord!'

NOVEMBER 26

"Be ye kind one to another."
Ephesians 4 v 32

Let's preserve shock of happiness. I'm all for a brusque upsetting of routine, now and again. Daily living can be tedious if we don't throw a stone through the grey window of boredom, now and again. It can work wonders. The occasional burst of joy when someone receives something they dreamed of, but certainly did not expect, will not do them one whit of harm. Waken up that ragamuffin of a day with a shock of happiness.

The rule about giving is to give more than expected. Knock the postman or the waiter or that cleaning lady off their feet with a sledge hammer of a tip. You won't go bankrupt and you'll get it all back. Believe me.

So often, for men, work is the place they pummel their brains but home becomes a place for not thinking. Not thinking can become a habit. And life is passing. Bring a shock of happiness home from work today for your children, or great Aunt Emma, or your wife. Try it and see what happens. You'll be amazed.

NOVEMBER 27

"For ye know the grace of our Lord Jesus Christ, that, though he was rich, yet for your sakes he became poor, that ye through his poverty might be rich."
2 Corinthians 8 v 9

Let's preserve a proper attitude to money. It's useful to pay bills with but it is crazy to make a god of it. In 1923 a group of the world's most successful financiers met at the Edgewater Beach Hotel in Chicago. Those present were: a member of the President's cabinet, the world's greatest wheat speculator, the greatest 'bear' on Wall Street, the president of the largest independent steel company, the president of the Bank of International Settlements, the president of the New York Stock Exchange, the owner of the world's greatest monopoly. Those men controlled more wealth than the United States Treasury held.

Forty seven years later investigation of these men brought up some fascinating facts. Were they all enjoying their wealth in a peaceful, comfortable old age? Don't you believe it. The following information was gleaned.

The member of the President's cabinet, Albert Fall, was released from prison so that he could die at home. The greatest wheat speculator, Arthur Culten, died abroad, bankrupt. The greatest 'bear' in Wall Street, Jesse Livermore, committed suicide. The president of the largest steel company, Charles Schivab, lived on borrowed money for five years and died, broke. The president of the Bank of International Settlements, Leon Fraser, committed suicide. The president of the New York Stock Exchange had just recently been released from Sing Sing prison. The head of the world's greatest monopoly, Ivor Kreugger, committed suicide. It makes you think? Let's do more than that.

NOVEMBER 28

"I lifted up mine eyes again, and looked."
Zechariah 2 v 1

Let's preserve the importance of the second look. Often in my life I have made a tragic mistake by failing to look at something a second time.
A writer was once on hoilday from university and told an interesting story:

'I was looking for what I called 'local colour' for use in a book I planned to write. My main character was to be drawn from an impoverished, shiftless community and I believed I knew just where to find it.

Sure enough, one day I came upon the place, made to order with it's rundown farms, seedy men and washed out women. To cap it, the epitome of the shiftlessness I had envisaged was waiting for me near an unpainted shack, in the shape of a shaggy bearded old man in faded overalls who was hoeing round a little patch of potatoes while sitting in a chair.

I started back to my boarding house, itching to get at my typewriter. As I made a turn in the dirt road which ran past the cabin, I looked at the scene from another angle. And when I did, I saw something which stopped me in my tracks. For from this side I observed, leaning against the chair, a pair of crutches, and I noticed that the man had only one leg. In that instant the lazy, shiftless character I had seen was transformed into a figure of dauntless courage.

Since that hour I have never judged a man after only one look or one conversation with him. And thank God that I turned back for the second look.'

NOVEMBER 29

"Marriage is honourable in all."
Hebrews 13 v 4

Let's preserve the spirit of our marriage vows each day. We said them, let's preserve what we said and remind our hearts of them, daily. 'To love and to cherish.' Have we begun to take each other for granted? 'In sickness and in health.' Do we complain when sickness comes instead of setting ourselves to help in every way we can? 'For better or for worse.' When the pressure comes millions flee to divorce. 'Forsaking all other.' What a binding important vow that is, meaning absolute fidelity. Do we preserve it or forget it?

To stand in a wedding ceremony and vow to be true to each other 'until death do us part' is a very serious business. The Bible teaches that Christian marriage is a reflection of the relationship between Christ and His Church. Would the Lord Jesus ever contemplate divorcing His Church? Would He ever throw her aside? Never. Let it be said of our marriages that not only did we say 'I will' but that we daily prove that 'I do'.

NOVEMBER 30

"In God I have put my trust; I will not fear what flesh can do unto me."
Psalm 56 v 4

Let's preserve trust in God. We are, in the fast lane of life, a nation of worriers. We get caught in a web of circumstances we didn't mean and worry that we'll never get out of it. Maybe some telltale gossip has upset the circumstances of life and we cannot see in any way in which to refute the lie he has spread. Or maybe we are like the woman who was worrying how her newly married son was getting on. 'What are you worried about?' said her husband. 'His wife is perfectly capable of caring for him and he for her.' 'Ah!', replied his wife, 'the plain fact is that I'm worried if I'm not worried.' Worry has an active imagination and the Devil would have us continually crossing streams that do not exist. An hour of worry is more exhausting than a day's work. As we move out of November and towards Christmas let's preserve our hearts a simple trust in God which in itself will prove profound. Do you believe He is able to deliver you? Trust Him then.

Self vindication shun! If in the right
What gainest thou by taking from God's hand,
Thy cause? If wrong, what dost thou but invite
Satan himself thy friend in need to stand?
Leave, leave all with God; if right He'll prove thee so;
If not, He'll pardon, therefore to Him go.

Be not men's servant, think what costly price
Was paid, that thou mayest His own bondman be,
Whose service perfect freedom is. Let this
Hold fast thy heart, His claim is great to thee,
None should thy soul enthral, to whom 'tis given,
To serve on earth with liberty of heaven.

DECEMBER

It is the season of the fireside. Beechwood fires are bright and clear. Oak log fires burn steadily. Brick and log fires burn too fast. Hawthorn, say the Irish, bakes the sweetest bread. Elm wood burns as if it's very flames were cold. Poplar fires give bitter smoke. Apple wood will scent your room. Ash, wet or dry, will be fit for anyone to warm their toes by. But out there in the cities and towns there is an almost 'mad' rush on.

'We have all been had!', said a lady as we contemplated the Christmas rush. 'It's far from the original story.', I commented. 'And what was that?', she smiled.

Let's spend this month contemplating the One who came all those years ago to Bethlehem. What better way to end the year together than to think about the Lord Jesus and the change He has made not only to history but to our hearts and lives. Come, let us adore Him.

DECEMBER 1

"Come, see a man ..."
John 4 v 29

The confusion is like a NASA countdown ... 20 shopping days to Christmas. I can almost imagine what is in your mind these days. 'What will you get Grannie and Grandpa, and Tom and Mary, and Charlotte (who has everything) and George (who appreciates nothing) and dear Fred (who would take anything!)?' Slow down, you're going too fast. Stop awhile, let it all pass for five minutes. Lift up your heart to Him who had no room to be born in, no boat to sail in, no penny to illustrate His sermon, nowhere to lay His sacred head. The foxes had their holes to go to, the birds could wing their way to their nest but the Lord of Lord's was homeless. But just think what He gave, unwrapped in Harrod's Christmas paper or the corner store's best: a smile to cheer any child's heart, a word, comforting as no other word ever did, a touch, an ill body would never forget. He was gentle, when others were rough. He was real when other men were pious. He was patient when others burning with ambition rushed on down the fast lane.

There was no fast lane at noon time by the well in Samaria. It was far from the bustle of the city with its occupying Roman troops but a woman was there who took a drink of living water and was refreshed beyond refreshment.

Now, calm down and go through this December with this song in your heart. 'All I ask is to be like Him!' You'll have a good day.

DECEMBER 2

"Let her alone: against the day of my burying hath she kept this."
John 12 v 7

The air hostess sat on the jump seat and, as the jet climbed, we all got chatting. We were all strangers. Suddenly one of the company got suggestive in his talk. I felt embarrassed for the hostess and although no hero, I suddenly heard myself saying, 'Now come on, let her alone.' Some men love to taunt women: even seemingly 'religious' men.

Judas said Mary's ointment poured on the Lord Jesus could have been sold and given to the poor. He taunted her but underneath it all he was a thief and wanted the money for himself. Extremely piety, in my view, is usually hiding something.

Is some Mary, some Hannah, reading these lines who has done something for the Lord which some 'religious' man has mocked? Hear the Saviour say those words to Judas, 'Let her alone.' No woman had ever had a great defender than the Saviour of the world. Let's defend the sacredness of womanhood wherever we go. The 'Men Only' philosophy is not ours.

DECEMBER 3

"i am that bread of life."
John 6 v 48

Whether it is in the form of a long French roll or an Irish soda farl, an English scone or whatever, bread satisfies hunger. But Christ is the 'Bread of Life'. Life is filled with disappointments. Every one of us has to trim our expectations before long. Most days bring a disillusionment of some kind. But who has ever been disillusioned with the Lord Jesus? He satisfies the soul with good things. He is the Bread of Life.

Can I bear a personal testimony? For ten months of the year, at this stage of my life, I have to feed one thousand hearts with spiritual food in a Bible Class in a city filled with division and fear, every Tuesday evening. I have

seen them come to feed of God's word through fog and
snow, the fear of bombs and bullets, rain and sunshine,
and many other distractions. It staggers me every week
to watch all those Bibles open, even before I get to
opening up mine; hundreds of young eager faces,
particularly, leaning forward to hear God's word. They
are spiritually hungry. The bread they desire is the word
of God.

One month I decided to change the fare, to 'lighten' the
study with a little Church history. I would do 'Great
Christian Lives', Tyndale, Luther, Jim Elliott etc. There
were plenty of people who came but there was no
power. I still meet folk who came to those two evenings
and went home hungry. Nobody said a word to me: they
didn't need to. I rose in the pulpit the next week,
cancelled the series and turned back to Bible exposition.
That evening a girl was converted to Christ. I hope I
shall never have to learn that lesson again. When folk
are hungry they do not worry about the name over the
baker's window: all they want is bread. Let's not fail
them.

DECEMBER 4

"But I say unto you ..."
Matthew 5 v 32

I heard Jonathan Dimbleby ask a professor who had
just done a series of T.V. programmes on the history of
'faith' what he would say to a teenager who wanted to
know about the authenticity of the Christian faith. He
replied that he would speak of the Nativity as a 'Jewish
folk tale'. The professor was an 'ordained minister'.
What will we say of Bishop David Jenkins and all his
doubts about the bodily resurrection of the Lord Jesus?
As John Scott said, with the support of the Church of
England Evangelical Council, 'Bishop Jenkins'
explanation so far does not mean any more than did

young Latin Americans when they shouted in regard to Che Guevaras 'Che lives.' The Apostle meant more than this. Does Bishop Jenkins?
No man ever spoke like the Lord Jesus. It was His authority that touched the people. He didn't speculate, He spoke with absolute, clear cut, finality. So, a word for us today from the great Bible Teacher, G. Campbell Morgan to all who preach God's word.
'A man has a perfect right to proclaim a theory of any sort, or to discuss his doubts. But that is not preaching. 'Give me the benefits of your convictions, if you have any. Keep your doubts to yourself; I have enough of my own.', said Goethe. We are never preaching when we are hazarding speculations. Of course we do so. We are bound to speculate sometimes. I sometimes say, 'I am speculating; stop taking notes.' Speculation is not preaching. Neither is the declaration of negations preaching. Preaching is the proclamation of the word, the truth as the truth has been revealed.'

DECEMBER 5

"And He began again to teach by the sea side."
Mark 4 v 1

What a teacher! Of course there are the Aristotle's, the Socrates, the Buddha's, the Jean Paul Satres, the Huxleys of this world: what makes the humble man of Galilee so different? What is that strange, indescribable, unheard of power that rams home His Words with such frank delicacy? Scribes taught tradition. He taught that people would perish or be saved according to what they did with Him. He would be the criterion of all judgement. Not service for Him but relationship to Him would be the issue. He didn't think of Himself as another prophet, He was the fulfilment of all prophecy. He didn't come to destroy God's law, He came to fulfil it.

Teachers want people to absorb their teaching but not
the Saviour: He wanted people not just to absorb His
teaching but to be devoted to Him, personally. Why was
He different? He was different because He was God.

'Trust Him when dark doubts assail you,
Trust Him when your strength is small,
Trust Him when to simply trust Him,
Seems the hardest thing of all'.

DECEMBER 6

*"And I saw .. in the midst of the throne .. stood a Lamb as
it had been slain."*
Revelation 5 v 1,6

A friend of mine, Bill Russel, rose one morning at a
Breaking of Bread service to speak about Christ. I
think the world of Bill, a converted drunkard, who
knows more of God than a thousand college trained men
put together. He had been in an abattoir and, with tears,
Bill spoke of a little lamb he had seen being slaughtered.
He said that the little thing had innocently turned its
head to the knife. Then Bill spoke of the innocent Lamb
of God who gave himself to the death of a cross.
Bill had captured the picture well because the word for
lamb in Revelation 5 v 6 is the word 'amion' which
means 'little lamb'. This means the meekest, gentlest,
most harmless and defenceless of all little animals.
Incredible, is it not, that John on being told that 'the lion
of the tribe of Judah' had overcome should now see that
'little lamb' approach the throne of deity and occupy it?
There is no more moving description of Christ in all of
Scripture. Behold the Lamb of God!

DECEMBER 7

"Christ Jesus came into the world to save sinners."
1 Timothy 1 v 15

It was in a hospital in 1934 that the young Prince Edward was being shown 36 injured veterans of the First World War. He chatted to all that were shown to him. 'But I have only seen 29 patients, nurse,' he said, 'I understand there are 36.' The nurse explained that the other seven were so badly disfigured that for the sake of his feelings he had not been taken to see them. The Prince insisted and stayed long enough to thank each soldier for the great sacrifice they had made. Then he turned to the nurse again, 'But I've only seen six men. Where is the seventh?' He was informed that no one was allowed to see him. The man, he was told, was blind, maimed, dismembered and hideously disfigured. He was isolated in a room he would never leave alive. 'Please do not ask to see him.', the nurse pleaded.
The Prince could not be dissuaded and with white face and drawn lips he looked down on what had been a fine figure of a man who was now a horror. The tears broke out and the Prince on lovely impulse bent down and reverently kissed the cheeks of that broken hero.
The Prince of Glory has stooped far, far lower to kiss, far, far worse ugliness. There never was a story to equal it. Christ Jesus came into the world to save sinners.

DECEMBER 8

"The hireling fleeth, because he is an hireling .. I am the good shepherd."
John 10 v 13-14

I stood in the Manchester Art Gallery and gasped. Holman Hunt's masterpiece, 'The Hireling', stood before me. There in a glass case underneath the mounting was a letter from Holman Hunt to the Curator of Art at the museum of his day: it explained what he meant to portray. He was aiming at men who said they were pastors of Christ's flock but who were anything but it. What a painting!

The young man in shepherd's garb in the painting was the hireling, brought in for a few pennies to stay with the flock for a short time. As he sits on a bank he is talking to a girl about a death head moth which he has in his hand, an object of superstition in England. While the hireling and the girl surmise what omen the moth has brought, two of the sheep are already in the cornfield eating the corn. They are as good as dead for if sheep eat corn they get blown stomachs and die. The image, the artist explained, was like pastors who claim to be shepherds of Christ's flock who speculate on mere superstition in their pulpits whilst their flock are going headlong to perdition and being given the wrong food all the time.

The sheep in the painting were all standing because sheep will only normally lie down when they feel safe and secure. This flock felt neither. There on the other side of the bank on which the hireling and girl are sitting are the little yellow marshmallow flowers. Marshmallow flowers only grow where the ground is marshy and wet. The hireling had got his flock on the wrong feeding ground and they will all develop footrot. You can imagine if a wolf came what the hireling would do. They would never see him again.

'His watchmen are blind.', wrote Isaiah. 'They are all ignorant .. they are all dumb dogs, they cannot bark; sleeping, lying down, loving to slumber. They are greedy dogs which can never have enough and they are shepherds that cannot understand: and they all look to their own way, every one for his gain, from his quarter.' (Isaiah 56 v 10-11)

Lord Jesus, Thou art no hireling.

DECEMBER 9

"Those that seek me early shall find me."
Proverbs 8 v 17

The Lord Jesus: no child will ever have a better Saviour to trust, a better friend to talk to, a better guide through life, a better master to follow.
With all my heart I urge the importance of teaching children their need of a Saviour who can meet their need of a Saviour and of the Saviour who can meet their need. Coleridge, the poet, once spoke very pointedly to a friend of his who had scoffed at the idea of teaching children God's word. 'Let them choose for themselves when they reach maturity.', his friend had quipped. 'Try that theory in your garden.', Coleridge challenged. 'Let the soil choose for itself. Don't pull out weeds and plant seeds in the soil, just let the soil choose for itself and see what happens.' Wise words. Those who seek the Lord Jesus, early, shall find Him. Get the seeds in early.

DECEMBER 10

"Philip findeth Nathanael ..."
John 1 v 45

A dog was run over by a car. A doctor hurriedly bound up the broken leg and took the dog into his own home. After weeks of care he was surprised to discover that the dog had just walked off and left him. He had some harsh words to say about the ungrateful dog. Two days later he heard a scratching at his front door; on the porch he found the dog he had healed - in company with another animal that had been hurt! Should ours not be a love like this? Have we not found One who can bind up our wounds and make us whole again? Tell others and bring them to the Lord Jesus. They will be extremely grateful.

DECEMBER 11

"In all points tempted like as we are."
Hebrews 4 v 15

When the Lord Jesus was a little boy, Herod persecuted Him. When the Lord Jesus grew to be a man the Jewish and Gentile civil authorities persecuted Him. Some in His own family did not believe Him. When the Lord Jesus was 33 one of His intimate friends sold Him for 30 pieces of silver. He faced it all and overcame it all as no man has ever done. The principalities and powers had never in history discovered someone who was so totally obedient to the Father's will. They could get no grip on Him whatsoever.

Are you persecuted at work for your stand for morality and truth? Has one of your intimate friends betrayed you? Are you being persecuted for your faith in your home and family? The Lord Jesus triumphed over all this in childhood and manhood, in all points. I recommend that you whisper constantly to yourself these words when you are persecuted and tempted; 'Unto Him who is able to keep me from falling.' I whisper them in my heart nearly everyday of my life.

DECEMBER 12

"Ye must be born again."
John 3 v 7

See that young fellow at university so keen for Christ? Why does Darwinism, or existentialism, or communism or whatever, not swamp His faith? His faith is higher than argument. See that older lady at the Church service singing her heart out with her eyes shut? Others may mock her but it does not worry her a bit. When people are truly converted you could not argue them out of their faith. Why not? Because they were not argued into it. A soul is never won to Christ at the end of an argument. Souls are born into God's Kingdom. If an intelligent person could argue someone into God's Kingdom, surely a more intelligent person could argue them out again. But it's not based on argument. It is not that God is unreasonable, it is that he is beyond reason: the new birth is an experience. One born again Christian is worth a thousand nominal ones who are a library of argument. I don't wonder that George Whitfield when asked why he was always preaching on the text, 'Ye must be born again.', replied, 'Because, ye must be born again.'

DECEMBER 13

"The greatest of these is love."
1 Corinthians 13 v 13

1   Love suffers long. This means when wronged, love patient and silent.
2   Love is kind. To be kind to the person who has done thee wrong is a triumph of grace.
3   Love envies not. Love is perfectly content with the will of God.
4   Love makes no parade. It never 'shows off'.
5   Love gives itself no airs. The person who is self satisfied is always contemptuous of others.
6   Love is not rude. Love is not blundering goodness.
7   Love seeks not her own. Love is not selfish.
8   Love is not touchy. There is no sin that so disrupts the Christian family than sheer bad temper.
9   Love thinks no evil.
10 Love is only gladdened by goodness.
11 Love bears all things. It gets under the load of life and bears it to the limit.
12 Love takes the kindest view.
13 Love never despairs of anybody.
14 Love cannot be conquered.
Who do you think all this is a photo of?

DECEMBER 14

"Ye shall know them by their fruits."
Matthew 7 v 16

Not to love the Lord Jesus is to reject the loveliest character of all creation. In Him is every possible beauty and those who worship Him get like Him. If we worship material things we become cold, ruthless and powerless. The fruits are inevitable.

Shortly before he died in 1950 George Bernard Shaw wrote, 'The science to which I pinned my faith is bankrupt .. its counsels which should have established the millennium have led directly to the suicide of Europe. I believed them once .. in their name I helped to destroy the faith of millions .. and now they look at me and witness the great tragedy of an atheist who has lost his faith.' Look what Shaw's faith produced: what does yours?

DECEMBER 15

"My strength is made perfect in weakness."
2 Corinthians 12 v 9

The pastor, A.B. Simpson, was approaching middle age, broken in health, deeply despondent and ready to quit in his ministry for God when he chanced to hear the simple Negro spiritual:

'Nothing is too hard for Jesus,
No man can work like Him'.

The message of those two simple lines carried faith and hope and life to his body and soul. He retired for a short season and got alone with God and then went out to serve the Lord in a life of evangelism for 35 years which reached out across the world.

The Lord has a set of scales. On one pan of the scales is the word 'as' and on the other is the word 'so'. As the problems of the day come down heavily on one side of the scales so God's strength comes down on the other side to meet those problems. The balance of the two is always perfect. 'As' your days 'So' will your strength be. That's the balance the Lord Jesus brings to any soul that trusts Him.

DECEMBER 16

"That ye .. May be able to comprehend with all saints what is the breadth, and length, and depth and height; And to know the love of Christ, which passeth knowledge."
Ephesians 3 v 17-19

How broad? Broad enough to stretch from the gates of heaven to the gates of hell. How long? Long enough to last for eternity. How deep? Deep enough to touch the inmost heart. How high? High enough to lift and place a sinner in heaven.

But notice that to have the power to comprehend all these dimensions we will only be able to do it with all saints. ('Saints' in Scripture is a N.T. word for 'believers'). The isolated Christian can know something of the love of Jesus. But his grasp is bound to be limited. To fellowship with other Christians, to hear their appreciation of the Lord helps you to see how vast God's love is. I've met them in Moscow and in South Korea, Paris and Cullybackey. Nazareth and Hyannis Point, in lean-tos and plush auditoriums, on mountain tracks and in city centres: people whose hearts the Lord has touched. I'm for the better for it: real Christian fellowship helps to measure God's love. And yet it surpasses knowledge: Christ's riches are unsearchable. In eternity with all saints we shall explore those inexhaustible riches of grace and love. Wouldn't it be good if we are going to be doing this together for ever to do a bit more of it down here and have less of the 'them' and 'us' syndrome amongst born again people? The false division of Christians is a scandal. How Satan must laugh at us!

DECEMBER 17

"They took knowledge of them, that they had been with Jesus."
Acts 4 v 13

I was in Nazareth and was having a meal with a gentle Arab Christian. He had lived in Nazareth all his life and was telling me about events at his work. Someone at work had lost their temper and had drawn out and hit him. He felt anger rise in him but resisted and went for a walk in the fields to cool down. When he returned his employer had sacked his assailant.

'Do you know?', said my Arab friend speaking of what his attacker had done, 'Only for ze grace of God I would have brought ze teeth out of his mouth!'

As I left Nazareth I thought that the little boy who had run its streets, the young man who had pushed his plane down at the carpenter's, the One who had been almost pushed down that nearby hill by a hostile crowd, the One who gave His life a ransom for many outside Jerusalem was now living in the power of an endless life. I had just seen evidence of it in a gentle Arab in the 20th century Nazareth. Will others see evidence of it in our place of work today?

DECEMBER 18

"For he saith to the snow, Be thou on the earth."
Job 37 v 6

As I write, outside my window the mantling snow is coming down in millions of flakes. My children are in the garden beside themselves and are little moving 'snow women' themselves. With my good wife I have been at the work of building a snowman and what fun we have had! It brings out that little boy and girl in us which we pray will never go away.

On one occasion some children were playing and decided to have a competition. They would see who could make the straightest set of footprints in the deep snow. They set off eagerly to the edge of the forest which was their finishing point. Only one set of footprints turned out to be straight. How had the boy walked in such a straight line? 'Easy!', he said, 'I fixed my eyes on one point ahead of me and walked towards it.'

So it is when we fix our eyes on the Lord Jesus, in the path of life, our feet always follow our eyes.

DECEMBER 19

"Husbands, love your wives, even as Christ also loved the church."
Ephesians 5 v 25

In this hectic run up to Christmas and the joys of children who are counting the hours to Christmas Eve, I want to concentrate on the effect the Lord Jesus has upon Christian parents. God put families together before He put Churches together and it is heart-breaking to see the incredible breakdown in marriage at the moment. I seem to have to counsel in this area almost every week of my life.

Is the husband's role like that of the widowed Captain Von Trapp in 'The Sound Of Music'? No. He is to be the leader of his wife, the head of his home, but it is to be a leadership of love. He is to love his wife as Christ loved the Church. How was that? Christ loved the Church to death itself. To be practical, how can a husband do this? Here are some guidelines.

1 He must know his wife to look out for her welfare.
2 He must keep the channels of communication open and clear.
3 He must set an example.
4 He must make sound and timely decisions.
5 He must encourage his wife's capabilities.
6 He must seek responsibility and take it.

Remember Cliff Barrows' motto for marriage: 'Marriages are held together by 12 words - I'm wrong! I'm sorry! Please forgive me! I love you!'

DECEMBER 20

"To communicate forget not."
Hebrews 13 v 16

How many husbands and wives have you heard use sarcasm scathingly to one another? If you want to know how far it can creep into your marriage just promise each other that you will not use one sarcastic word in your conversations as husband and wife for one week. See what happens! The lowest form of wit seems to have a high position in millions of marriages. Communication can be fun, of course! I remember a Church secretary announce once that he wanted to take 'a wee run over the sick'! My good friend, Val English, who has such a great ministry for the Lord, told me he was once announced in a Church with these words: 'I

would like on your behalf to worship Val English!'
Communication in marriage can be fun too but let's
watch how we communicate. Take the man who said,
'Darling you've been working so hard all week, cooking
and cleaning and taking care of the children. Tonight I'm
going to take you out for a good dinner!' His wife burst
into tears!
A tone of voice, a posture, a raised eyebrow, a
drumming of the fingers on the table, a turning of the
head can communicate poison. Our Lord Jesus never
communicated poison in a movement in his life: neither
should we.

DECEMBER 21

*"The ornament of a meek and quiet spirit, which is the sight
of God of great price."*
1 Peter 3 v 4

When Gerry Fitt, former M.P. for West Belfast,
entered the House of Lords, he was asked what
he thought about his wife now being named 'Lady Fitt'.
'She has always been a lady!', replied Lord Fitt.
What is a wife? Some women could answer that she is a
cook, laundry woman, chauffeur, seamstress, partner,
counsellor, financier, student, electrician, travelling
companion, philosopher, entertainer, receptionist, and
slave all at once! Mrs. Everything.
It may often seem like that, yet there is only one quality
God looks for in a Christian wife which is more
important than any other. It is an imperishable quality: it
is named 'the inner person of the heart'. This is the New
Testament's description of a wife's attitude which is
precious in the sight of God.
If a wife's attitude is 'meek and quiet' does this make
her a sandwich maker and a baby machine, docile and
no part of the decision making process? Is she to be

reduced to a whimper? God forbid. It means she is inwardly clothed with strength and character and confidence. She is not shallow, loud or cheap. She is tranquil and under control. She has genuine humility and does not fight against God or others. I can tell you there are mighty few men like this and they boast of being the stronger sex! What a lady is the lady of 1 Peter 3 v 1-9: once, twice, three times and all her days, a lady in the sight of God. She's got class.

DECEMBER 22

"Redeeming the time."
Ephesians 5 v 16

The most precious commodity you can give to your child is your time. The Lord Jesus gave so much of His time to children: how could we do less? As Christmas approaches electronic toys may fascinate and lots of money spent on presents may seem to please children but they will not ultimately judge us as parents by such things. Did we or did we not spend time with them? This question will weigh heavily in their judgement of us.

Father, busy in your office plush,
Rushing around so much, you cannot touch,
Your child's heart that way,
Oh! it may buy him food or toys,
But you must give him time,
Your time, if you would ever say,
'I've made my child's heart glad.'

Mother, who daily makes the mould,
In those first years, edged by fears,
Fears of how he'll fare,
Makes yours the encouraging word,

And hold his love, even when he rebels,
Always care, always care,
And you'll make your child's heart glad.

Then when he's left his parents care,
Leave the nest, and the rest, to make his own,
When you are old and that childhood's gone,
Far from your grasp and reach,
He'll say of you in truth,
'They made my childhood glad.'

DECEMBER 23

"Rejoice with the wife of thy youth."
Proverbs 5 v 18

In counselling I come across parents who are having a
rough time in their marriage and they speak of their
children as being the welds that holds them together.
Children were never designed to be the weld that holds
the home together. If parents establish a relationship
which revolves around their children rather than their
mate then it is very unfortunate. Insecure parents who
find in their children what they should have found in
their mates cannot cope when the time for releasing their
children comes.

Ask the Lord of the Christian family to truly help you to
love your mate more and your children will greatly
benefit. There is no more secure place for children than
with a mother and a father who love one another. Don't
try to make your child the person you always wanted to
become. Block such feelings. Make sure when your
children leave the nest that you already have a deep
relationship with your wife which can then become even
deeper.

DECEMBER 24

"When Herod the king had heard these things,
he was troubled."
Matthew 2 v 3

His nickname was 'Red'. It was all because he sold his birthright for some red vegetable soup. His real name was Esau and he had many relations; Herod was one of them, an Edomite ('Redite'). Herod heard about the little baby to be born at Bethlehem and knew very well that He was the Messiah. But Herod wanted immediate power, he did not care about some future spiritual blessing: he was right in the Esau tradition. All that 'spiritual thing' in the future wasn't as exciting as political acumen, friendship with Rome, the roar of the crowds that were his, now. He chose the immediate like his ancestor had chosen before him.

What happened? The scene in Bethlehem as Mary awaited the birth of Christ was dreadful in comparison to the luxury of Herod's palace. But where, oh where, is Herod's palace now? It is mere Mediterranean rubble. And where is the baby of Bethlehem? He is exalted far above all.

DECEMBER 25

"For God so loved the world, that he gave his
only begotten Son."
John 3 v 16

Christmas is not a happy time for everyone. For many it means the awareness of an empty chair at the Christmas table. For many a childless couple it means as other people's children rip their presents open it almost rips their hearts open. In fact, for more people than we imagine, Christmas brings great sadness. Just last Christmas I had to visit a home where a dear father had died just as he was buying his turkey. The presents in the corner of the room seemed threatening rather than a joy. Christmas for that family will never be quite the same again. It means separation.

So it is for all sad hearts on what for many will be a happy day, I write. As in your heart you muse on the scene around you please let me remind you that for God Christmas meant one thing: it meant 'a son away from home'. He understands.

DECEMBER 26

"Be not drunk with wine, wherein is excess; but be filled with the Spirit."
Ephesians 5 v 18

Is alcohol a stimulant? Pharmacologically (what a big word!) speaking it is classified as a depressant. It depresses the highest centre of the brain controlling judgement, balance, wisdom and the power to assess anything.

What of the power of the Holy Spirit? He always stimulates. Let Him guide you and you will be amazed at how He will stimulate your mind, your heart and your will. Alcohol dehumanises but the Spirit of God draws us to Christ. He never speaks of Himself, He always speaks of the Saviour. We cannot have a thought of Christ without the Holy Spirit. Don't be filled with wine today but be filled with the Spirit, Christian. But 'Am I not allowed a little wine for my stomach's sake?', you ask. My answer is that a lot of people must have terribly bad stomachs!

DECEMBER 27

"A time to keep silence, and a time to speak."
Ecclesiastes 3 v 6

The New Year is beginning to loom on our horizon. This little book will probably be put aside and you and I will have to part. I have so enjoyed writing to you these last 360 days and I want to sign off with five prayers from my heart, for us. Here is the first. 'Lord, this is an interesting week we are in. A lot of people seem to be eating turkey sandwiches and these children, Lord, they seem to be playing mostly with the boxes their presents came in! Calm us, Lord, in this holiday week and teach us to set priorities for the coming year. Give us, Lord, one thing which in this year we have not always shown to others: sensitivity. Help us to get our sensitivity antennae up high. Help us when to speak and when to keep quiet. Help us to know when to offer aid and when to allow independence, for, at different times one is as important as the other. Above all, Lord, help us to be sensitive to the leading of the Holy Spirit for five words in the Spirit is better than 10,000 in an unknown tongue. Keep us sensitive, Lord. Amen.'

DECEMBER 28

"The faithful God."
Deuteronomy 7 v 9

Lord as this year slips away help us to 'backward cast our eye' and rejoice. Help us at some time today to think over the past year and pinpoint those times when we saw Thy hand overruling in tight corners. Help us to see ways that were made straight, rough places, plain. As the nation spends this week watching television or attending sports meetings, help us, Father, as our black friends put it, 'To steal away Jesus'. Thank you for leading us through all the labyrinth of ways. Lord, we can see a straight line from today right back to January 1st, but it didn't look so straight the other way round. Great is Thy faithfulness. Help us in the coming year to know that Thy faithfulness will be unchanged. Thy word is our candle on the water. Help us to have this priority in the New Year that we will ever look to Thy word because it is a light which will never go out. Help us to know that knowledge of that word never comes by intuition. Amen.'

DECEMBER 29

"Before honour is humility."
Proverbs 15 v 33

'Lord, in this New Year give to us a new appreciation of humility. The whole philosophy of the world at the moment seems to be to get us to think well of ourselves. Pride is choking millions. As Augustine said, Lord, 'It was pride that changed angels into devils; it is humility that makes men as angels.' From pride of face and pride of place, deliver us.

Help us, Lord, in these coming days not to lift a finger to exalt ourselves. Help us never to stoop to manoeuvring or applying for promotion: help us to do well what lies at hand and in due time Thou wilt bring about changes for our good. If Thou doest not bring about changes, then, Lord, help us to realise we are better off without them. No good thing wilt Thou withhold from them that walk uprightly.

And, Lord, just remind us as this Christmas week comes to an end that there is something we can swallow which will never lead to indigestion: pride!'

DECEMBER 30

"Forgive, and ye shall be forgiven."
Luke 6 v 37

'Lord, one thing more: make us in this coming year a forgiving people. We want to thank Thee for Thy forgiveness which reached down to the pit of our lives and lifted our feet unto a rock. Forgiven! The sweetness of it leads us right into Thy presence. But, Lord, how easy it is to know Thy forgiveness and yet to hold grudges against other people. Lord, when we think of the crimes of our tongues: dishonesty, unkindness, flattery, impurity, blasphemy, slander, pride, criticism, exaggeration, temper, greed, boasting: what a change if we, who have been forgiven so much, could use these tongues of ours to say to someone, 'I forgive you!' Help us, Lord, not only to forgive but to forget. Help us never to harp on the old string to the forgiven person by saying 'But do you not remember you once said, or did...?' Lord, we are never more like Thee than when we forgive. Help us. Amen.'

DECEMBER 31

"Did not our heart burn within us?"
Luke 24 v 32

'Goodbye, my reader. Thank you for walking through the seasons with me. We have become good friends but time, our old enemy, has come to part us. I must take my leave and face another season, like you, not knowing what lies in it for me or my loved ones. If they ever mention my name to you or yours to me let's remind them that we were seasonal companions, once, and that a third figure drew near and walked with us in the way. Let's tell them how our hearts burned within us as He talked with us and expounded in all the Scriptures the things concerning Himself. He was the Man 'For All Seasons'.

For all those who are trusting in Christ alone for salvation, the journey will soon end: the gates of the Celestial City will soon appear. The seasons of Spring and Summer, Autumn and Winter will be no more. It will be a timeless haven, it will be eternity. Soon and very soon we are going to see the King. Goodnight, I'll see you on that morning.'